MW01221717

The Kingdom Of Christ

THE

KINGDOM OF CHRIST:

OR

HINTS

ON THE

PRINCIPLES, ORDINANCES, AND CONSTITUTION

OF THE

CATHOLIC CHURCH.

IN

LETTERS TO A MEMBER OF THE SOCIETY OF FRIENDS.

BY

A CLERGYMAN OF THE CHURCH OF ENGLAND.

VOL. I.

LONDON:

DARTON AND CLARK, HOLBORN HILL.

J. Green and Co., Printers, 13, Bartlett's Buildings.

CONTENTS.

LETTER I.

A 2

LETTER II.

LETTER III.

CONTENTS.

V

Page

LETTER IV.

CONTENTS. v

PREFACE.

THE nature and object of these Letters are sufficiently explained by their title. They treat of the Kingdom of Christ; they profess only to be a collection of hints; and they are suggested by the history and present circumstances of the Society of Friends. But it may be well to state, in a few words, why the Author has entered upon so vast a subject; why, if he thought himself fitted to discuss it at all, he has not discussed it more fully and learnedly; why he has connected it with the proceedings of a particular sect.

1. It seems to me, that whatever may be the temper or education of theological students, and thoughtful men generally, in this day, or to whatever point they mean to direct their studies, the questions,—Is there a Catholic Church? what are its principles

and constitution?—inevitably force themselves upon their attention, and in some
sense take precedence of all others. We have
most of us known persons who determined,
at the outset of their course, that the cultivation of personal religion in themselves
and their brethren, should be the sole object of their solicitude. "Some men, they
said, might be needful to defend the out-
works of Christianity; in general, those
who had least right to be esteemed in the
church, the most to be honoured in the
world, would take that office upon themselves; the Christian who understands the
secret movings in his own heart, the temptations to which he is liable, the aids and
deliverances which he may expect, has a
higher and more awful vocation. To watch
over the seeds of life which are planted
within him, till they have taken root downwards, and borne fruit upwards, and are fit
to be transplanted into another soil, and,
so far as he may, to teach others how they
may exercise the like care and husbandry;
this is his task, from which he must on no

account turn aside to notice the movements of the world without, or to investigate the mechanism of visible institutions." Some use this language from lively convictions, sustained by little knowledge of themselves; in some it is the utterance of a deliberate, inward conviction, of which greater experience may modify the shape, but cannot alter the substance. The former soon discover how little they counted the cost; what mighty influences are at work to urge them out of the quiet haven of contemplation into outward and definite action; what plausible excuses there are for yielding to these influences; how impossible it is to preserve the texture of their spirits in that fineness and delicacy which they once thought so necessary, but which they now hardly think desirable; how needful it is to act upon vulgar men, by vulgar motives which alone they can understand; how dexterous and cunning it is to turn the instruments which the world has invented, and of which it deems highly, to the service of

that religion which it hates. But the
other class are led, by nearly the same
experience, to very different reflections.
They perceive that it is, in some important
sense, the condition of our receiving wisdom, that we should impart it; they wonder, if there be such a law, how it happens
that the spiritual energy and vitality of each
person, should be diminished by the pains
which he takes to quicken his brethren;
they inquire whether there is no divine
scheme which shall accomplish both purposes at once, — no great machine, the
wheels of which move, because the Spirit
of the living creature is in them? In other
words, whether there is not, or has not
been, or shall not be, a Catholic Church?

Again, a man starts from the very opposite
position to that which we have been considering. He regards the phrases spiritual
and personal religion with some suspicion.
Though he is aware that they have an important meaning, he fancies that they are often
indexes of a restless and factious temper;
he thinks that they express a discontent

with what is quiet and orderly, an inclina-
tion to what is exciting, piquant, and exclusive; he thinks it best for individuals,
that there should be a certain established
tone of mind, to which they should con-
form themselves; and essential for society,
that a love for peculiar notions should not
set the different portions of it at war with
each other. At different periods, different
methods may be useful to check this tendency. Toleration may do that most effectually to-day, which restraint and severity
would have been used to accomplish in
times gone by. The principle in both cases
is the same,—to prevent the order and harmony of society from being disturbed by
the friction of individual sentiments and
speculations. Now, if we suppose this habit
of mind not to be the result of mere con-
stitutional laziness, but, as it certainly must
often be, of a hearty and honest reverence,
and even passion for order,—a reverence
and passion which manifest themselves in
a faithful fulfilment of the ordinary relations of life,—and if we suppose it to be

accompanied, as it generally is, with somewhat of practical shrewdness and observation, it must, I should think, be much as-
saulted by such reflections as these:—"After
all the contrivances that men have resorted
to for the purpose of hindering these out-
breakings, which I feel to be so dangerous,
what have they accomplished ? Persecution
provoked the spirit which it strove to ex-
tinguish.   Have compromise and liberality
succeeded in repressing it ? Is this age, in
which all opinions are so commonly believed to be indifferently true, less fruitful
of party notions and animosities than any
previous one? Do men find fewer excuses
now than formerly, for quarrelling with
each other, and hating each other ? Would
it not be more correct to say, that our modern liberalism means permission to men
to quarrel with and hate each other as
much as they please ; a tacit repeal of the
edict, which had been found in all ages so
troublesome, but had never before been
formally abrogated, that each man should
love his neighbour as himself ? If this be

the case, what is the meaning of that order
of which I have dreamed? Was I altogether wrong in fancying that it was possible? If so, everything within me and
without me is a contradiction; confusion
and perplexity lose their names and their
natures,—they become the *law* of the world.
But if there be such an order, must it not
be deeper than all these outward edicts
and decrees, which have been constantly
asserting its necessity, and have been utterly unable to preserve its existence? Till
I understand the principles of this order, is
it possible to understand why any of the
rules which depend upon them are violated, or how they may be maintained? Is
it not a childish sentimentalism, utterly
unworthy of a practical man, to whine because men chuse courses for themselves,
when I have not yet ascertained whether
there be any constitution with which there
were meant to be an agreement, and what
it is?" Thus, men of this class, also, are led
to inquire, whether there be any divinely
ordained and universal society for men,

which is superior to all mere positive law
and arbitrary convention ; in other words,
they are led to examine into the nature and
principles of the Catholic Church.

Once more : There are some who have
been led to perceive, that all the mighty
machinery of the world around us, and the
more subtle and wonderful machinery of the
world within us, cannot exist merely for their
own sakes and for ours. " To cultivate the
religious principle in ourselves, to preserve
society from falling into disorder, may be
great objects, but they cannot be the ultimate object ; for the glory of God, for the
manifestation of His character, the system
of nature, the operations of mind, and the
course of history must have been contrived. This is the only end which can account for the existence of all inanimate
nature ; this is the only end in which
the conscious and voluntary creation can
find satisfaction and repose. If we would
enter into the designs of God, if we would
not live in constant contradiction with ourselves, we must forget all minor considera-

tions, we must count as secondary and subordinate, the education of our own hearts, and the regulation of society; we must draw all our thoughts, desires, and hopes to this centre." A man who has adopted this grand and unselfish principle, for the rule of his inward and outward life, is likely for a time to acquiesce in it as something which not only surpasses, but supersedes all other feelings and speculations. But after a while, he is compelled to perceive, that there is a danger in this case too, of substituting words for realities, and of making his principle abortive, by making it exclusive. If there be no great scheme through which God is manifesting forth His own glory; if we are to invent the schemes for promoting that glory, we soon become the objects of our own worship. If it be merely in nature that God hath made a manifestation of Himself, we may see power and order; goodness and truth we cannot see. But it is questionable whether even this power and order be not discernible there, because we have had

indications of them on some other ground;
whether we do not impute them to nature,
because they are necessary to man.   If,
again, the manifestation of goodness and
truth, as the foundation of order and
power, be only made to a few minds here
and there, then also the principle is set at
nought; the glory of God cannot be the
end implied in the constitution of man.   Is
there not, then, some spiritual order, answering in universality to the order of nature, in and through which, it has pleased
God to manifest His perfections? Is there
a Catholic Church?

In these three cases, (and I think it will
be allowed that they include most of the
forms of thought which prevail among us),
we have seen that men who would have
been naturally indisposed to consider the
subject of these letters, are nevertheless
drawn to it by the circumstances of the
age in which they live, and by the necessity of following out their own principles.
Let us next consider in how many ways
the question which is excited in their minds

is wont to be answered. The words RES-
PICE, CIRCUMSPICE, PROSPICE, contain
the three dogmas of our day respecting
the church. " Look back, says one class
of thoughtful and intelligent divines, look
back to the centuries which immediately
followed the coming of our Lord in the
flesh. In these ages lived the men who
conversed with Christ's own apostles, received their traditions, imbibed their spirit,
suffered their persecutions; then the church
was one in itself; the heretics who rose up
within it, were distinguished from its true
members, and soon cast out; then men
received mysteries without speculating upon
them; then they understood their great
powers, and proclaimed them to the world;
then doctrines were believed because the
church asserted them; then the ministers
spoke as those who had authority, and the
people thought that it was their only function to receive the words which they heard,
and to bring forth the fruits of them in
their lives; then sacraments were reckoned
of mighty dignity, and the ordination of

the priest, and the consecration of the elements, gave them their validity; then the
conditions and methods of a holy life were
understood, and men who desired spiritual
blessings fashioned themselves according to
the rule of the church, and not according
to their own caprice. Then the church
was indeed a church, then it was indeed
Catholic. Since then it has fallen into divisions; the Eastern has been opposed to
the Western; the Western has become
split into Papists and Protestants; each of
these, especially the latter, into numberless
other divisions; the vestiges of a Catholic Church are scarcely discernible. But
it may be restored; the early ages are the
pattern in the Mount, after which it is
to be built again; all modern innovations
must be discarded, all modern speculation restrained, and men must labour to
arrive at the unreasoning innocence of
childhood."

" Look around you, say the teachers of
another school, and wonder at the amazing blessings and privileges of the age in

which you live. Now first is the church
showing herself in her real freedom and
power; now have men learned to combine,
for the promotion of great spiritual objects; the barriers which superstition and
prejudice raised to the progress of the
Gospel, the notions of a particular sanctity
in places, forms, and offices are gradually
disappearing, and all that machinery which
has been found so useful in forwarding
secular purposes, is converted to the service
of the sanctuary. We have failed to secure
uniformity of opinion, but we are beginning
to secure uniformity of purpose; all is not
yet as it should be, for a number of inconvenient usages and antiquated restrictions
stand in our way; but all is becoming
right. We have at last got into the true
line and scheme of action; the church is
approaching every day nearer to the condition of a great co-operative society, aiming at the conversion of the world, and
certain, at no distant time, to accomplish
its aim."

" Look forward, say a third party; every

thing behind you, except in the days of the
apostles, is dark; everything around you
is cheerless; the church began to decline
when its first preachers left the earth; it
has been degenerating ever since, and has
reached its lowest point of degradation
now.   But a new dispensation is at hand;
the prophecies, which, by one class of critics, have been supposed to be fulfilled in
the first coming of our Lord and the establishment of the church, by another have
been turned to mere private and personal
uses, all point to its arrival; then, indeed,
a kingdom will be set up on earth, then,
indeed, Christ will reign among His an-
cients gloriously.   Our present duty is to
wait and wish for the time; to keep aloof
from all institutions and societies, by whatever name they may be called, whether
confessedly of human origin, or claiming
apostolic derivation, which have been de-
filed by earthly sin.   In due time a church
will appear; the new Jerusalem will descend from above, as a bride adorned for
her husband; and, by terrible judgments,

the earth shall be purged of the enemies of her and of her Lord, and shall thenceforth be the obedient subject of those over whom she has been the cruel tyrant.

Now, for those who do not feel the necessity of examining into the nature of Christ's church and kingdom, I do not write; for those who are perfectly contented with any of those views which I have described, I do not write; lastly, for those who want some new and startling view to set them all aside, I do not write. But in saying this, I believe that I do not exclude any very considerable number of readers. I have explained why I think that very few considerate men are indifferent to the subject. I am persuaded that almost as few are so content with the system which they prefer, that they are not at times ready to abandon it as untenable, and at times to see a reasonableness in each of the others; and I feel quite sure that most men are sufficiently weary of systems and schemes, to resist the intrusion of any new one, affecting to displace its

predecessors.   What remains ? I answer,
to look at the facts of the case as they are
presented to us by these disputants, and to
see whether they do not give us some hints
of an older and simpler doctrine, which excludes neither the Respice, the Circumspice, nor the Prospice ; but declares that,
only in the union of the three can we find
a church which shall satisfy the wants of a
creature who looks before and after, shall
present the image of an order abiding from
generation to generation, and be a mirror
of the glory of Him which was, and which
is, and which is to come.

2. My object, then, is only to trace the
" Hints" of this doctrine. A learned treatise is necessary for the justification of
either of those particular views on which I
have commented ; a learned treatise would
be necessary to expound some original
view which should set them aside ; but
what seems to me most necessary, for the
circumstances of our time, and the wants
of our minds, is, that we should be
taught how to profit by the writings of

men who have seen certain sides of truth
very strongly; how we may be prevented
from rejecting what they rejected. At present, most of our books are written against
some past or prevailing notion; Papists write
against Protestants, Protestants against Popery; the supporters of the *Via Media*
against both. It is impossible for men
holding one view, to read the works written on the opposite hypothesis, except for
the purpose, of finding fault with them.
It is impossible for those who adopt none
of the views, to gain quiet and comfortable
instruction from the writers who have defended them. Thus three-fourths of our
time for reading is spent in finding out
what we may abuse; and numbers seem
ready to abandon reading altogether, because they find so little with which they
may agree. Surely this state of feeling is
most mischievous; surely there must be
that in the writings of all the three classes
which I have described, from which we
might derive a blessing; and there may
be a blessing in each one, which the other

cannot give. What we want, is to be brought into a point of view, in which the fair and illuminated side of each doctrine, and not its dark side, may be presented to us. When we have been familiarized to its beauty, its deformity will be far more disagreeable and appalling to us, than it ever can be while we are perpetually conversing with it alone.

How easy it is to misrepresent this desire, and to give it the most odious character, I am well aware. By the very slight and moderate injustice of representing the student as one who wishes to place himself above all sects and parties, that from a calm elevation he may behold their errors, and smile at them with the complacency of the great Epicurean poet, and not as one who wishes to place himself where he may receive the light from them all, because he feels himself so dark and ignorant, that he cannot spare one ray of it, he may very plausibly be described as the most self-conceited of human creatures. It will be seen from the third of these letters, that the

Author is not unprepared for such imputations, and that he has taken some pains to examine how far they are reasonable. Merely on his own account, it would have been absurd to interrupt the discussion of the subject for the sake of repelling charges against the writer; but, seeing that his whole purpose was to discover a method which may assist himself and his readers in examining the question of the church, and in studying the theories of those who have written ably and profoundly upon it, it was essential that he should not be supposed to have adopted a false method at the very outset of his work. It was needful for him to prove, that he was not putting himself in the place of a teacher, but of a learner; was not assuming to be wiser than his neighbours, but was anxious to sit at their feet; was not angry with them for anything which they presumed to teach him, but only because, instead of taking the vocation of teachers, they formed themselves into a police to hinder the entrance of all wisdom but their own. I have not complained of the antiquarian theologians, because they reverence that which is past; but because they are cold and discouraging in their treatment of the desires which men feel in the present day, and cheerless respecting the future. I have not complained of those who look with admiration upon the present age, because they think that God has a great work for it to do, and has endowed it with gifts suitable to that end; but because, by rejecting the wisdom of former ages, and making light of men's pantings after something better than the routine of things around them, they forget their function, and make abortive their gifts. I have not complained of those whose eyes are wearily watching for the morning, because their hopes are too bright and gorgeous; but because they will not acknowledge that the day which they long for is already risen, and will be seen whenever it please God to disperse the mists and fogs by which the eyes of men have been hindered from discovering it. To shew that the half-scholastic, half-popular de

crees by which the realm of theological
thought has been portioned out into the
two provinces of Doctrine and Discipline,
and practical Christianity into the two
provinces of the Inward or Spiritual, and
the Formal or Ecclesiastical, rest on no
adequate foundation, of authority or of
reason; that we must go back to the
old principle of the church being a Kingdom, and steadily keep that principle in
sight, in all our studies respecting it—that
the Gospel is indeed the revelation of a
kingdom within us, a kingdom, of which
the heart and spirit of man can alone take
cognizance, and yet of a kingdom which
ruleth over all, and to which all other
kingdoms, even now, are reluctantly doing
homage, while they most struggle to
resist it—that the outward badges of this
kingdom are not inconsistent with its spiritual character, but uphold that character,
which would perish so soon as they were
removed—that this universal kingdom or
church is not the adversary of national
order and family life, but is the sustainer

and consummation of them both—that this church is not the adversary of man's reason and will, but is the appointed trainer of them both, for a state and a knowledge which, without her, they could never acquire; that she forgets her commission and underrates her powers, when she strives to crush them, and not rather to bring them forth, and give them the highest developement of which they are capable; and that they sink into a low, grovelling, despicable condition, when they refuse her guidance, and do not aspire after the glory to which she promises to lead them — this I thought not a needless undertaking in these days, and yet one in which a person who is himself only seeking for knowledge and light, might be profitable to others; because he who is willing to state his own difficulties, and sympathize with ours, is sometimes better able to help us, than those who are so much above us to be surprised at our ignorance, and impatient of our dulness.

3. Though it is impossible to convince all

readers that I am sincere in these professions, yet it was right to take all means for avoiding the appearance of self-conceit or presumption.　It seemed not easy to devise a better means than to connect my observations on these great and universal principles with certain events that were passing in the heart of a small, and comparatively unknown religious society.　A less ambitious mode of setting forth truths, which I believe to be important, than that of embodying them in " Letters to a Member of the Society of Friends" did not suggest itself to me.　But this, was not my chief motive for taking that course.　I felt deeply interested in the crisis which that body has reached, on account of its own members; I could not imagine one more strikingly illustrating the truths which I wished to assert, or one more full of instruction to ourselves ; and it was also very important to the object which I had proposed to myself, to show that my views were capable of a practical application ; that they explained the relation be-

tween the English church and the bodies
which have separated from it, and that
they hold out the very best hope of a reconciliation, without the sacrifice of our
position, or of any one real principle maintained by them.

There are only a few facts necessary
to support this opinion, with which the
Letters themselves will not sufficiently
acquaint the reader. That a body rose
up in this country, during the first half
of the seventeenth century, which assumed a more exclusively spiritual character than other sects both in its doctrines, its ministrations, and its discipline;
that it is distinguished by particular
badges of dress and speech; that it protests against wars, against worldly amuse-
ments, and against national worship; above
all, that it entertains a somewhat different opinion respecting the Scriptures from
that prevalent among Christians generally,
and that it has utterly renounced the
use of sacraments; that the members of
this body were much persecuted in for-

mer times, and are now rather popular in society, enjoying some immunities which do not belong to the other sects, and no longer regarded by those sects with dread or dislike, these facts, are notorious to all. The more recent events, of which the general reader cannot be supposed to be equally well aware, may be stated in a few words.

Every one knows, that the largest and most powerful settlement of Quakers is in America.   In that country, a few years ago, a man arose among them, who maintained that the modern Friends had departed from the maxims of their ancestors, and were approaching far too nearly to those of other religious bodies. " You speak of the doctrines of the Trinity and of the atonement," said he, " like the members of any common sect ; you are beginning to magnify the written Word far beyond its real worth ; you are forgetting all that your founders taught you respecting the Invisible Teacher and the Universal Light." This Elias Hicks preached many sermons,

in this strain, and made a number of converts to his opinions. After some conflict, they were disowned by the Quaker
body, and are now treated as schismatics.
But the spirit of inquiry which the American Quaker had excited, spread to England; and here it produced exactly the opposite effect to that which he would have
desired. A portion of the Quakers who
had mixed with other sects, and adopted
many of their habits and feelings, became
alarmed at the passages which he quoted
from their ancient oracles. They began
to assert more and more loudly, that
Hicks was indeed a heretic as to the
doctrines of Christianity, but had too much
pretence for calling himself an orthodox
Quaker. These statements awakened a
spirit which had been long dormant in the
elder members of the Society. They
affirmed that Quakerism, as taught by Fox
and Barclay, did not impugn the doctrines of Christianity, but presented them
in their highest and most spiritual form;
that, as soon as their teachings were for-

gotten, the Society would perish; and
that the restless disposition of the young
members was the most striking confirmation of their great doctrine, that spiritual
knowledge can only be acquired by the
submission of the heart and understanding
to a Heavenly Teacher. Between these
two classes there lies, of course, a large
body of moderate men, who endeavour to
explain away each of the extreme views,
and by all means to save the Society from
the dissolution which threatens it.

From this short statement, it will, I
think, be perceived, how much the great
experiment of the Quakers, its origin, progress, and results, may teach us respecting
our own position and our own controversies—respecting the best method of maintaining the one and settling the other—
respecting the power which we possess of
blessing those who curse us, if we will first
understand ourselves, and the certainty of
our deserving all their curses, and reaping
the fruits of them if we are heedless of
their, example, and emulate their divisions.

This volume, the reader will see, is a collection of letters already published in separate numbers. It will therefore contain some repetitions and recapitulations which may seem unnecessary. I perceive, also, that there are many slovenly phrases and disorderly constructions in it, of which I am sorry to have been guilty. A writer on theology is bound to keep the well of pure English undefiled, and to study diligently and observe carefully the laws of universal grammar, for he knows better than any other can, what frightful consequences have arisen from ignorance in the use of words, and from the habit of casting them into loose and popular moulds. The only excuse, (and it is a very insufficient one,) for any error of this kind which I may have committed, is, that I felt it a kind of impertinence to take pains with the composition of this work as if it was destined to live and be remembered in times to come. The words FUNGAR VICE COTIS, &c. express the height of my ambition.

If I should be permitted to give a brighter polish and finer edge to any sword in Christ's armoury, I shall be abundantly satisfied; what any one thinks about the material and fashion of the whetstone can signify little.

In the present volume I have discussed the SACRAMENTS of the Church. My great object has been to shew that in them the idea of Christianity as the revelation of a spiritual and universal kingdom, is set forth, that it depends upon the prominence given to them, whether this idea is upheld or lost, and that with the utter loss of it all the practical fruits of Christianity will disappear. In the next volume I propose, with God's permission, to examine the Laws, Government, and Order of the Kingdom, its Powers, and its Prospects; these will gradually exhibit themselves as we consider those great endowments of the Church,—the Scriptures, the Ministry, her Forms of Prayer, the Literature and History which she has been accumulating from age to age. In the third volume I propose to consider the Relation of this Kingdom to the different Kingdoms of the Earth, to Civil Government, to Social Life and Education.

ERRATA.

Page 3, lines 13 and 14 from bottom—*for* servant of servants, the slave, *read* servants of servants, the slaves.

" 3, line 6 from bottom—*for* the, *read* this.

" 5, line 12—*for* learning, *read* leaving.

" 18, line 9 from top—*for* denial, *read* deniers.

" 24, heading—*after* answer, *insert* to their difficulties.

" 36, line 7 from bottom—*read* so I believe it is—needful for, &c.

" 50, heading—*for* Lock, *read* Locke.

" 52, line 15 from bottom—*after the words* Dr. Cabanis, *insert* or have adopted the Eclectical Philosophy of Reid and Stewart.

" 63, line 4—*for* its, *read* their.

" 82, line 8 from top—*for* should, *read* she.

" 93, line 4 from top—*for* Son, *read* Sun.

" 97, heading—*before* Notions of repentance, *insert* introduces false.

" 100, line 8 from top—*omit* if

" 136, line 9 from bottom—*for* word, *read* Word.

" 153, line 13 from top—*for* men, *read* him.

" 164, line 1 from bottom—*dele* actually.

" 178, line 6 from bottom—*instead of* I was very fearful of two results—one was of impugning that grand truth of which, *read* I was very fearful of impugning two grand truths— one that of which, &c.

" 179, line 2, *dele* was.

" 204, heading—*for* the idea—*read* its idea.

" 225, heading—*for* raised, *read* caused.

" 236, heading—*for* preface, *read* purpose.

" 244, line 6 from top—*for* this Sacrament, *read* those Sacraments.

" 252, line 6 from top—*for* it, *read* their authority.

" 303, heading—*for* dogmas, *read* danger.

" 308, line 7 from bottom—*for* obligation, *read* abrogation.

LETTERS TO A MEMBER

OF THE

SOCIETY OF FRIENDS.

BY

A CLERGYMAN OF THE CHURCH OF ENGLAND.

No. I.

ON THE PRINCIPLES OF QUAKERISM,
AND THEIR CONNECTION WITH THOSE PROFESSED BY
OTHER SECTS AND BY THE CHURCH.

LONDON:
W. DARTON AND SON, HOLBORN HILL.

ERRATA.

Page 5, line 12.—For *learning* read *leaving*.

„ 36, 7 lines from the bottom.—Read, *So I believe it is —*
needful for, &c.

„ 63, line 4.—For *its* read *their*.

ADVERTISEMENT.

As these Letters may fall into the hands of persons who are not members of the Society to which they directly refer, it may be necessary to mention, that a sect has for some time existed in America, which maintains the doctrines of the early Quakers, respecting the Indwelling Word, and the Universal Saving Light and denies the doctrines of the Atonement and of the Trinity, in the sense in which they are generally received among Christians.

These persons, called Hicksites, are disowned by the Quaker body. Nevertheless a considerable number of the English Quakers affirm that the Society is not sufficiently explicit in its acknowledgment of what they consider the peculiar doctrines of the Gospel, especially that of Justification by Faith, or in its belief in the supremacy of Scripture over all spiritual communications and revelations. They contend that the Hicksites had good grounds for claiming the early Quakers as supporters of their tenets. They plainly signify their intention of renouncing fellowship with the Society, unless it formally disclaim those passages in the writings of their teachers which are capable of this interpretation.*

The Society is now nearly divided into those who hold these opinions—those who assert Quakerism to be the highest and purest Christianity, because it maintains spiritual life and teaching against forms, doctrines, and and the mere letter of Scripture—and those who wish

* A few of this class have already ceased to be Quakers.

to keep the Society together, by combining the views of the early Quakers, somewhat explained and modified, with those which are so strongly asserted by the discontented members.

The reader may suppose that these letters are addressed to a person who has adopted the views of any one of these parties, or is hesitating to which he should belong, or is equally dissatisfied with all.

The following list of books will give some notion of the activity with which this controversy has been carried on :—

The Beacon, by Isaac Crewdson.
The Beacon Controversy between the Society of Friends and Isaac Crewdson.
A Lamp for the Beacon.
Holy Scripture the Test of Truth, by Richard Ball.
The Truth Vindicated.
Strictures on the Truth Vindicated, by J. J. Gurney.
A Letter by John Wilkinson, on his resigning his Membership of the Society of Friends.
A Letter to John Wilkinson, by the Author of the Truth Vindicated.
A Letter to John Wilkinson, by Samuel Tuke.
Defence, &c., in Reply to the Beacon, by Dr. Hancock.
A Remonstrance to the Society of Friends, by B. Newton.
Appeal to the Society of Friends, by Elisha Bates.
Address on the Subject of Christian Baptism, by Elisha Bates.
Correspondence between Elisha Bates and Members of the Society of Friends.
Sermons, by Elisha Bates.
The Repository, a Periodical Publication, by Elisha Bates.
Report of the Proceedings of the Yearly Meeting, 1835.
            Ditto   Ditto   1836.
The Doctrine of the Inward Light considered, by J. E. Howard.
The Crisis, Parts I. and II.
Three Essays, by William Boulton.
Declarations by the Yearly Meetings of America.
Letters, by Philo and others, in the *Christian Advocate* and *Patriot* Newspapers.
Philo answered, by the Author of the Truth Vindicated.
Extracts from the Writings of the Early Friends, Published in Numbers,—&c. &c.

LETTERS

MEMBER OF THE SOCIETY OF FRIENDS.

No. I.

MY DEAR FRIEND,

IF the books and pamphlets which you so kindly
forwarded to me had been all written by members
of your Society, I should not have offered a word
of comment upon the subjects discussed in them.
As a private Christian, and as a student of ecclesiastical history, I must have been deeply interested in the controversy ; but I should have feared
to take part in it, lest I might excite your alarm,
and render your own inquiries less manly and less
effectual.

But I find that I should not be the first in-
truder. The Christian Observer and Eclectic
Review have volunteered their advice and encouragement to your disaffected members. Dr. Wardlaw of Glasgow, and Mr. Newton of Plymouth,
have made a formal attempt to detach them from
your communion. If I had agreed with them, I
would have left you in their hands.

B

I cannot, of course, pretend to their talents or their reputation, and in many respects I must be far less agreeable to your Society than they are. They meet you as members of a brother sect in committees and societies. I know you only as individuals with whom I have had much agreeable intercourse. Two of the four, probably, would account you allies in politics, — me, *ex-officio*, at least, an enemy. Moreover, in all questions respecting the dignity of Sacraments,—the connection between the constitution of the Church and the idea of Christianity, and the importance of Episcopal Ordination to Ministers, and of Apostolic Succession to Bishops—they would all agree with you in denouncing my opinions as antiquated, bigoted, and ridiculous.

But I do not approve of the method which these writers have adopted in addressing you. I dislike it from taste, from experience, from principle. To inspire men with contempt or indifference for those whom they have been taught from their infancy to admire and love — from the accounts of whose deeds and whose sufferings they have acquired their first perceptions of moral courage, and beauty and dignity of character,— from whose teaching they have probably first learnt to love their brethren, and revere the operations of their own spirits,—seems to me at all times a most heartless proceeding. I know the phrases that are used to defend it. I know what they say about the paramount worth and preciousness of truth. In my heart of hearts I own that preciousness, and hope that I may die rather than part with the sense of it. But I believe a tender and reverent spirit is inseparable from the love of truth. I never saw the last permanently strong where the other was wanting; and I·believe that anything which tends to weaken either, weakens both of them. I do not believe that those of your Friends, who are tempted by their own hearts, or the sneers of others, to think scornfully of their ancestors, will be half so zealous and affectionate in their determination to risk everything for the truth's sake, as those who retain a fond admiration for their beauties, and are willing to throw a veil over their deformities. I cannot forget that Ham was cursed though Noah was drunk. I cannot forget what his curse was; —the most affronting to the proud spirit of independence which dictated his crime—" A servant of servants shall he be." And a servant of servants—the slave of every fanatic, who is himself the slave of his own delusions — do those high-minded persons most generally become, who, after his example, commence their career of free inquiry with detecting and exposing the absurdities of their earthly or spiritual fathers.

A moral instinct would lead me to the conclusion; all the experiments that I have seen or heard of abundantly confirm it.

I have known persons, brought up in your Society, tempted by such arguments as Mr. Newton's pamphlet contains, to join our church. I

saw no reason to question their sincerity or their
zeal. But I observed that their views were always
more negative than positive; that they were led to
embrace a doctrine, not so much because they believed that to be true, as because they perceived
its opposite to be false; that they could perceive
what was inconsistent much more quickly than
they could recognize what was orderly; that their
minds were unquiet, unharmonious, and ricketty.
In a few years our proselytes departed, gone, as
we ought to have expected beforehand, to join or
establish some newer sect, denouncing us now, as
they have denounced you before ; destined shortly
to become as discontented with their present notions
as with either. I say it in sorrow, not in bitterness ; in reproach to *us* for seeking converts, by
exciting unhallowed feelings, not that I dare to
pass uncharitable judgment upon them. There
are instances equally recent and better known, of
some, high in cultivation, and, as I am well assured, in feeling and in honesty, who had fled to
us, from what most would consider, a much worse
faith than yours,—a faith which almost every Dissenter, Quaker, and Churchman thinks himself at
liberty to scorn and satirize. We raised a shout
when they joined us ; we listened with delight
while they laid bare the gross abominations of the
body from which they had escaped ; we thought
it a mighty compliment to our faith, that such
sagacious champions should adopt it ; we thought
we had a security for the permanence of their
convictions, which scarcely any other circum-

stances could have afforded us. Time showed
what sage prophets we were. These learned and
able Neophytes were as little constant as those
ardent ones; they soon left us, proclaiming to the
world as the reason of their departure, the grand
discovery, so often made before, (never, perhaps,
since the days of the Athenian sophists announced with equal boldness), that that only is
true which seems so to each man. Nothing can
abate the grief which we feel on their own account for their change. To us they have made
abundant compensation for our loss, by learning
us the lesson, never to be conned over or prized
too much, that the mind which is continually
dwelling on the falsehood of any system, even
though it do not in the least exaggerate the
amount or evil of that falsehood, contracts an incapacity for welcoming or perceiving truth, in
that or any other system.

On these grounds, if on no other, I should
have disapproved of the method which several
churchmen and dissenters have taken in their
recent addresses to you. All seem to make it
their business to undermine your respect for
your founders, and your belief in the *positive*
principles which they taught. I say positive
principles, for the Eclectic Reviewer, and Dr.
Wardlaw and Mr. Newton will be ready to
exclaim, ' we agree with George Fox and his
friends most entirely, in their denunciations
of your church, though their language may seem
to us occasionally too uncourteous, and though
we may believe that they pushed their objections

too far, when they attacked all pecuniary provision for the support of ministers.' These were their *negative* doctrines ; in these I am perfectly aware that they may find admirers and supporters in every vestry-room and tavern. But I need not inform *you*, that your early Friends rested their opinions on these subjects on certain principles relating to the heart and spirit of man. Whether they were good logicians in linking together these premises with these conclusions, is a point upon which you and I may differ, and upon which I may have occasion to speak hereafter. But this at least is certain, that they never for one moment severed in their minds the results from the principles. You are well aware, that in their mere hatred of Episcopacy, and of all the ecclesiastical institutions that had been connected with it, they would have found allies and abettors enough among the Presbyterians, Independents, Anabaptists, of the age in which they arose. Yet you know that they acknowledged no fellowship with these men, but denounced their doctrinalism in language as merciless as that which they used against our forms ; and that in turn they endured persecutions from them, at least as severe as any which they suffered from us after the Restoration. Why do I say these things ? not with a design which would be much more foolish than cunning, (and for my purpose quite unnecessary), of leading you to dread and dislike those who bear these names in the present day—but to show you, that they have no actual ground of sympathy with you, merely because they agree with you in detesting a third party. The reasons and principles upon which your Friends based their opposition to our priesthood and liturgy, are those very reasons and principles which Dr. Wardlaw and the Eclectic Reviewers would persuade you are utterly false and heretical, and inconsistent with Christianity.

Now here is the point on which I join issue with them. I say these principles were not false and heretical, and inconsistent with Christianity. A number of phrases and notions may have been appended to these principles, of which I utterly disapprove. In support of these principles, your friends may have declared themselves at war with everybody, and everybody at war with them. With this conviction on their minds, they may have denounced opinions as inconsistent with theirs, to which I most inwardly and heartily subscribe. They may have used language respecting the persons who maintained these opinions, which I think most extravagant and unreasonable; and a sense of the necessary connection between their doctrines and their denunciations, will have become stronger in their minds in proportion as their opponents identified the two together, and considered themselves as much bound to deny what the Friends asserted, as to assert what they denied. But through all this confusion, I perceive certain great truths maintained by these Friends, with a power and vigour which have scarcely been surpassed, and for the sake of which, I, for my part, can well forgive all the hard language used by them against institutions that I believe to be not only of incalculable benefit, but of divine appointment. Nor do I take any credit for this forgiveness. Every right-minded man must feel that one, who, from a sound and honest heart, directing a somewhat less sound understanding, curses him or that which he supposes to be him, is at all times to be loved rather than disliked. In such days as these, he will find it not only very pleasant, but very useful to compare such men with those who rave at him on no principle at all, or with those, still more odious, who, with a simpering face and civil compliments, are seeking to undermine him, because he is a witness for principles which they hate.

But this is not all. I maintain, that those truths which your early Friends asserted, lie at the foundation of the institutions which I love. In recognising those truths, I believe that I am upholding those institutions, and showing on what an immoveable basis they rest. It is nothing to me that Fox and Penn did not perceive this; it is nothing to me, that those who fought for these institutions against them, did not perceive it. Such contradictions and perplexities are not new. All history—ecclesiastical history most especially—is full of them. One set of men is busy in maintaining certain great and permanent bulwarks for truth, which, if they were taken away, the truth would be left without power, and without a witness. This is their task; they do not perceive exactly what they are defending, or why they are defending it. They often, therefore, fight ignorantly, blindly, passionately; but they do God's work, and future generations have reason to bless them.

On the other hand, it is given to some to perceive with great power the truth, or at least a portion of it, which is the secret foundation of those institutions, which is the living principle embodied and expressed in them. Such men often conceive a furious rage against the institutions themselves, as if it was they which kept the truth from manifesting itself to men—as if there were no way to exhibit it but to tear them away. For a long while this strife continues; one party doggedly upholding forms, the other vehemently asserting the Spirit independent of these forms. At length a time arrives, which is marked out by evident indications of Providence, for the termination of the controversy. Those who had been so diligent in upholding forms wax faint and feeble; they begin to think, that, after all, it does not so much signify to mantain this thing or that; concessions are very desirable; a little must be given up to keep the rest. On their side every thing is weak, flimsy, temporising; you see that they had no reason for defending that which they are now willing to abandon; you suspect (not unjustly or uncharitably), that they have exceedingly little reason for defending that which they wish to maintain.

Meanwhile, how fares it with the other party? Are the Spiritualists become more spiritual, now

that the defenders of forms have begun to care
less about them? I have told the truth respecting
us—you will not wish me to disguise it respecting you. You will not say that the Friends of
this generation, are as spiritual as those of the
first age. You will not contend—I think none
of your Society will contend—that there is as
clear a perception of the meaning of the words
by which you describe your faith, as there was
among those who first gave these words currency.
Do you not feel that the coin has been damaged,
and defaced, and depreciated; and when you pass
it, is it not with a melancholy thought, that it
had a real value once, only a conventional value
now? I find these acknowledgments in the writings
of Friends of all your parties, each, according to
their different temper or tendency, expressing them
differently. Your moderate party laments that there
is not the spirit of peace and unity among you
that there once was; the more decided of your
orthodox friends say, that there is not the submission to the voice of the Spirit, the humbleness,
the waiting, the self-annihilation that there used
to be; Mr. Howitt says you have lost all your
boldness and zeal; the Hicksites say you know
nothing of the sentiments of your early friends;
the Seceders say you know nothing of the doctrines of the Gospel. I should not myself have
ventured to say one of these things; but I find
them written and printed, and supported by the
testimony of persons who can be found to agree
on no other point. If, then, it be true, that there

has been a decay in the spiritual life of those who assert that which is purely and nakedly spiritual, coincident with a growing indifference to forms, among those who esteem forms, have we not reason to suppose, that a crisis is approaching? What if this state of things should continue? What if all outward witness should disappear from the world, just at the moment that the inward witness is most weak and ready to die? You have at once the Millenium of infidelity, that to which every man who wishes for the misery of his species—who wishes to see men changed into brutes—is looking forward with prophetic hope and exultation.

You see it must be so. If you look merely to us, you may exclaim with good reason,—' See the hour is approaching, which our great men told us of, when forms shall be universally contemned and trampled under foot.' But if you turn your eyes inward, have you not cause to exclaim,— ' The hour is coming, the dreadful hour, which those Friends would have contemplated as the Egyptian night of the world, when all apprehension of a spiritual principle is perishing out of the hearts even of us, its appointed witnesses.' What if these two facts, apparently so contradictory, should really be the joint indication of our state, and of the will of God concerning us? What if they should be saying to those churchmen who are willing to cast away forms,—' You are despising forms now, because you never knew the principle and the meaning of these forms; because you adopted them merely as traditionary heirlooms; because you did not own that there was a spirit and life in them.' What if they are saying to the Quakers,—' You have been fighting all along against that which was the standing witness, the divine scheme for asserting those spiritual truths, and sustaining that spiritual life, of which you thought that your own hearts were the safe depositaries;—now, if you would not see everything that you have accounted most precious wither before your eyes, you must turn to these forms for the preservation of them.'

I hope I have explained sufficiently how entirely my views respecting your present position, differ from those of the churchmen and dissenters who have hitherto addressed you. Instead of wishing to dispossess you of your patriarchal faith, I lament to see that that faith is not stronger and deeper. Instead of thinking you too firmly rooted in the principles which George Fox promulgated, I would, if I could, establish you more thoroughly in them. Instead of availing myself of the dissatisfaction which I see prevailing amongst certain members of your body respecting these doctrines, and saying—' See how nobly we support those other doctrines, to which you suppose they are opposed,'—I would do my utmost to persuade these persons, that the truths which they are just beginning to perceive, and are embracing with such a first-love ardour, are not inconsistent with the views which they are inclined to abandon, but can only be held soundly and

firmly when associated with them.   I wish to
make each one of your parties perceive, that it
has hold of a principle, which it must not for
all the world abandon; and I wish then to show
you by what means only you can uphold each of
these principles without mutilation, with real
power, and in harmony with the rest.   In plain
words, I wish not to unquaker you in order to
make you churchmen, but to teach you how to
be thorough Quakers, that you may be thorough
churchmen.   And this power of interpreting to
you your own position, of leading you to be what
each of you in some sort is striving to be, I possess, not in virtue of any talents or insight which
belong to me as an individual; — I possess it, because God has been pleased to place me on the
high ground of a church polity, from which I can
look down and see the directions that you are
taking, and show you to what point they are
leading.   This is the revenge that I wish to take
for any little insults that you or your fathers have
put upon us; this is the compensation that I
wish to render you for the injuries real or fancied which they or you may have endured at our
hands.

I consider George Fox a great man and an emi-
nent teacher.   Do not mistake me.   I do not
think George Fox had a commission to preach
the Gospel.   I do not think that, in the strict
sense of the word, he *did* preach the Gospel; but
I think that he was raised up to declare a truth,
without which the Gospel has no real meaning,

no permanent existence. All around him, George
Fox heard men preaching the doctrines of Christianity — preaching justification, sanctification,
election, final perseverance, and what not; exhibiting amazing logical subtlety; making nice distinctions, building parties upon them;—his heart
required something which none of them could tell
him.   All these doctrines were about God and
man,—all talked of a connection between God
and man; but all their theological skill, and all
their theories on human nature, seemed to George
Fox only to make the distance wider between
the poor man and his Lord. Impassable gulfs
of speculation intervened. There was a voice in
the heart of this mechanic which told him that
this could not be. As he studied his Bible to
understand that voice, he found continual encou-
ragements to believe that it could not be. At
the same time, the darkness that was over his
mind, his incapacity for realizing that communion which he felt must somehow be possible —
told him that the teachers of the day were in
some sense right, — that there is a deep fountain
of corruption in man, and that man, unless raised
out of that corruption, could never apprehend
God. The tumult within him becomes more and
more awful, till at last the bird of calm lights
upon the waters, and the day begins to dawn.
He perceives that man is a twofold creature;
that there is a power always drawing him down,
to which he is naturally subject, and to be subject
to which is death; but that there is also a power

drawing him up, a light shining in darkness, and
that to yield to that power, to dwell in that light,
is life and peace. To this conclusion he was
brought himself, and this, with the earnest zeal of
a lover of mankind, he longed to tell to all the
world,—' My brother, there is a light shining in
the darkness of your heart—the darkness has not
comprehended it,—Oh believe in that light, follow in that light, and be happy!'   Dare I say
that one atom of this belief was deception? Dare
I say that he was not taught this truth from
above?   Not till all the deepest and most sacred
convictions of my own heart have been resisted
or have perished; not till I become a traitor to
God's house, and deny all his discipline; not till
truth and error become hopelessly confounded
and intermingled in my mind.

In this part of Fox's life, in this part of his
discoveries, there is not one symptom of fanaticism or mysticism. Fanaticism glorifies its own
notions, and seeks to build a sect upon them;
but Fox spoke of a light which lighteneth every
man that cometh into the world.   Mysticism
glorifies its own feelings and revelations; but
Fox considered that the revelation to himself was
only the discovery of a truth which belonged alike
to all his brethren.   Am I to say with some of
your Friends at the Yearly Meeting, or with some
of other sects who have addressed you on your
errors, this only meant the natural conscience,—
only meant that! And what does that mean? It

is darkening counsel by words without knowledge, to substitute one phrase for another phrase. It is a cruel mockery of man, to tell him that a conviction which has been ripening in his heart through solitude and anguish, and almost despair; which has haunted him by day and night; which he has felt that the sin within him kept him from realizing; which, at last, when it has been born within him, he has embraced with more than a mother's joy:—I say it is cruel mockery of man, and a contempt of God, to say that this only means something to which you attach no meaning at all. Would it not be far more correct to say, that the conscience means this, and that the facts of the conscience can be explained on no other principle? Would it not be far more right to say, that precisely that which does awaken all thoughts, and reflections, and remorse in man whatever, and has its seat in what he rightly calls his conscience,—does arise from the presence of this Divine Word, and is the consciousness of that presence, and of His right to command us?

Does such an opinion sound startling to some men of this generation? I know that it does; I know that it must; but let me tell them, that it is a scheme of philosophy which they have adopted;—not, perhaps, from study; for there is a philosophy which dwells in the market-place as well as in the school, and which, when some great name has given it currency, becomes the inheritance of all, whom a

higher wisdom does not teach to reject it:—that
it is a scheme of a philosophy, and not their
religion which makes it offensive to them; for
had they looked into the writings of the oldest
and holiest men of the church, they would have
found that this tenet was no new-fangled one of
George Fox; but was part of the old faith of
Christendom. Nay, that the belief of a conscience which was natural, and not the sign of
something *supernatural*, would have been treated
by the wise men of old, as only a subtle form of
Pelagianism. For their minds, honest, yet quite
as reflective as ours, thought in this way,—That
in me which reproves sin—condemns sin—cannot
be sin. There is something in every man not
utterly hardened, which does reprove and condemn sin; if that something be natural, nature
has a good principle in it. This belief is Pelagianism. But if these reproofs of sin do not
arise from nature, they must arise from the connection between man, and a Being above man.
To talk, indeed, of this truth as an invention
of George Fox, betrays a lamentable ignorance
of the history of the church and of the world.
It is this feeling of a twofold life in man,—
of a struggle upwards and a tendency downwards, a stretching after, a yet unseen and un-
manifested friend of man, who seemed to be
upholding him against the enemies who were
continually striving to overwhelm him, against
his own nature, against the world around him,

which has in every age given an interest to the philosophy, and even to the mythology, of the old world. And what, if it could be proved that traditions sent from the east—from the chosen people —gave birth to these feelings? They were actual feelings, still; not merely expressed in books, but agitating, tormenting, and cheering the hearts of living men.

And if the denial of Fox's opinion betray an ignorance of what those men in past ages have experienced, who were not taken under God's especial training; they shew a still greater ig-ignorance of those seers and prophets, whom He raised up to be the teachers of His own peculiar people, respecting their condition and their relations to Him. For to what end was He training these holy men, by so many secret processes, and by such sore discipline; but to know Him as the secret Lord of their hearts,—to hold fellowship with Him by day and by night,—to recognise Him as the King of their nation, who directed all its plans according to justice and truth; to declare Him to their countrymen, as the Lord to whom they must submit their hearts, if they would not sink into slavery to their evil natures, and to the world around them;—the Lord, who by judgments and invitations was leading them away from the idols of sense, to seek Him and to find Him.

I say, he who does not perceive this, in the Jewish prophecies, is not alone wanting in spiritual discernment; he must despise and set at nought the letter of them. And surely, if these prophets were not mistaken, if they were not misled by their Great Teacher, the whole economy of the Jewish nation, the mysterious rite of circumcision, the law, the forms by which they were kept separate from other nations, were devised (not solely indeed, but mainly) for this end,—to guide the people out of sensible carnal worship, into that worship of the Lord of the spirit, who is spirit and who is truth. They who do not connect this notion with the belief of the oneness of God, and put forth the preservation of that truth, as the main purpose of the Jewish commonwealth, fall into great and hopeless cofusion; they fancy that the One Everlasting God, whom the Hebrews were taught to worship, was a God of Nature,—was some presiding power over nature; such as a Chaldean, Magian, or a Greek Pantheist might have reverenced; and not the God of Abraham, and Isaac, and Jacob,—emphatically, the God of Man.

Will it be said,—'But this Jewish people were the chosen of God; this revelation to them was a peculiar revelation. Fox was still wrong in speaking of this Word as dwelling with all men:' I ask, what was the promise made to the father of the Jewish people, but, "that in him, and in his seed should all the nations of the earth be blessed?" And when did the hope of the fulfilment of that promise dawn upon the Jew, but

when the unseen Word began to reveal himself to
his servants the prophets? Then, when they
began to feel their own real connection with this
Being, did they feel the possibility of all nations
being brought into the covenant; then were they
able, though dimly, to anticipate the manifestation
of this great Lord of their nation, as the King
who should reign over the Gentiles, and in whom
the Gentiles should trust. They felt that their
Lord was the Lord of Man; and that, as such, he
would be revealed.

You see with what earnestness I maintain the
truth of that doctrine of your founder, which he
has of late, by members of your society and of
other societies, been so denounced for upholding.
You see that I do not wonder he should have
asserted this truth with such passion and vehe-
mence. You see, that I acknowledge it as that
which is implied in all Christianity; and the utter
loss of which, out of the minds of men, seems to
me to involve the extinction of Christianity itself.
You see that I base these conclusions,—not on
the witness of my own heart, merely, answering to
his heart; not on the evidence, merely, of Pagan
records, shewing that men through many ages
were straining after this idea, if haply they might
feel after it and find it;—but upon the revelation
of God himself,—upon the evidence which the
records of Scripture furnish, that it was by leading men into this truth, that He prepared them
for the kingdom of his Son. And can I help

feeling joy, and wonder, and thanksgiving, and new assurance that we are living under the dispensation of a Gospel addressed to the poor, when I see a truth, which the wisest and best men of the old world,—which the Athenian Plato, which the Alexandrian Philo, (though a Jew, and living almost on the borders of the Gospel kingdom,)—were only toiling to find, proclaimed aloud by a poor, untaught English handicraftsman; to hear the fact announced by him to English peasants, with more confidence than either Isaiah or Jeremiah dare have assumed, in speaking to their own Israelites; that GOD, in very truth, is not far from every one of us; but that in Him we live, and move, and have our being.

But you observe how I have limited all my language upon this subject. I have said, that this great truth is the preparation for Christianity, that it is involved in Christianity, and that, though it may not be the first apprehended by every Christian,—nay, may not be formally apprehended by him at all; yet lies at the root of all his spiritual life. But I have not admitted that it *is* Christianity itself. I will illustrate this distinction, in reference to what I consider the three great ideas of Christianity,—Justification of the conscience, the Atonement for mankind, and the Trinity.

I. Let us consider, what were the actual wants and anxieties of the men in the old world, who experienced the struggle between the light and darkness of which we have spoken. Must not such thoughts as these have been continually present to their minds:—Here are two powers struggling within me, one good, one evil; sometimes one prevails, sometimes the other; sometimes the darkness seems about to be scattered, sometimes the light seems almost quenched: but I, who am I, in the midst of all this awful struggle? Do I belong to the light, or to the darkness? Of which have I a right to call myself the child now; of which shall I be the child for ever? The consciousness of evil, of rebellion against a power continually exerting itself for my good, testifies against me; my belief in the graciousness, in the mightiness of the Being who is on my side, speaks in my favour: but then, what awful outward facts seem to corroborate the former conclusion! All the outward sicknesses, sorrows, troubles of the world, seem to be lifting up their voice to condemn me,—to be proving that my unseen Friend is either not omnipotent, or that His forbearance with my often repeated disobedience will at last have a limit;—and what is that limit? May not Death at last decide this struggle? may he not be God's permitted minister, to decide it against me? These thoughts do not imply the least unbelief of a future state; that was not the anxious question of the Heathen, as all their mythology proves: but it was, What shall I be, in that state? Some etherial particle in me may mount up and enter into rest, and even be united to the divine essence;—but will it be myself? I cannot believe that I shall die, in the sense in

which all the things about me die. Whenever I
feel that I am at all, I feel that I am immortal; I
may lose the thought while I am speculating;
I can never lose it while I am acting and living.
But this is the point,—shall good or evil, shall
light or darkness be that to which I am united,
when all the spiritual energies, by which I seem
to have asserted my connection with something
better than myself, shall be as much crushed by
pain, and weakness, and death, the great consummation of them, as the energies by which I eat,
and drink, and walk? These, I think we may
perceive satisfactorily, were the real, the practical
questions which agitated the minds of the better
men (nay, in some sense of all men) in the old
world.   Scholars have not at all times perceived
that this was the real jet of their inquiries, partly
because they have not been sufficiently conscious
of the same anxieties within themselves, to be
capable of interpreting them in others; partly,
because they have been misled by the language
of Cicero, and those who lived at a time when
philosophy was pursued rather to gratify a taste,
than to satisfy a want; and, consequently, when
questions respecting the permanence of the
spiritual part in man, the existence in him of
something immaterial and indiscerptible, took
place, of the far more deep and interesting pro-
blem—Who am I? What will become of me? The
Jews were taught, by their divine Trainer, to experience precisely the same difficulty, only with
still greater power and reality, only with a

brighter and better hope as to its solution. They felt in themselves this struggle; but then, taking hold of the covenant, with Abraham, Isaac, and Jacob, they were able to believe that the righteous Lord, who revealed himself to their hearts, was indeed their Lord, and would be so for ever and ever; and coming with the appointed sacrifice, at the appointed time, in the appointed place, to the appointed priest, they were able to believe that that covenant had not been destroyed through their iniquity; that they still had an inheritance in the King of their nation; that they should behold his face in righteousness; and thus, when his glory was manifested to the whole earth, they should partake in it. Yet it was a hope still;—still the doubt rested upon their minds, and at times would gain a dreadful ascendancy,—Is this evil and accursed nature which belongs to me, my ownself? Are not its evils imputed to me? Are not they counted a part of me? Will not death destroy that nature; and when he destroys it, shall I be spared? These questions, we say, must have occupied men, not because they did not possess the light which lighteth every man that cometh into the world, but because they did possess it;—yea, according to the degree in which that light was revealed to them, or in which they followed it. And it is on this ground that I say that the doctrine of George Fox is not *itself* Christianity; while I argue just as zealously, that it is implied in Christianity; and, that they who would deny it, must be

driven to great shifts to explain what Christianity
is. For I say, that when the Word was made
flesh, and dwelt among us; when, in that flesh
He passed through the trials, and troubles, and
conflicts of man; when in that flesh He died
a real death; when He rose again triumphant
over that death; that he answered these dreadful doubts and questions of the spirit of man
at once, and for ever;—and that no other
answer whatsoever could have satisfied them.
Then was that question, Who am I?—am I to
account myself the child of light, or the child of
darkness?—am I to believe that God looks upon
this evil nature as myself, or as my enemy?—am
I to believe that He regards me as His child, or
merely as His servant—as one whom He wishes
to save from death and sin, or one that He is
only content to save if I please him?—at once
resolved by the most wonderful demonstration
that men or angels ever saw. By death He condemned sin in the flesh—by His resurrection He
justified all that believe. Here is the grand distinction at once established which men had all
their lives been crying after; here is that justification of the person of man—here is that condemnation of his nature which he requires; here
is the assertion finally made, man united to
Christ is a holy and righteous creature—man
separated from Christ is married to his evil
nature, is under a curse. Here is God, by
raising up Christ from the dead, justifying men
from all things from which they could not be

justified by the law of Moses—assuring them that
this is their true and proper state, that which
every man, since Christ has died and risen,
may claim for himself, and that, by claiming it,
he looks upon his sins in their proper light—as
plagues from which he hopes to be separated for
ever; upon Christ's righteousness as that which
he enjoys now and hopes to enjoy for ever. Now,
I say that this view of justification is that which
brings peace to the heart and spirit of man—
is that view of it which a sinful man, under the
goadings and anguish of conscience, embraces
with such delight and rapture;—that this is the
doctrine set forth in the Epistle to the Romans,
and the progress to the discovery of which is
brought out with such wonderful power and life
in the seventh chapter of that Epistle. Nay, I
will venture to stake the truth of this assertion
upon the acts and records of convictions, and
conversions, and experiences, whether found in
the writings of Quakers, or Methodists, or Calvinists. I will be bold to say, and I am ready to
make good my assertion by actual proof, that if
you separate in those records that which the
confession of the party shows to have actually
brought peace to the conscience, from the notions
and opinions which the teaching of particular
doctors may have identified with it, you shall
perceive that it was the belief, that one whom the
heart had long been struggling to find,—with
whom it had felt that it had the most intimate
connection,—whom it felt had been reproving

it for its sins, offering it peace and life,—had, by
a series of outward acts, demonstrated that the
struggling spirit was acknowledged by Him,—
that he was on its side in the dreadful battle that
was fighting,—that the battle in fact was His
own, and that He would, in time, trample all its
enemies under its feet,—that it was this belief,
and no other, which brought them to comfort,
and confidence, and hope.

In what way, then, is this faith inconsistent
with the doctrines of G. Fox, and your early
Friends? It is inconsistent with them in this
way—that they consider the acts which the Word
did, in the flesh of man, were chiefly valuable as
they showed what acts he would be doing in the
heart of each man. " The humiliation and sufferings, which were the great characteristic of
His work, is that which the Word is seeking to
produce in you and in every man. You see here
the type of what he would be doing in you,
crushing, extinguishing all selfish powers, feelings, exercises, bringing everything into obedience and captivity." Now this is excellent, if
only the man first understands himself; if only
first he knows what his relation to this divine
Word is ; if he only knows that that which will
be put down within him is not himself but his
enemy ; if only he were taught beforehand that
he himself is united to Christ, and is an object of
His complacency. Without this, all these notions
of crushing and extinguishing self become mere
burdens to the conscience ; they convert every-

thing that a man does, or thinks, or speaks, into
sin,—make him regard all the operations of his
faculties, and even of his affections, as unholy,—
make him at the same time feel that he is unholy
for not exercising those feelings and faculties,—
make him despair at last of attaining the final
end of complete self-annihilation. This has been
the effect upon all honest men and women, whether Romanists or Protestants, of *substituting* the
doctrine of the Word in man, for justification by
the death and resurrection of Christ.

But having made this concession to your seceding Friends, I must tell them frankly, that
when they set up this doctrine of justification
against the doctrine of the Word speaking to
man and in man, instead of merely saying that
one is not included in the other, they are at once
cutting away the foundations of their own truth,
and doing what in them lies to hinder themselves
from ever attaining the knowledge of any other
truth.

I speak earnestly on this subject, because I see
with grief, but not surprise, the course which
those Friends are taking. They have felt the
need of something that your early writers do not
supply them with, for the peace and satisfaction
of their consciences. So far well; it is their
duty to " seek for peace and ensue it;" and if
they find their brethren are neglecting the only
means of attaining this peace, they are right
to warn them. If they see any sect arising up
among you here, or in America, which not only

overlooks these doctrines, as George Fox in a
great measure did,—but which sets the doctrines
of early Quakerism formally against them, which,
generally speaking, he did not,—they are right to
show the necessity of that which these men reject. But here ends their commission. When
they take upon them to say, that certain principles are not true, because they have discovered
some to be true, which other people fancy to contradict them ; when, in order to accomplish this
work, they not only set at naught all their own
authorities, but venture into depths wherein, I
must plainly tell them, they need more learning,
as well as more spiritual insight than they at present possess, to advance a single step ; — talking
about the doctrines of the fathers of the Christian
church, and at one swoop denouncing them all as
men ignorant of the Gospel, merely because they
maintained a truth which St. Paul preached to the
Athenians,—then I do begin to tremble for these
Friends, for that they seem to me to confound
that which they have felt with that which they
have acquired from very untrustworthy sources,
and for that their faith seems to me very slightly
mixed with humility. Yet I should not have un-
dertaken the office of counselling them, if I did not
perceive that they were choosing for their guides
persons who, I know, can only mislead them.

There are some supporters of the Establishment, with a little sprinkling of philosophy, belonging to the school of Mr. Scott and Mr.
Newton, but without possessing any of the

heartiness and simplicity of those excellent men,
who seem to make it their object to prove to the
world, that whatever principles are found in other
men's writings, if agreeable to what they taught,
are useless—if different from them, are mischievous. They begin with affirming, that the
doctrines of the Reformers are merely those promulgated by these doctors of the eighteenth century, and then they proceed to contend, that any
thing that was held before the age of the Reformation is worse than suspicious.

In this feeling, Mr. Osburn's book against the
Fathers seems to have originated, and it pervades
our religious newspapers and magazines. Such
writers as these offer themselves as very natural
allies to the discontented or factious of any party;
but woe to those who seek light from them! It
is not merely that they will never be able to pass
beyond a very narrow circle of views and opinions,
—it is, that even these views and opinions will,
in an exceedingly short time, be converted into
mere words and phrases. The men I speak of are
not merely unjust to the Reformers and the Fathers,
they are unjust to the teachers whom they idolize.
There was a life and sincerity of devotion about
those teachers, with which every good man must
sympathise. He may not think them great theologians; he may think, that when they tried to
systematize that which they had experienced, they
fell into considerable perplexities, did injustice to
others, and very often misrepresented themselves.
But he will not for that cease to honour that

light in them, which he sees to have been from
above, or doubt that they were raised up to do a
good work, which, with more enlarged perceptions, they might not have accomplished so well.
It is only when their names are used by men on
whom scarcely a skirt or rag of their mantle has
fallen, not to uphold precious principles concerning the life of man, but to upset other truths and
principles also most precious, interfering it seems
with the system in which those principles are embodied, that we feel even tempted for a moment
to speak slightingly of them. These observations
you, I am sure, will feel to be applicable to the
present crisis in your Society. Your seceding
Friends are setting up the doctrine of justification
by faith, against the belief of the Word dwelling
in the heart of men; the two, they say, cannot
exist together. But I say, that the fact of justification which St. Paul taught,—the fact of justification which Luther proclaimed to the world,—
the fact of justification in which Scott and Newton, and all other men, have found peace and satisfaction, is not at variance with this belief, but
necessarily linked to it, and is beautifully in-
terterpreted by it. Nay, I will even venture
what may seem strong and startling assertions,—
that the men of whom I speak are undermining
the doctrine of justification by faith; that the
cause of the discontent with which it is viewed
by many holy and good men, who in their hearts
recognize the principle of it, is, that it has
been severed from the doctrine which George Fox

taught; and that we shall never understand how necessary it is to the personal life of every man, until the connection is re-established. When once the idea of union with Christ ceases to be at the foundation of this doctrine, the phrases that we are accounted righteous for Christ's sake; that sin is not imputed to us; that the righteousness of Christ is imputed to us; — immediately assume a form which may well seem frightful and dangerous to one who worships a God of truth, and feels that the acknowledgment of truth in Him is essential to any truth and sincerity in our own minds. Vainly and impudently do men pretend that these fears are the effect of carnal reasoning, and the unwillingness of the proud heart to stoop to God's revelation. The persons who most abhor the notion of God being guilty of a fiction, are those who are most willing to receive that revelation as their teacher, and would be most ready to own that they should not have had that abhorrence, at least in nearly the same strength, if their love of truth had not been cultivated by its pure and holy instructions. Yet I am most willing to allow, most anxious to assert, that these words are not objectionable; that we cannot dispense with them; that we cannot, without the greatest peril to sound divinity, explain them away; that all their seeming evil has arisen from the carnal and intellectual notions with which persons who boast of high spirituality, and of humbling their understandings, have encompassed them. Once admit, that by

the very constitution of humanity, a man, is
righteous only as he is united to Christ, that all
righteousness in self is a contradiction in terms,
and the notion of a sinner being accounted
righteous is converted into the sternest reality.
His Divine Judge looks upon him according to
his true state, not according to that fictitious,
anomalous, monstrous state, to which by sin he
has reduced himself; his Divine Judge calls upon
him to believe in the light, that he may be the
child of the light; to assert that position, to
claim that union which has been asserted for him.
Rejecting this glorious invitation, he believes in a
lie,—he makes a lie. The light is come into the
world; he loves darkness rather than light, because his deeds are evil. Hearing the proclama-
tion of his freedom, and believing it, the sins
which have held him down, and of which he
seemed to be a part, become separated from him,
—are no more treated as himself. He enters into
the mind of God respecting them; he hates them
as God hates them; he abjures them, for he feels
that the same love which embraces him loathes
them. He becomes the inheritor of a righteousness which is his own and is not his own; which
is his as the light of the sun is his, because he enjoys it, is warmed by it as long as he walks in it; but
which, the moment he claims it as his property,
deserts him as the light and heat would desert
him, if he thought that the stock of sunshine
which was given him yesterday would serve him
for to-day. If you meditate upon the thought

c 5

which I have just set before you, you will see, I
think, that no language so well as that which has
been constantly employed in all formularies since
the Reformation, describes this justification, or
explains the connection between the justification
of Christ, by God raising him from the dead, and
the justification of each man's conscience by his
belief in Him who raised Christ from the dead.

But you will perceive also, I believe, that this
life-giving truth in the mouths of those who seem
to assert it most vehemently, has been changed
into a dead and spiritless dogma. The justification by faith, taught by the modern Calvinists,
and not less by the Arminian Methodists, is not
that justification by faith which wrought such
wonders at the time of the Reformation; it is a
hard notion, galvanized occasionally by the hatred
of its supporters to some other truths which they
fancy opposes it, but at other times dry, withered,
cheerless. Your seceding Friends will find, whether they expect it or no, that those to whom they
fly for refuge from the unsatisfactoriness of Quakerism, instead of being carried, as Luther and
the Reformers were, out of themselves, by this
faith of union with the righteousness of another,
are debating all day long questions which begin
in self and terminate in self; questions about the
nature of faith and the degree of assurance ; how
much apprehension, and how many spiritual experiences go to establish a man's claim to be a
child of God, or whether some strong belief, some
inward witness that he has been elected to eternal

life, do not supersede the necessity of such inquiries altogether. In either case, what becomes of that truth with which Luther shook the Seven Hills? Witnesses, apprehensions, assurances!— how he detested the words! How utterly Popish they sounded to him! But, again and again I ask, How have these notions intruded themselves, under cover, too, of that creed which was once used for the very purpose of setting the conscience free? Is it not because the doctrine of an actual union of the spirit of man with Christ has been lost sight of? And is not this also the reason why the distinction between the flesh and the spirit in man has been so forgotten and misinterpreted,—why the conflict described in the 7th of Romans has been a subject of such fierce controversy,—why the blessings and curses of God, the Gospel, and the Law, are not directed against different parts of the same man,—the blessings to himself, the curses against the evil nature to which he has no right to be in bondage,—but against two sets of persons, whom the minister assumes the divine prerogative of defining? And has not the same cause produced another effect, perhaps more melancholy?

Is not the union of the spirit of man with Christ treated as some high esoteric doctrine, a part of the Christian cabala, to be spoken of for the benefit of the initiated; but with which few have any concern. Such a view of the subject is inevitable, when this union is supposed not to be an actual *fact*, but only what may *become* a fact, if men are enabled by diligent striving, or by the mere favour of God, to realize it. But who can tell the miserable effects produced by this view? When that which should cheer the labourer, as he walks in the morning to his plough; which should be with the weaver, at his loom; which is the only comfortable security for the honesty of the shopkeeper; which only can give cheerfulness and hope to the physician, in his ungrateful toil; which should go to the desk with the attorney, if he is to be anything better than a pettifogger;—is kept for those who aspire to the very heights of saintship—alas! what must become of the faith and life of a nation?

Surely, every step taken in religious notionality and dogmatism, where this habit of teaching and feeling prevails, must be only a step into greater self-delusion; surely, it may not be without truth, that men of experience say, that any servant, or workman, or physician, or attorney, may be more safely trusted than one who has the phrases of the sanctuary in his mouth, and is able to turn them to the purposes of his craft.

II. The Reformers declared the doctrine of which I have been speaking to be the *sine qua non* of the church's life. So I believe it is—needful for each man, and therefore necessary to a church composed of men. But there is an easy transition from this true and sound assertion to one which I maintain is utterly unsound and false; that justification is the foundation of a church.

The Calvinistic bodies, here and on the Continent, identify these two propositions: see the consequence.—The justification of my conscience, by belief in Christ as the crucified and risen Saviour and Lord, is that which I mean by this doctrine: consequently, this being the foundation of the church, the church comes to mean a certain number of men whose hearts and consciences have been purified by faith. This sounds very well; but now for the practice. The question arises,— Who are these men;—how is it to be ascertained that they have formed right apprehensions respecting their own purification of heart and conscience? Here begins a controversy. One party says,—the acknowledgment of the doctrine of justification, and of such doctrines as are necessary to it, is the bond of our union: another says,—no; the mere doctrine of justification is not justification; you must ascertain the reality of each person's faith in Christ, or you cannot admit him to your communion. The arguments of each side against its opponents have been admirably borne out by facts: those who have set up the creed or notion of justification, as the bond of fellowship, have made it evident by their practice how vast the difference is between the literal acknowledgment of a notion, and the practical belief of a truth. Those who have adopted the other method of ascertaining, by an examination of convictions, experiences, signs of faith, who is the true, and who is not the true believer, have confirmed all that their opponents prophecied, as to the substitution of something else, for the faith which is assumed to be so self-sufficing. All the history of sectarianism, from the Reformation downwards, may be said to be little more than a series of expedients to obtain tests of one kind or the other, which should be satisfactory; or to reconcile the two kinds of tests together. The dogmatists find, one notion after another must be taken into their creed, in order to guard this tenet of justification; but the more bulwarks they raise, the more do their opponents proclaim them to be the enemies of spiritual life. The men of experiences and apprehensions invent new and more subtle tests, to determine the state of the affections and feelings of their worshippers; and the other side cry out, that they are either running into the most extravagant fanaticism, or framing snares for the conscience, or substituting feeling for faith. Now it seems to me, that all these things have happened inevitably; that the notion of building up a church upon the assertion of a fact, expressly concerning the distinct life of each man, is an absurdity and a contradiction which, in the first place, tends to destroy the meaning of that doctrine itself; in the second place, leads to interminable strife and separation. I say, that the life of a church is based upon a deeper foundation than this, even upon that foundation upon which the doctrine of justification itself is based,— the ATONEMENT made for *mankind*, in the person, and by the incarnation and death, of Jesus Christ.

In this assertion, as far as it is opposed to the doctrine of particular redemption, i. e. a redemption made for those who believe in the redemption, I am supported by your early Friends. They spoke of an universal saving light, given to mankind; and they said, that the church was called out, by the Spirit, to be a witness for this light, and that it could not be built upon individual notions and conceits. These are two grand principles—like the one of which I have already spoken, I conceive very imperfectly carried out; but, nevertheless, hinting at the principle upon which the universal church is grounded.

My complaint of these doctrines is, that, instead of leading us forward to the privileges of the new dispensation, they throw us back upon the old. If the Friends were right, as I believe, in their assertion, that the Word lightened every man that came into the old world, what did the death of Christ, if it only procured a universal saving light, obtain for men more than they possessed already? This question has often been asked by the Calvinist, and I fear no satisfactory answer has been given to it. Surely, the mere words, *universal* and *saving*, are not worth much, in pointing out the difference between the new state and the old one: and yet they are worth something in another way, as pointing out a very important distinction, which both Fox and Barclay seem to be aiming at, but not clearly to perceive; which their Calvinistic opponents entirely overlook. I have shewn already, that the same Word who revealed himself to the hearts of particular men, as their

Lord and Friend, revealed himself also as the King and Lord of a *nation*. From the moment that the Jewish commonwealth was constituted, according to the divine plan, we see the idea of a Mediator beginning to dawn through its various institutions.

It is not in any artificial types, in the interpretation of which so much perverse fancy may be exercised, that we recognize this idea. It is implied and involved in the whole constitution. God reveals himself to his people, as an absolute Lawgiver, frowning upon sins,—sins which they have actually committed; and yet these sinners are still partakers of His covenant; they constitute a holy and righteous nation. How are these two ideas compatible? How shall each man feel himself to be a sinner, and yet feel that the body to which he belongs is a pure and holy body? The Jewish mind, educated by its divine law, is itself taught to answer the question; the feeling is awakened in it, of the necessity of a Mediator between it and God; the reason is taught to feel that there must be such a Mediator, that it must be in Him that the nation is constituted; and that each member of the nation is pure and holy, —not in himself separately, but as he views himself in connection with his nation, and so in connection with its Head.

Thus David and Isaiah learned to feel that their glory was not in being David and Isaiah, not in being prophets chosen and appointed of God; but in being *Israelites*. All their privilege of drawing nigh to God, belongs to them in that capacity; they renounce it when they set up any individual distinction or glory. All the way through the Jewish history, we shall find this idea of the nation subsisting in a Mediator,—perfect, holy, and righteous in Him,—coming forth with greater life and clearness, while we see a few gradually led to understand who and what this Mediator must be; that His character must be the same as the character of the Absolute Being with whom he connects man; that He must, in the highest and most wonderful sense, be one with Him; yet that He must be also perfectly one with the creatures whom he unites to their Maker.

If by the light of this idea, and of the other, which you see is included in it,—that all unity as a nation only lasts while the members of it regard themselves as one in this great Being,—you study the institution of *Sacrifices*, you will be at no loss I think, to perceive the meaning of an ordinance, which, when it is disjoined from men's position in a commonwealth, and is refered merely to their individual state, becomes utterly unintelligible. The Jewish nation, being united together in one Head, is a holy and righteous nation. Every act done by any man in disobedience to the Law of God, is renouncing his connection with the Head of the nation, and with the other members of it. It is setting up a selfish life, it is renouncing the privileges of a Jew. For this act, he comes with the sacrifice appointed by God, offering it, through the Priest, and with confes-

sion of his sin; he is pardoned, and admitted back
into the privileges of a member of the whole nation.   The sacrifice he offers is determined by the
Law, not by his choice; he may not offer a heca-
tomb instead of a single ox, —value is not the criterion of worth.

If you carry the hints which this study has
afforded you into an examination of the Pagan
records, you will find the same idea of mediation,
mixed with grosser hints and anticipations of an
incarnation; you will find sacrifices an essential
national institution; and you will find the grand
difference to be, that the Jew has a knowledge of
the character of the Being he worships,—worships
a God of righteousness; looks upon his own nation as selected to be a witness for the character
of that Being; looks upon the Mediator as partaking in the feelings of man,—not because he is
less righteous than the Absolute Being,—but because his righteousness is best manifested through
those feelings and that sympathy; and, as the
consequence of all these views, considers sacrifice
as an appointed means of restoring communion
between himself, his fellows, and his God.   That
the heathen, starting from a wrong view of God's
character, — looking at him primarily as a God
of power, — turned for sympathy to mediators
who shared in their weaknesses and sins, —
turned to sacrifice as a means of averting the
wrath or conciliating the favour of a capricious
being.

Now the necessity for this Mediator, and all

the ideas connected with Him, did not grow out
of that belief of a Divine Word dwelling within
each particular man, but were the ground of it.
That principle which had relation to the commonwealth, went before that principle which had relation to the individual.   An apprehension of this
truth, I suppose, is indicated by the distinction
which your Friends draw between the universal
saving light, and the revelation of the Word to
each particular heart.   And their error is exactly
that which I have pointed out already, that they do
not see that the yearning in the hearts of men before the coming of Christ was not for a light, since
that they had already, but for that to which the
light pointed—for a personal manifestation ; for
some one who should bind men together in one
commonwealth, by binding them first to God,—
one who should appear as the Head of the race,—
to establish a communion between the race and
its Father, and by doing that, should bind the
members of the race to each other.   The more
light men had respecting their relations to each
other, the more they will have felt the want of
this ; the more they will have sighed for perfect
communion with God and each other ; the more
will they have felt that none could effect this
communion but He who was revealed as the
Head and bond of their society, and at the same
time as the Mediator between it and God ; and
the more they will have expected that when
this Being did come, He should identify himself thoroughly and perfectly with man, and

that He should offer some real sacrifice to God.
All this, we say, was accomplished wh en
was made flesh, when He passed through all
the stages of human life and human suffering;
when he offered up the perfect sacrifice, holy, acceptable, and unspotted to God and to his Father.
By never committing one act of selfishness,—by
identifying himself perfectly with the meanest of
the race, He proved himself to be the Head of
the race; and he was perfectly acceptable and
well-pleasing to God, in that he was the perfect
image and express likeness of His own love.
The only sacrifice with which God could be
pleased—the only offering that could satisfy His
righteousness and His love, was made upon Cal-
vary, and by that act, we say, God is reconciled
to mankind,—mankind is shown to be constituted
and established in Christ, and, through Christ, it
is possible for God to maintain a perfect fellowship with man.

These ideas of sacrifice and satisfaction, and of
Christ reconciling the father to us, have often excited the displeasure of your writers, and of late
have been almost denounced by good and able
men among ourselves; but you will find, I believe, that all that is reasonable in the displeasure
which they occasion, has arisen from the shameful perversion of these words, by those who have
refused to consider the atonement as made for
mankind; have refused to connect the atonement
with the idea of a commonwealth or society; have
altogether overturned the very idea of it, by con-

sidering it as performed to deliver some individual
men from the wrath of God. In consequence of
these notions, the three views of satisfaction, each
of which, when distinguished, is good, have been
confounded into one hideous, and well-nigh blasphemous notion. The satisfaction offered to the
perfect love of *God,* by the perfect and well-
pleasing sacrifice of Christ, — the satisfaction offered to the *Law* by giving up the body to death,
(a satisfaction which, in some sort, the death of
every man makes, but which was only complete
when the Head of the race gave himself up to
death), and the satisfaction offered to the *evil
spirit,* by giving up to him all that he can rightly
claim, while all that is real and precious is redeemed out of his hands;—these three notions
have been horribly mixed together, and that which
Bishop Hooper, (the most Genevan, be it remembered, of all the Reformers), called a satisfaction
to the devil,* has been described by persons who
pretend to adopt the theology of the Reformers,
as a satisfaction to God. In like manner, the
idea of a sacrifice to reconcile the Father to us,—
an idea which becomes actually necessary when
we consider on what conditions it is possible for a
perfectly loving Being to hold communion with a
sinful one; and when we make communion the
end of the reconciliation, is changed into the

* I am happy to see that this passage in Bishop Hooper's sermons, is retained for the instruction of the religious world, even in
the mangled edition of the works of the Reformers, published by
the Religious Tract Society.

dreadful doctrine of Dr. Watts' hymn, about
" the rich drops of Jesus' blood, which calmed
the Father's frowning face."

But to wind up my remarks upon this subject,
it is upon this ground of an actual reconciliation,
effected for mankind in the person of Christ, that
we say a church universal only can stand. This
being once effected, the Spirit of God can come
down and dwell among men; and we agree with
you, that it is the Spirit only who can call forth
a church, and establish it upon this basis.

But then, we say, that the Spirit has done this
work; that the Spirit did come down on the day
of Pentecost, and gather together the church, and
united it together in the name of the Father, the
Son, and the Holy Ghost, and that he has never
deserted it since. The universal church, we say,
stands, the great representative of mankind,—redeemed and restored mankind,—and this it would
do, though it had but a dozen members, and
though but one of those members really understood his position. The unbelieving world, separated and dividing, and each following his own
interests, is altogether an anomalous, monstrous
body,—it is a practical contradiction and lie. This
is our correction of your notion of an universal
saving light over the world. We say that the
church is that saving light to mankind; that it
speaks peace to every man as a man; but that it
tells him he must enter into the conditions of a
man, — must take up the position of a man, —
must renounce his individuality, — must become

member of a body, in order that he may enjoy all those privileges which Christ has claimed for him, and which are laid up for him in Christ.

On the other hand, to those sects which set up the notion of individual faith and a particular redemption as the ground of a church, we say, —You are no witnesses to mankind; you proclaim yourselves enemies to mankind; you separated yourselves to be witnesses for separation, not for union; you deny salvation to the world, and yet you adopt the principle of the world in your own constitution. And we say further, in this faith of an universal atonement, and of a church grounded thereon, we uphold the doctrine of personal justification, as you never can do; we show what right a man has to account himself righteous in Christ, and how he never can be righteous in any other way; and we testify, that the enjoyment of this righteousness, and a full communion with God and his brethren, is the salvation which he is to seek, which in his selfish carnal nature he can never enjoy.

Again, then, I would ask your Friends to beware how they reject the Quaker doctrine of an universal light, for any of those partial and selfish notions upon which the sects are built. Let them take care, lest, while they fancy they are asserting the doctrine of the atonement more explicitly than your old Friends, they lose the very life and meaning of that doctrine altogether. And since they cannot stay where they are,—since the doubts, once excited in their minds, can never

be quelled till they have obtained full satisfaction,
—let them enquire diligently, whether there is not
some way of reconciling their old faith with their
new discoveries and obtaining the perfect fruit of
both. And when you have understood yourselves
on this point, you will understand also the true
meaning of that tenet of Quakerism respecting
the immediate influence of the Holy Spirit of
God, which the dissenters are so apt to deride.
Those who believe in a church and communion,
established in a complete atonement, complain of
you, not for what you assert, but for what you
fail to assert, on this point: not for saying, that
the Spirit is an occasional Teacher; but for saying, that he is not a constant Teacher: not for
saying, that there are occasional lapses and visitations of the Spirit; but for saying, that He does
not dwell constantly and habitually with men: for
saying, that the whole church of God, and the
body of each man who will live as a member of
that church, and renounce his individuality, is not
the temple which He delights to hallow: not for
saying, that He occasionally opens men's lips to
speak in his name; but that every power, and
gift, and faculty of man's body, soul, and spirit,
are not under His regulation, and intended to be
used for His glory: not for saying, that He has a
particular class of ministers, whom he intends to
be teachers of his people, and to whom he sends
gifts and inspirations for that end; but for saying, that He has not carefully preserved such a
race in every age, by whom he has promised to

teach his church; making it the sin of the minister not to believe that he has this continual power and guidance with him, and to cultivate every faculty as if he had it; making it the sin of the people not to believe that his teaching shall be effectual for their greatest good.

III. In the remarks which I have made hitherto, I have wished to shew you how the refusal of religious people, to acknowledge the great mystery of man's connection with the Word, has driven them to all kinds of shifts and inventions to explain the truths which they felt necessary to their well being. I have shewn you how, in treating the doctrine of justification, they have resorted to notions which outrage the truth of God; how, in treating the doctrine of the atonement, they have resorted to notions which outrage the love of God; and I have shewn you, that, by restoring this mystery to its proper position, we are enabled to get rid of these awkward tricks and devices of the carnal understanding, and to place the great truths which they have disguised on a firm and real foundation. I have shewn you, that, in taking this course, we are not only doing no violence to Scripture; but that we are exhibiting the connection between one part of Scripture and another; enabling you to understand them literally, without the aid of a number of glosses, which the (so-called) literal interpreters unconsciously introduce and, at the same time, teaching you that Scripture is not merely a collection *of texts,* but

D

the exhibition of a grand and coherent scheme, by
which God has trained man to the knowledge of
his true position, and of Himself.

Indeed, I feel bound to say again, as I have
said once before, that, let religious men deceive
themselves as they will, it is not reverence for
Scripture, but reverence for a system of philosophy, which makes them unwilling to acknowledge
this mystery, and ready to adopt any clumsy and
disingenuous artifices in order to get rid of it. It
is Locke's Essay on the Human Understanding,
and not the Inspired Volume, which leads them
to denounce all notion of a communication to the
heart of man, but what comes through words and
letters, and the organs of sense. They may talk
of caring nothing about philosophy, of despising
metaphysics; and they may be quite sincere in
saying we know very little about them: but the
carnal notions which lie under this system of
metaphysics, and make it so natural and so plausible, may pervade the mind, and prevent the
heart from expanding, where formal knowledge is
entirely wanting, or has been sedulously avoided.
That the most thoughtful men of Europe, whether
Christians or infidels, have been driven to reject
this system, from the sheer impossibility of reconciling it to facts and reason, I need not tell you.
But it is worth remembering, that it was attacked
on its first formal promulgation, as undermining
the principles and premises upon which the
church universal stands.

There are some letters usually prefixed to
Locke's Essay, which, his admirers boast, caused
the death of Bishop Stillingfleet, to whom they
were addressed.   Whether their idol deserves
the credit of that achievement, I cannot say. But
a prophecy of Stillingfleet's, which is treated with
bitter scorn in these letters, has been proved by
the experience of a century and a half, to be rather less childish than it seemed to his antagonist.
The Bishop says, that whenever the notion should
gain currency, that all the principles of human
thought are derived from sense and experience,
the doctrine of a Trinity must be discarded.   You
remember, with what a shout of laughter Locke
replies to this remark. " I believe in the Trinity,"
cries the philosopher; [there is a pious fraud in
words,—but let that pass;] "I believe in the
Trinity, because it is a doctrine laid down in
Scripture; the bishop may do as he pleases."
And his admirers, among the orthodox English
dissenters, have been shouting in full chorus, ever
since,—" We believe in the Trinity, because it is
written of in Scripture; let the bishops do as
they please."   Were I writing to some infidel
opponent, who thought that the church is based
on a contempt of reason, and that Locke and the
dissenters are the best defenders of it, (till a hap-
pier era shall come,) I should call his attention to
this plain avowal, that they believe in a doctrine utterly contradictory to all the principles
of human thought which they recognize, be-

D 2

cause they find it set down in a book; that we, on the other hand, the supporters of implicit faith, the alleged enemies of all reason, have maintained in the person of one of our most illustrious bishops—and do maintain, by our forms at least—that the Bible, being the exposition of the mind of Him who is perfect reason, will not contain anything contrary to the real principles of human thought. And I should then ask him to look at the history of metaphysics, from Locke downwards, and observe that this great teacher, who was supposed to have entirely confounded our bishop and our church, has now actually not one genuine follower left, except among the English dissenters; for all others, have either followed his principles to their legitimate consequences, as they are developed by Condillac and Dr. Cabanis; or else have acknowledged that there is one faculty in men for judging of things within the realms of sense and experience, and another for judging of things beyond them.

But, writing to you, I will take another course, and suggest to you a comparison between the remarks of Stillingfleet on Locke, and those that William Penn published, not many years before, in his " Sandy Foundation Shaken." You will then be able to perceive, in reference to this third great idea of Christianity, how the doctrines of your early Friends bear upon those of the English dissenters, and of the church respectively. Penn's work would probably be given up, by

most of your modern Friends, as at least a rash
and dangerous publication. But I am not disposed to believe that he did harm to the church,
or to the world, by the very wild language which
he used on this subject. He did, indeed, in a
most furious and reckless manner, make war
upon that belief of the distinct personality of the
Father, Son, and Spirit, without which the doctrine becomes, I conceive, mere mist and vapour;
but he did, at the same time, so shake the
notion of a Trinity, grounded upon the mere
words of Scripture, and not possessing a reality
for the life and heart of man, that I almost dare
to claim him as a supporter of the truth which he
seemed inclined to assail. I believe there were
sandy foundations to shake; and that, whether
Penn succeeded in shaking them or no, they were
destined to a tremendous shaking afterwards.
Look at Geneva, according to some, the source of
all spiritual illumination; look at the reformed
bodies on the Continent; look at Moses Stuart
and the American sects; look at the English dissenters ; and say whether there were not and are
not some *very* sandy foundations. Among the
last the doctrine tarries, I know:—they will tell
you that it must be believed, however seemingly
contradictory to reason; that we know little about
grasses and strata of earth, and consequently
are likely to know still less about heavenly things.
—' It is not impossible; and we want it, in order
to make good some other important doctrines;

therefore we cannot abandon it.' I do not say
that this last feeling is a wrong one; I do not say,
that if a humble man feels that he needs a Father,
a Redeemer, a Sanctifier, he may not on that
ground cleave mightily to this truth; and say,
that he will not give it up for all the arguments
and reasonings in the world. But I do say, that
when men, while resting on this ground, are
taught to regard every thing else which they
cannot understand, as unworthy of their belief,
they run a very great risk of losing this confidence;—run a very great risk of confounding the
operations of their minds, with the persons to
whom they attribute those operations;—run a
very great and tremenduous risk of looking upon
the Father, Son, and Spirit, not as objects of
devout adoration, but merely as persons performing certain offices for their welfare. Let the
records of recent ecclesiastical history, especially
in England, say whether these fears are unreasonable; let them say, whether men, who have begun
to look upon the mystery of God, and the Father,
and Christ, merely as the mystery of their election,
and redemption, and sanctification, have not sunk
into a frame of mind, from which all distinctions,
all unity, have been banished;—have not tried to
invent some notion of the Trinity, which would
do as well for their personal life, and be more
agreeable to their understandings;—have not
tossed about from Sabellianism to Arianism, and
from Arianism back to Sabellianism, and at last

ended with discovering that they had no ground
for the soles of their feet to rest upon,—no sun in
the heavens for their eyes to gaze upon. But, if
that be true which I have said on the last head,
all the personal feelings and faith of man are
unsafe, unless they rest upon the ground of an
universal atonement. Unless each man feels
himself to be a member of a body, reconciled and
united to God in Christ, he has no clear and
definite indications of his own relation to Christ:
his mind will be continually fluctuating and disturbed. On the other hand, unless this belief of
an atonement rests upon the faith of a Trinity, it
is unmeaning and baseless. The union of the
whole body to the Father, in the Son, by the
Spirit, are the very terms of the constitution.
Unless there be an Absolute Being, the ground of
all being,—unless there be one in whom that
Being beholds the church, and in whom it beholds
Him,—unless there be a Spirit, uniting together
all the members to each other, and to their Head,
the source of their faith, the inspirer of their
worship, the originator of all their acts, the ruler
of all their powers,—the idea of a church has no
consistency, the idea of an atonement no possibility. Thus are we driven to this principle, as the
ground of our society,—the only bond of our
fellowship, — the only foundation for universal
communion,—the only source of life, and distinctness to each person in it. And yet this, which is
the first ground of all faith, is also the termination

of all.   This mystery of a Father dwelling with
the Son in one Spirit, is the grand resting-place
and repose of the reason, the feelings, and all the
faculties of man;—that for which they are ever in
search, and can have no peaceable home or resting-place until they find it.   This is that blessed
and perfect unity, for which the announcement,—
" Hear, oh Israel! the Lord thy God is one
Lord," is only the preparation;—that consum-
mate unity of God, which is the real ground of all
unity between men, the real ground of all unity
in our own hearts, transcending all things, yet
sustaining all things, the perfect love, the ineffable glory in which the saints delight, and
yet which compasses the cradle of every baptized
child.

I have thus arrived at the point to which all
my observations have been tending,—to the connection, I mean, between the constitution and
order of a church, the principles of Christianity,
and the personal life of each man.   I have written
to you the more cheerfully on these points, because I perceive in your Society a sense of the
difference between a sect and a church, and a
groping after the idea of a church not based
upon human caprice, which I do not find among
other dissenters.   I need not tell you, that there
are many among them whom I esteem and love,
and that I believe there are principles and truths
in their minds, which will never be satisfied till
their sectarianism disappears.   But I find that

the phrases, ' the church is a voluntary association,' — ' the church is either the whole invisible,
body of true believers or the particular body
met together in a particular congregation :'—
I find, I say, that these phrases have got such
possession of their minds, and are so worked into
the very tissue of them, that it is very difficult to
make them understand what we mean when we
say, God has established a kingdom upon earth,
and that it is a real kingdom, based upon principles which cannot be affected or undermined by
the inconsistency of those who belong to it, or
the unwillingness of any to partake of its privileges.   I am quite aware that they have abundant excuses for their want of comprehension, —
that the ordinary language of churchmen, and
our great ignorance of our principles, are quite
sufficient to confirm them in it.

But the same incomprehension ought not to
exist among you. All the protests of your fathers
against self-seeking ; all their denunciations of
mere dogmas, ought to prepare you for entering
into my meaning. I can see good reasons in the
purposes of Providence why your Friends should
not have been able to perceive that the church,
which they thought it was the pleasure of God to
set up two centuries ago, and of which George
Fox was to be the founder, had been set up some
sixteen centuries before, and built upon a foundation which the gates of hell cannot destroy; —
I can quite understand why they may have been

allowed for a time to remain in ignorance of the
fact, that the church, if it is based on some permanent principles, must be upheld by some permanent institutions,—the true testimonies for the
fixedness of God's plans, and the power of God's
Spirit against the rashness and self-will of men.
But I say again, the time is come when these
truths, however obscured by the ignorance and
passion of man, must be perceived aud realized by
you, if you would retain your principles, otherwise than in mere name and notion.

You say that you do not like the doctrines of
the Trinity, and the Atonement, and the Incarnation to be turned into mere dogmas.   Hear, then,
how they have been turned into dogmas.   A universal church is found existing, acknowledging
the Trinity, acknowledging the Atonement as the
foundations of its being.   These great truths are
expressed in Sacraments ; their relation to the
constitution of the church and of society gradually unveiled in the written word ; their meaning interpreted to the people, by a ministry connecting one generation with another ; their
meaning expressed in various acts of allegiance,
and offices of thanksgiving, intercession, communion.   The members of this church become,
to a great extent, ignorant of the principle upon
which it is founded.   They will not suffer the
written word to interpret those principles to the
people; the idea of a spiritual constitution becomes
hopelessly lost in naturalism and sensuality ; the

principle of an universal kingdom is abandoned, by one of the officers of that kingdom usurping dominion over the whole. Here was conduct, and here were notions so contradictory to the idea of a kingdom, that they must have destroyed it, if God had not been its protector. But he raised up men who perceived the necessity of a written word, to interpret to us the constitution into which we have been introduced, and to interpret each man to himself,—perceived the eternal distinction between the flesh and the Spirit—the right of every man by his spirit to claim union with Christ, the Lord of his spirit—the inconsistency of a visible and mortal head, with an universal and imperishable kingdom. They protested against these principles as subversive of the idea of a catholic church; they affirmed the reality of this church; they affirmed, that in each particular nation or kingdom, constituted under its appointed head, this church must be recognized as the foundation and upholder of all political institutions, or else those institutions would lose their character, and become mere instruments of internal oppression or external aggrandisement. Thus the church, the kingdom of Christ, remained established in its sacraments, its ministry, its forms, with a new witness of the divine protection and government exercised over it. A large portion of its members, however, continued to assert principles incompatible with the universality and unity of the church, and anathematized all who would not ac-

knowlege these principles. With them there
could be no communion, for they would not have
it; they remained a seceding, separating, apos-
tate body. Other bodies of men, as I have shown
you, renounced the idea of an universal kingdom
upon other principles. They established voluntary (more properly arbitrary) associations,
grounded upon the notion or belief which each
member had, that he himself, and the other members, were true believers in Christ; or if not constituted on this ground, constituted on one
merely of opposition to some other body, upon
the assertion of some particular notion, or the
non-assertion of some other notion. Here begins
dogmatism. Personal salvation or safety is made
the groundwork of the society; just so much of
the doctrines asserted by the universal church is
to be believed, as seems necessary to that safety.
Hence the questions, — How much is to be believed? What portions are to take precedence of
the rest? Hence strife, battle, rage; hence also, I
am bold to affirm, persecution; for whenever the
church catholic has persecuted, it has done so because it has taken itself for a party; because it
has not understood that it was standing on certain eternal and immoveable principles. In asserting the doctrine of the atonement, we assert
redemption, liberty for mankind, union with God,
union with each other. We denounce the denial
of that doctrine, because we say, that to deny it is
to take away from man that which in all ages he

has been sighing for,—communion with God, communion with his fellows. When we assert the doctrine of the Trinity, we do so, because we believe it be the grand foundation of all society, the only ground of universal fellowship, the only idea of a God of love. As different notions and heresies arise respecting these points, we are obliged to exercise the faculties which God has given us, to draw subtle distinctions, to refer to ancient experience, to call in all aids of philosophy, and philology, and history. But this we do, because they drive us to it. All we want is to maintain a principle, without which, we say, men would be divided from each other; a principle which, while we maintain it, enables us to claim fellowship with every man who will not disclaim it with us. For the sake of the poor man, — for the sake of the denier of these truths, — for the sake of Jews, Turks, and Infidels, we assert and uphold them; for we find them to be the key-notes to all the harmonies of the world, and that without them all would be broken and dissonant.

These are my reasons for feeling that you, the assertors of spirituality, the enemies of mere dogmas, if you would uphold those principles of your Society which your orthodox members are asserting; if you would maintain those principles of unity which your moderate party are asserting; if you would combine these with the truths and facts concerning the personal life of

E

each man, which the party that calls itself
Evangelical, is asserting, you must manfully
cast away your prejudices, and inquire calmly,
rationally, and under the teaching of the Spirit
of God, into the foundations of the catholic
church. In this inquiry I am anxious to assist
you.

I propose, with God's permission, in my next
Letter, to address you on the subject of Baptism ;
in the third, on the Lord's Supper; in the fourth,
on the Written Word; in the fifth, on the Ministry;
in the sixth, on Creeds and Forms of Prayer ;
in the seventh, on the Universal Church, and its
Preservation, by means of these, through every generation since our Lord ascended ; its Present
State, its Future Hopes. In the eighth, I propose
to consider the relation between this Church
and Kingdoms of the Earth; how National and
Church Life are connected together in the purposes of God ; what relation the one bears to the
other. In the ninth, I propose to inquire into
the Effects of this Relationship, as to the conduct
of the State towards the Ministers of the Church,
towards its Ordinances, &c. In the tenth, I propose to apply these considerations to the position
of Existing Sects, and especially to the position of
the Friends. In the eleventh, I mean to enter upon
those particular Testimonies which Friends have
been supposed to bear against the Evils of the
World, and to show that if they would bear these
Testimonies usefully, and not mischievously, they

must be content to unite themselves with the rest of the church catholic, and with that portion of it which upholds the idea of the church catholic in its own country.

I must entreat your pardon for this unreasonably long letter, and subscribe myself

Yours very faithfully.

LETTERS TO A MEMBER

OF THE

SOCIETY OF FRIENDS.

BY
A CLERGYMAN OF THE CHURCH OF ENGLAND.

~~~~~~~~~~

No. II.
ON BAPTISM.

~~~~~~~~~~

LONDON:
W. DARTON AND SON, HOLBORN HILL.

ERRATA.

Page 82, line 8 from top—for *should* read *she*.

  ,,   100, line 8 from top—omit *if*.

  ,,   136, line 9 from bottom—for *word* read *Word*.

  ,,   153, line 13 from top—for *men* read *him*.

ADVERTISEMENT.

An Advertisement was prefixed to some copies of the First Letter in this Series, the substance of which it may be adviseable to repeat.

The doctrines of Fox, Penn, Barclay, &c., respecting the Indwelling Word, the Universal Saving Light, and the Immediate Operation of the Holy Spirit, have for some years past given rise to great controversy, in the Society of which these remarkable men were the founders. The dispute began in America. A party of Quakers called, from their leader, ' Hicksites,' openly renounced the doctrines of the Trinity and the Atonement, as incompatible with the peculiar doctrines of their Society. The members of this sect are disowned by their brethren. But, more recently, many English Quakers have contended, that their founders disparaged the doctrines of the Gospel and the authority of Scripture; that their writings involve, if they do not express, the Hicksite heresy; and that they ought to be disclaimed by the Quaker body, The Society is now nearly divided into those who hold those opinions, (though they appear to be rapidly seceding from it), those who assert primitive Quakerism to be the highest and purest Christianity, because it maintains Spiritual Life and teaching against forms, doctrines, and the mere letter of Scripture; and those whose chief object it is, by compromise and conciliation, to preserve the existence of their sect.

These Letters are respectfully dedicated to all the parties here described. They suggest the only method by which, as the Author believes, the important principles asserted by each, can be reconciled, and the lovers of truth and unity in the Quaker body delivered from hopeless dissatisfaction and division.

At the same time, the Author does not pretend to conceal his desire, that the members of his own Communion also may consider the arguments in these Letters, and especially in the one which he now presents to them,—may be led by them better to understand, and more to prize their own principles,—may discover from them that their principles, instead of being the cruel " fetters"* of a foregone age, offer the only hope of freedom to those who are groaning under the heavy bondage of the present.

February 1.

---

* See a letter from Lord John Russell, his Majesty's Principal Secretary of State for the Home Department, to the Earl of Burlington, Chancellor of the Metropolitan University.

LETTERS

MEMBER OF THE SOCIETY OF FRIENDS.

No. II.

My Dear Friend,

In my last letter I endeavoured to shew you that your Friends had been the assertors of some great principles to the disparagement of certain great outward facts—that other sects had asserted these facts to the disparagement of the principles —that the separation had been violent and unnatural—that *you*, in your attempt to resolve all facts into principles, had made your principles inoperative and almost unmeaning—that *they*, in order to uphold the facts without the principles, had been driven to inventions and notions unsupported by Scripture, and inconsistent with themselves. I argued, that the grand doctrine of the union between the spirit of man and Christ, is deprived of its efficacy by you, because you do

F

not see the importance of Christ's death and resurrection in justifying man—is set at nought by
them because they oppose a formal notion of justification to the truth of the word revealing
Himself in the conscience of man.   I contended
that this idea of the union of each man's spirit
with Christ, is grounded upon a deeper truth
which has reference to mankind; and that this
truth is imperfectly shadowed forth in your doctrine of an universal saving light — is utterly destroyed by their notion of a Redemption effected
for particular individuals, not for the race.   I
maintained that this idea of an atonement for
mankind as the establishment of a communion
between God and His creatures in the person of a
Mediator, necessarily involved the idea of a Father,
Son, and Spirit,—their distinct personality—their
essential and absolute unity.   This idea, I shewed
you, had by your friends been converted into a
mere spiritual conception—had by the Dissenters
been converted into a mere notion or dogma; re-
taining a real and precious meaning so long as it
was connected with the personal life of him who
believed it, but always in danger of losing its reality—of being held, not as an eternal and glorious
truth, but as an opinion which must be acquiesed
in lest he should suffer from the want of it.
From all these premises, this conclusion seemed
to follow, that a church, based upon the acknowledgement of a Trinity, and of an atonement
for mankind, is the true foundation for the per-

sonal life of each man,—the only reconciliation between spiritual principles and outward facts,— between the truths which are presented to man by God and the heart which receives those truths from God,—between our private and our social relations,—between both and our relations to God. Hence arose the inquiry, Is there such a church? If there be, what are the signs of its existence, and on what grounds has it pleased God to constitute it, by what instruments to uphold it? We are thus led to the subject which I proposed to consider in my present Letter.

The ground upon which Fox and Barclay rejected Baptism and the Lord's Supper was this: That Christ came to establish a spiritual kingdom, and that in the idea of a spiritual kingdom is involved the abolition of all ritual observances. For, a while they say the Apostles were permitted to indulge their Jewish notions; the light had dawned upon the world, but it had not yet perfectly risen. On some it shone brighter than on others; the Apostle of the Gentiles rejoiced that he had only baptized two Corinthian families, and evidently intended to intimate, that the followers of Apollos and Cephas, who probably exalted these formal acts very highly, were in a low spiritual state. But when the Jewish polity, according to the Divine purpose, passed away, the only plea for such institutions ceased; a new era began, or ought to have begun; and it was the sin and carnality of the church, which still kept it in bon

dage to the elements of the world. These notions,
or some such as these, are, you know, part of the
faith of your childhood; they grow with your
growth, and strengthen with your strength; they
cannot, I conceive, be wrenched out of your
minds, without peril to much that is most precious
in them.   It is easy to tell you that you ought to
pay a literal obedience to the commandments of
Christ; to say that his words are very express;
to show that you have resorted to methods of explaining these away, which you would not like
to apply to any ordinary document containing
the wishes and injunctions of a friend.   It is easy
to do this; the argument has been tried with you
again and again : but in general it has not succeeded.   I am not sure that it ought to have succeeded; I am not sure that those with whom it
does succeed are really the most submissive to
Christ, or the most ready to follow him whither-
soever he goeth. Why so? Because this reverence
for the commands of Christ, if it be the result
of anything but a superstitious fear, must be
grounded upon a feeling that you are connected
with him, that he is your Lord and your friend.
But if through education, or whatever other circumstances, you have been led to think that the
notion of Christ as the Lord and friend of your
spirits, is inseparably connected with that other
notion of his delivering you from bondage to formal and external precepts,—I am mightily afraid
that these exhortations, reasonable as they seem,
reasonable as, I conceive, in one sense they are,

—may overturn the very principle and life of that obedience which they seek to promote. For my own part, if I succeeded in upsetting any of the arguments, — sophistical as I deem them, — by which you uphold your disbelief in the sacraments, until I had first detached that disbelief from all the truths with which it is intertwined, I should regard my triumph with sorrow and humiliation; I should believe that for the sake of my logic, I might have gone far to destroy some brother for whom Christ died, by weakening feelings which God had implanted and carefully nourished within him, for the very purpose of guiding him to the knowledge of himself. On the other hand, if I shall be permitted to show you, that these truths stand firm without the denial which accompanies them, nay, will never stand firm till it be removed, — I am in no fear of your texts and arguments. No dialectician will be needed to explode them; they will drop off as easily and as completely as the hard skin of the chrysalis from the living and ascending butterfly.

I take my stand, then, on the very ground on which your teachers have taken theirs. I say Christ did come to set up a universal spiritual kingdom, that he did come to deal with men as spiritual, and not as fleshly creatures; that he completely accomplished these purposes; and that a church which does not stand upon the fact that these are his purposes, and that he did accomplish them, has no foundation, and when the rains descend and the winds blow, must be shaken and must fall. By this test I claim, that the church to which I belong shall be compared with all existing sects, your own included. To this test I bring the ordinance,—I do not yet call it by what I conceive its only fitting name, the Sacrament of Baptism,—and I affirm, that because you have neglected this ordinance, your witness for a spiritual kingdom has been a feeble and ineffectual witness. Again, that for want of the belief in an established spiritual kingdom, the notion of Baptism which prevails among the sects, and among those Churchmen who are willing to account themselves members of a sect, is a confused and carnal notion.

You will scarcely be surprised at the first of these allegations, strange as it may appear; for you will remember that in my first Letter, I distinctly maintained that Barclay's idea of an Universal Light, though most sound and true, was in fact the idea of an elder dispensation; and that in striving to substitute that idea for its fulfiment in a personal incarnation and atonement, he was throwing us back upon that dispensation,—converting us into Jews, without giving us the law, and the sacrifices, and the covenant, by which the faith of a Jew in a brighter and better era was kept alive. Of course, this language is not to be taken without some qualification. I do not mean that it was possible for a good and wise man like Barclay, not to see many truths far more clearly than the best and wisest Jew could have seen them. In his writings I find, and rejoice to find, indications that Christ has come into the world; yes, that he has established a church in the world; and that the fact of that coming, and the teachings of that church, have raised Barclay to a point of view which enabled him (at times, not by any means always), to make light of both. But yet I do say, that taking the mere principle of Barclay nakedly, — divested of all those blessed accidents with which, by reason of his position, it became surrounded,—it will be found to be—not a false, not an unimportant principle,—but one which belonged to a person living under the covenant of Abraham, Isaac, and Jacob, which was known long before the Son of God was revealed in human flesh, long before he sent the Comforter from the bosom of the Father to guide his disciples into all truth. If, then, I shall hereafter endeavour to show you, that Baptism is not only not opposed to the doctrine of a spiritual dispensation, but that without it no belief in a spiritual dispensation can tarry long among men, I am only following up a proposition which I have already endeavoured to make good, that you, the rejecters of Baptism, have even, when you are most right, still held principles which are only in their first germ, not in their full bloom.

But when I come to the other branch of my proposition, — when I undertake to ascertain what is the idea of Baptism, and to show how those who have practised the rite have yet overlooked its power and meaning,—you will be ready to exclaim, Yes! if you do that! but *hic labor hoc opus.* And this, perhaps, with a look of melancholy compassion, is all that your kindness and courtesy will permit you to say of my rash attempt. There are others, you well know, who are not in the habit of exercising such self-restraint. They will begin at once to exclaim, " Now for awkward dilemmas, dishonest shuffling, base equivocation; and yet the ugly truth peeping out through them all, — that it is not the sects which have a hundred different notions, but that you, you of the United Catholic Church, are at war upon this, your own choice and favourite subject. —High Churchmen, Evangelists, followers of Mr. Budd,—each with his own notion and fantasy, each alleging the authority of the church and of Scripture. Happily you cannot keep us in ignorance of this secret. Do not suppose that you have been fighting in the dark, that we have not been looking on, and taking note of every manœuvre and every onset of the generals and troops on each side. And when this confession has been reluctantly dragged forth, *another* must follow it. This writer, who takes such a high tone, and assumes to be a teacher of others, must be good enough to tell us to which of these parties he himself belongs; if to any one, then he must be so gracious as to explain how it happens that the other two have come into existence; whether they are utter heresies; if they are, how they came into *the church;* if not, why we must bow our minds to a particular view of this doctrine;

why we may not have the same liberty of thinking, which, it seems, is permitted in *the church.* Or there is still another alternative, — our letter-writer, an anonymous individual, may set up a scheme different from all these; and then, exquisite modesty! require our assent to that to which, perhaps, nobody in England but himself subscribes, and this by way of asserting a catholic doctrine ! Any way, if you watch him well, you will find that he is smuggling in the opinion of some party or some individual; calling that the church's opinion; calling the church's opinion the Scripture opinion; and, by these different pretences, forcing a doctrine down the throats of those poor persons who are wise enough to open their mouths for the purpose of receiving it."

Such, you are well aware, will be the language, mixed, of course, with many smartnesses, which, through poverty of invention, I am not capable of anticipating, with which the religious newspapers will accost me, if they chance to become aware of my project. In a somewhat different style, I will meet each objection separately. It is fancied that a Churchman must wish to disguise the fact, that there are serious differences of opinion among those who belong to his communion on the subject of Baptism. If it be meant that he will not speak of such divisions with levity; that they cost him many a bitter tear in secret; that in his best moments he could count his life a cheap sacrifice if he might heal them;

—the charge is one which he can bear very well,
—which he only fears is too honourable for him,
—which he prays may become truer every day.
But if it be meant, that it is his particular interest as a Churchman to hide these facts (seeing
they exist) from the world, he begs to ask, For
what reason ? If he were very zealous in maintaining that the Church of God is a voluntary association, dependent for its existence solely upon
the faith, the holiness, and the unity of its members, concealment of facts which indicate too
plainly that this faith, and holiness, and unity are
not what they should be, (are lower, perhaps,
though on this point it must be absurd to express
an opinion, than they were in any former age),
would be almost a virtue, so greatly would the
promises and truth of God be endangered by the
disclosure. But if this is exactly what he does
not maintain, exactly what he is at such constant
pains to prove is not the case ; if the burden of
his song from morning to night is this, ' God is
true though every man be a liar ;—he has established permanent symbols and witnesses of his
truth ; all men are admitted to partake the blessings of these symbols ; and if they do not, it is
their loss—the truth remains :' why should he,
of all men in the world, be most anxious to conceal the most striking, most appalling evidences
of his own position ? I protest, if we did not believe that arguments are made for man, not man
for arguments, and, consequently, that the interests of our species must not be sacrificed for the

sake of making good any conclusion; and if we were not convinced that it is injuring our fellow-men to present them continually with instances of confusion and evil, instead of leading them to think on whatsoever things are pure, lovely, and of good report; and if we were not ashamed to attack crimes in other men, from which we feel that we are not exempt ; and if it were not better to confess our own sins and theirs to God than to men, — we should be always parading forth the errors with which church history abounds ; so mightily do they make in favour of that principle which we, as Churchmen, are labouring to establish. But again, it is said, that I must either adopt one of those notions which are current in the church ; or else, which is more presumptuous still, set up a notion of my own, to supersede them all. With submission, I will do neither of these things. I will consider each of these opinions ; I will attempt to show how and wherein each seems to have denied the truth of the others. I will attempt to show how that which each really prizes, that which he feels he cannot part with, will unite in a principle—larger, deeper, more satisfactory, than any of the three, yet freed from the perplexities and contradictions which each has felt in the opinions of the others, and occasionally in his own. Will this be choosing any of the opposing notions which prevail, and putting myself to the necessity of explaining how the others still exist ? Will it not be accounting for them all, and justifying them all ? Will it be setting up a

crotchet of my own in preference to the opinions of
wiser, better, and more experienced men ? Will it
not be rather refusing to set up my judgment
against any of them; refusing to determine to
which of them I shall not render the respect and
homage which I feel that all have a right to claim
from me ? ' But at least, I must on my own authority determine this view to be that of the
church.' Not until I have brought you to confess,
that each of these parties was right in reading its
own view in the forms of the church; not till I
have shown that each has failed, palpably failed,
in identifying its own views with those of the
forms of the church; not till I have shown you,
that it is by the forms of the church, and not by
my own wit, that I have been led to see how
truly each of these views includes a portion of the
meaning of Baptism, how its full meaning is only
expressed by the union of them all. ' But then, I
must assume the Scripture view and the church
view to be the same.' Not if you can find another
that coincides equally with the letter of Scripture,
the spirit of Scripture, the scheme of Scripture.
' But, after all, this view is to be forced upon you,'
Not unless you want it. If there are no wants in
your mind and heart which require such an idea
of Baptism, and will not be content without it, I
know that I may allege the union of discordant
opinions, the authority of the church, the consistency of Scripture, in vain. If there be, you will
seize it, though the person who offers it to you
be the silliest man in Europe. In your case I

know there are such wants. I therefore set before you that which I believe will satisfy them. In the case of the writers in religious newspapers, whose craft is to make paper shrines to the great goddess of opinion, which the religious world worships, I do not suppose that there are any such wants. They have their own peculiar wants; the spirit of strife and division caters to them abundantly. We have no command to supply them with food; on the contrary, the injunction is very peremptory, ' Give not that which is holy unto dogs, neither cast ye your pearls before swine, lest they trample them under their feet, and turn again and rend you.'

I need not tell you, that our formularies speak of a baptised child as *regenerate*. All churchmen, therefore, who acknowledge and use these formularies, of course, believe that in some sense or other the child is regenerate. The question is, In what sense? Here the dispute begins to which I have alluded. Those who, in honour or derision are called High Churchmen, maintain that the words are to be construed strictly,—that they denote a positive change in the moral and spiritual condition of any person to whom they are applicable, and fix Baptism as the period of that change. Those who, in honour or derision are called *Evangelicals*, affirm that no moral or spiritual change can take place in an unconscious subject; that the word regeneration, in its highest sense, signifies such a change, and describes the state of a man who has actually and consci-

ously passed from the death of sin unto the life of
righteousness; but that in a lower and not illegi-
timate sense, it may signify merely an admission
into the privileges of the Christian Church.   The
followers of Mr. Budd (I know not whether they
have yet acquired any nickname), maintain, that the
child of a parent who truly believes the covenant
of God, is certain, in virtue of that covenant, to be
hereafter brought into Christian faith and obedience; and therefore, by a very allowable prolep-
sis,—present and future being one in the eyes of
God,—may be called, even in the highest sense,
already regenerate.   I may not have quite satisfied the supporters of any of these opinions in the
description I have given of them,—of course the
modifications of each are very numerous, and at
their extremities they touch upon each other;—
but to all intents and purposes I believe you will
find my classification a sufficient one, and you will
find it hard to invent any fourth opinion which
shall not fall under the principle of one of them,
unless it shall comprehend them.

The second of these opinions is the one which
will present itself to you as the most plausible, so
far, at least, as it is an explanation of the fact de-
signated by the word regeneration.   You may
possibly find it hard to understand,—and all the
Dissenters, I believe, feel the same difficulty,—
how the word can ever come to mean merely a
possession of outward privileges.   You may wonder what outward privileges of a religious kind a
baptised child enjoys, which he would not pos-

sess if he were unbaptised; and if a little grace is supposed to go along with these privileges, you wonder how persons so accurate in the use of language as the Reformers generally were, — so little inclined to look upon words as mere counters, should, in documents carefully superintended by them, and intended to form the hearts and the theology of future ages, have sanctioned the application of so solemn a phrase to so very inconsiderable a matter. But, leaving these points, with which you do not feel that you have any particular concern, to those who are obliged, for the comfort of their own minds, to settle them,—you think that the so called Evangelical party, has abundant reason to rejoice that it has, under circumstances somewhat disadvantageous, ascertained that really precious sense of the word, which, so long as they keep it, makes their evidently reluctant admission of another formal sense comparatively unimportant.

This opinion you would ground, no doubt, upon the evidence of experience and fact. Scripture, you of course believe to be on the same side; but the experience of a transition from an evil to a righteous condition, is that, you think, which determines the meaning of Scripture; and ascertains the doctrine of baptismal regeneration in any but a formal sense, to be a falsehood and an impossibility. As this is the ground which you, and hundreds of others take, I cannot do better than ask you to study attentively the actual recorded cases of conversion. ' For what purpose, you inquire? To prove that there are numerous, confused, superstitious, or fantastical notions in the minds of those who experienced them? I am willing to admit so much. But after all deductions, and allowances, and special pleadings, there will remain a startling positive fact, the most amazing in its history and its consequences, which no artifice can get rid of.' But, my dear friend, I do not want to get rid of one fact; I do not mean to special plead a single history of the kind; I take them as I find them; I assume their truth. And what then? Why, I find in every one of these narrations expressions such as these: ' Then I was first *awakened;* then I was first brought to a knowledge of the truth; then I first felt and understood the love of Christ.' These, you will allow, are recognised phrases, and they are phrases, thank God, from which, after ten thousand distillations, the meaning has not wholly escaped. I will be bold to say yet farther, that you may estimate the sincerity of the person who describes these spiritual processes by no test more surely than this, — if it appear evident that these phrases are *significant*, and not merely phrases of course,—if the writer recognises the existence of certain facts before he became conscious of them, and acknowledges that he had been struggling and closing his eyes against the light, you cannot avoid the conclusion, that, let external circumstances or fantasy have lent what aid they may to the colouring of the story, it is the story of an actual and mighty transaction.

If, on the other hand, you see that these phrases mean nothing; that awakening does not imply having been asleep ; that acknowledging the truth does not imply that there was a truth which he had previously denied; if the words, first understanding the love of Christ, do not express his belief that the love existed before he felt it, you will be generally able to detect from other signs, — perhaps from an extreme accuracy in the detail of impressions, and a great anxiety to put everything in its proper place, — that the writer has been a very diligent student of religious experiences and biographies, and a very indifferent student of himself.

There is another criterion of sincerity in these histories, which seems closely connected with the former. If you find any narrator describing the perception of a relationship to a mighty Friend and Saviour, as the reward of all his sorrows and anxiety, and the commencement of a new life to him ; you will generally find other most touching proofs of his meekness and honesty ; you will find in the midst of some cant, perhaps some indications of an exclusive feeling, which accord very ill with the rest of his language, — such utterances of affection for his fellow-sinners, and especially the friends of his youth, and such inward life and joy, as it is most humbling and heart-cheering to read. On the contrary, if the man talk chiefly of his change of nature, — thank God that he is not what he was, or what other men are, — indicate that it is the confidence of

having taken a new start, and of having got
some feelings which he had not before, rather
than trust in Christ and the belief that he has
died for him, which gives him a hope of happiness here and hereafter, in such a case, I put
it to you, whether that charity which hopeth all
things, has not to dig through heaps of religious
jargon and pharisaical contempt before should can
arrive at one vein of that precious ore which
she is searching after, and is determined to
find.

The more you meditate on these observations,
the more interesting, I am persuaded, they will
be to you, and the more you will be persuaded
that a conversion must necssarily presuppose a
state, into accordance with which the man at
a particular crisis is brought, which he is
obliged to call his true state, from which he is
obliged to speak of himself as having departed.
Try as hard as he will, he cannot so frame his
expressions that they shall not denote his belief
that the condition into which he is now brought,
though not his natural condition, is yet his own
proper condition. He knows that all his acts are
inconsistent with themselves; that he was in contradiction with himself while he did not recognise
this as his state, and that his acts will become
inconsistent again, and he again at variance with
himself, when he forgets that it is his state. All
the time till he had arrived at this conviction he
was asleep, blinded, ignorant of the truth. Now
he has *come to himself*. And what is this state?

Not one of independent virtue and excellence, —
that is not intended for any man or angel, for any
being except God,—but a state of union with another, *this* is his proper state.   When he knows
that it is so, and acts as if it were, he becomes
what he was meant to be ; otherwise he is living
as perverted a life as if he were striving to walk
upon his head instead of upon his feet.

But, supposing this to be the case, supposing a
man who believes himself a child of God, a member of Christ, an heir of the kingdom of heaven ;
holds that belief which alone can enable him to
do consistent and reasonable acts ; which view
would seem to be, *prima facie*, most extravagant
and absurd; that which tells a man that he is not
this, or that which tells him that he is this ; and
that it is his sin not to act upon the supposition ?
Observe, I am not yet explaining the principles of
that assertion ; I am merely removing an *a priori*
objection.   The Evangelical party say, if there be
such a thing as conversion, it cannot be that a
man, previous to conversion, was a child of God, a
member of Christ.   I say, if the records of conversions be true, there is the strongest possible
difficulty in *not* ackowledging that to have been
the state of each man previously, which he then
claims and affirms to be his.

Do not suppose that there is the slightest no-
velty in this view of the question.   The Evangelical party has accustomed itself to look upon the
doctrine which pronounces men children of God
before they enter into the acknowledgment and

enjoyment of that wonderful relation, as something which is at war with all spiritual Christianity, most especially at war with the doctrine of justification by faith. See whether the great preacher of that doctrine so considered it; see whether he did not as much insist upon a ground for his faith to stand upon as I have done; see whether he did not as much speak of Baptism, as that which gives this ground, as any High Churchman among us. I take up Luther's Sermons, and select passages almost at random, to prove this point:—

" But that this might be easier for us to do, even Christ hath taken it upon himself, he suffered himself to be baptized and took his cross and carried it, not resisting or gainsaying, and so was obedient to his Father unto the death, even the death of the cross, as Paul saith, Phil. ii., that he might deliver us from sin, and might appease his heavenly Father, which he did of his mere grace without any desert of ours: whereof we have baptism a sign and pledge, as Paul saith unto Titus, iii. 4: "But after that the kindness' and love of God our Saviour towards man appeared, not by works of righteousness which we have done, but according to his mercy he saved us by the washing of regeneration, and renewing of the Holy Ghost, which he shed on us abundantly, through Jesus Christ our Saviour : that being justified by his grace, we should be made heirs according to the hope of eternal life." Secondly, the Holy Ghost appeared here in the likeness of a dove, when Christ is baptized, whereby is signified, that we also receive the Holy Ghost in our baptism, which ruleth and guideth us according to the will of God, which is present with us, and helpeth us in bearing the burden of the holy cross, which exhorteth us, which is instant upon us, enforceth us, and, when we yield to the burden of the cross, is present and helpeth us ; if we fall, raiseth us up again, and is with us a certain faithful companion in our journey. He also maketh the burden of the cross light, which we were very unable to bear, if he did not put his help. If so be that thou fall into sin, remember to go back unto thy baptism, for this is the only ship wherein we pass over.

" Wherefore take heed of them which make two tables whereby we pass over the sea of sin ; namely, baptism and repentance : believe them not, whatsoever they handle, it is mere delusion : baptism is the beginning of repentance. As often therefore as thou fallest into sin, have recourse unto thy baptism, there thou shalt again obtain the Holy Ghost, who may be present with thee. —*Sermon on the Epiphany*.

" He setteth forth the grace of God given to us in baptism, with words very full of praise and commendation : he calleth baptism a washing, whereby not the feet and hands, bu tthe whole man is once washed, purified, and saved.

" There is need of nothing but only faith in this grace of God, that it may remain and be acknowledged the work of grace alone, that we are saved without all our works and merits, and so also there may remain in us pure love, praise, giving of thanks, and glory of the divine mercy, without all glory and pleasing of ourselves in our own strength and endeavour, as it hath been often said and at large. Human righteousness is also a washing, but not whereby the whole man is so washed, but that Pharisaical washing, whereby only the apparel and vessels which are outward are made clean, whereof it is spoken, Matt. xxiii. 25. Whereby it cometh to pass that men seem unto themselves pure, but inwardly they remain full of filthiness. Therefore he called baptism not a corporal or outward washing, but the washing of regeneration or new birth, by which not those things that are outward are washed, and only the outward man made clean, but the whole nature of man is altered and changed into another nature; that is, the carnal nativity is thereby destroyed, with all the inheritance of sins and perdition."—*Sermon on Salvation by Grace without Works.*

" And hereby the nature of a true and right faith is taught; for it is nothing which some say, ' I believe in God Almighty,' as the Jews and many others are wont, and do therefore receive corporeal benefits of God; it is a true and lively faith, whereby thou believest in God, howbeit by Jesus Christ. First, that thou doubt not that God is become a merciful father unto thee, which hath pardoned all thy sins, and in baptism hath adopted thee for his son and heir, that thou mayest certainly know that thou art saved; again thou must also know this, that that was not done gratuitously, neither without satisfaction made to the divine justice, for there can be no place in thee for the divine grace and mercy to work salvation, and to give thee eternal good things, unless the justice of God be before most fully satisfied : for Christ witnesseth, Matt, v. 18, ' One jot, or one tittle shall in no wise pass from the law, till all be fulfilled."—*Same Sermon.*

" Wherefore if he should any thing doubt, he should procure exceeding ignominy and reproach to baptism which he hath received, and to the Lord's supper, and also reprove the word and grace of God of falsehood; wherefore take heed that thou nothing doubt, that thou art the son of God, and therefore righteous by his grace,

let all fear and care be here away, Howbeit thou must
fear and tremble, that thou mayest persevere such an
one unto the end : Thou must not, being in this case,
be careful that thou mayest become righteous and saved,
but that thou mayest persevere and continue ; neither
must thou do this, as though it consisted in thine own
strength, for all thy righteousness and salvation is only
of grace, whereunto only thou must trust : but when
thou knowest that it is of grace alone, and that thy faith
is also the gift of God, thou shalt for good cause live
in fear and care, lest that any temptation do violently
move thee from this faith."—*Sermon on being under the
Law and under Grace.*

The idea, then, of a holy and righteous state
for a man, as belonging to him before he claims
it, though rejected in our modern Evangelical
theology, is involved in all the facts of which that
theology professes to be an exposition, and is
formally admitted and asserted as essential to his
doctrine, by the founder of the Evangelical school
in Germany. Let us then attempt to set this
party right with themselves, and see whether, by
so doing, we do not bring them into nearer accordance with the brethren whom they despise.
They say that Baptism means only an admission
into the visible church. The question then oc-
curs here, which I asked in my last Letter of
those who said that the light, spoken of by Fox,
meant only the conscience, What does that
mean? Our Catechism answers in plain terms.
It means that you are a child of God, a member
of Christ, an heir of heaven. Surely you will not

put such a fraud upon me as to translate these
words back into the very phrase of which they are
given as the explanation ! But, are they a fair and
legitimate explanation of it ?   Supposing they
were, those facts of conversion would not be less,
but much more intelligible than they are; supposing
they were, we should not have to suppose that
Luther was quite ignorant of the truth which
he lived to preach.   But what warrant have we
for saying that they are ? I have answered this
question already in my last Letter.   I maintained
that Christ, by whom, and for whom all things
were created, and in whom all things consist, has
made reconciliation for mankind ; that on the
ground of this atonement for mankind, God has
built his church, declaring men one family in
Christ ; inviting all men to consider themselves
so ; assuring them that only in Christ they are
or can be one family ; that, separate from him
they must be separate from each other.   Therefore
we, believing there is such an atonement, and
that such a declaration has gone forth, and that
it is a sin for men to account themselves separate
from Christ, and separate from each other, when
God has, by such a wonderful act, declared them to
be one body in him ; and believing that the mark of
that universal body or fellowship, appointed by
God himself is Baptism, do, without fear or scruple, asseverate of ourselves, and of all others who
will come to this holy Baptism, of all who bear
the marks and impress of that nature which Christ
took, in his birth, of the blessed Virgin ; that

they are admitted into these high and glorious privileges; that they are brought into a state of salvation; that they are made sons of God and heirs of everlasting life; and that for this they are to give thanks to God unceasingly, and to look to Him who has introduced them to such a dignity to keep them in it even to the end.   And in saying this, we contend that we give honour to the free grace and redemption of God; that we give faith, the faith of the child, the faith of the boy, the faith of the man, a ground upon which to stand, and which otherwise it cannot have.   We say, hereby we are able to teach little children, that a Father's eye is upon them in love; hereby we are able to tell the young man, who is beginning to feel that he carries within him an accursed nature, which is not subject to the law of God, neither indeed can be, that by union with Christ he may rise out of that nature, and trample it under his feet; and this whether he has always maintained a fight against that nature, leaning upon the promise of his Baptism; or whether he has sunk under its dominion, and become the slave of the sin out of which Christ delivered him; for in the last case, as much as in the first, we say he must be taught that he is united to Christ; and that by not claiming that union, by trusting in himself, by thinking that he was something when he was nothing, he has become the servant of the devil, not of his true Lord; consequently, that if he would not continue in sin, he must assert that glorious privilege of which, by his own

G

act, he has deprived himself. Lastly, hereby we enable a man, in the midst of the world's conflict and bustle, not to spend his life in fretful and selfish questionings and debatings whether he is a child of God or no, but boldly to take up the rights of one, and enter into communion with his Father; and to seek for the knowledge of God, which is eternal life; and to do his will from the heart, by his spirit dwelling in him, and to look or the manifestation of Christ from heaven, when the redeemed body shall rejoice with the redeemed Spirit, when all evil shall be cast out for ever from the kingdom of God, and when God shall be all in all.

Thus have I justified the truth which the Evangelical party assert respecting Baptism, and cleared it of the contradictions with which it seems to me that they have encompassed it. I say you are right that Baptism is an admission into the visible church. Only understand what that implies, what it must imply, in order that your justification and your conversion may have any meaning; in order that your preaching may have a power and reality, in which now, alas! it is grievously wanting; in order that you may not be perplexed with perpetual puzzles about the degree in which you may encourage your people to believe themselves what God has declared them to be; in order that you may not keep their consciences in perpetual bondage, while you pretend to set them free; in order that you may not exalt those whom God would humble, and make those sad whom he

has not made sad; in order that you may not
hinder your hearers from drawing nigh to God
with a pure heart and faith unfeigned, and receiving the blessings which God has promised to
all who seek him.

I now turn to the High Church view of Baptism, against which, I hope, you may feel somewhat less prejudice than you did when I commenced the discussion.   You will, I think, be
inclined to believe that those who hold this view
may not be " all (with possibly a few exceptions,)
open sinners. self-righteous Pharisees and dead
formalists," as Mr. Philpot, late of Worcester College, kindly reports of them; or in the more gentle
and humane language of the Record Newspaper,
(though it, I believe, does not acknowledge the
possibility of any exceptions), " soul-destroyers."
This is all I desire ; for, as I told you in the beginning of my letter, I am not about to set up
their notion as the true and exclusive one.   I
mean to show you wherein I think it inconsistent
with itself and with the idea of the church, and
how that inconsistency must be removed from it
before it can be reconciled with the views of the
other parties, and can contribute an element to
that grand idea of Baptism which will, I believe,
result from their union.

The doctrines of this party, which are nowhere
so ably and so eloquently expressed as in the tracts
of Dr. Pusey, (published the year before last,) entitled " Scripture views of Baptism," turn, as
I have said, mainly upon the principle that God,

G 2

of his free will and mere grace, does, by the operation of the Spirit, in the act of Baptism, change
the nature of the person partaking that ordinance,
and thereby constitute him his child, the member
of Christ, the heir of heaven. If you read Dr.
Pusey's tracts, you will see at once, that no other
notion of regeneration except that which is implied
in the words Change of Nature, has ever struck
him as even possible; or if it has, that he has at
once rejected it as inadequate. This is the point
which I wish now to examine.

In older and simpler times, every thoughtful
man felt deep thankfulness to our Lord for the
wonderful blessing which he conferred on us by
teaching us the phrase *New Birth*, or *Birth from
above*. To be taken out of the region of abstrac-
tions, to be presented with a fact of every day
occurence, yet still amazing and mysterious, as
a key to this deeper mystery,—to be able to
translate words into life,—this was exactly what
every man who knew his wants felt that he
needed. It was a fulfilment of the promise, that
the Lord would teach his people a pure language,
a language which they might interpret, not by a
dictionary, but by another part of his own scheme,
a part of it known to all tribes of the earth, to
rich and poor, learned and unlearned alike.
Therefore, understanding this to be the intent of
Christ, they meditated on the obvious facts of ordinary birth, and thus they felt that their minds
became clearer .respecting the more transcendent
truth. That the body passes from the dark night

of the womb into the light of ordinary day, was
the simplest view of physical birth; that the
spirit comes out of the womb of nature into the
light of the Son of Righteousness, was the corresponding view of the *New Birth*.   Now, in the
full belief that God, by Baptism, takes the child
into covenant with himself; that he adopts it
into Christ's holy body; that he bestows on it
his Spirit;—it was most just and reasonable that
the word $\phi\omega\tau\iota\sigma\theta\epsilon\iota\varsigma$ should be applied to the baptised man.   If he did not afterwards walk in the
light, and seek fellowship with the light, he would
die in his sin.   But still the light is come into
the world; the man is brought into the light;
God himself has brought him into it; and any
sinking hereafter into the dark flesh,—the womb
out of which he has been brought,—is the voluntary abdication of a glorious privilege.   Such is
the view, I conceive, most present to the mind of
the fathers of the church : and to this view, you
perceive, there is nothing hostile in any of those
facts respecting a passage from darkness to light
in mature age, on which the Evangelical party
dwell; on the contrary, one assertion rightly understood, sustains the other.

Neither is there anything contrary to what God
had been previously teaching man respecting his
own condition.   For he had been teaching him to
know that he was a spiritual creature, and that
he had a nature; he had been teaching that his
spirit was united to the Divine Word, that his flesh
was chained to earth; he had been teaching him,

lastly, that the Divine Word had claimed a union
with him, and had gotten the victory over his
enemies.   If, then, it pleased God to claim the
man as a spiritual creature united to Christ, and
by Baptism to stamp him as such, it is pure mercy
and grace indeed; but it is mercy and grace according to a Divine order; it is a mystery, but it is
a mystery into the fellowship of which, God, with
infinite wisdom and prudence, has been all along
conducting his saints.   But if for the words, ' New
Birth' you put ' Change of Nature,' Christ's beautiful analogy, which he has with such pains and
love made known to us, is altogether set aside;
for no man in his senses can find anything like
a change of nature in ordinary birth.   Again,
the order of God is violated; he does not deal
with man as he hath been doing with him; he has
been preparing man, hitherto, by a wonderful
process, for the kingdom of his Son, and now
he sets up that kingdom on a principle of which
he had given no hint before-hand.   Baptism is
not the consummation of a foregone scheme; it
satisfies no wants previously excited, it makes
useless all former dispensations.   But it is a graver
fault still, that by this notion the idea of a sacrament is destroyed; for in the idea of sacrament is
necessarily implied, that all the virtue and life of
the creature consists in its union with a Being
above itself.   It is dead of itself; it lives in him.
Suppose nature, as such, to become anything
pure, or holy, or righteous, by virtue of any
change wrought in it; or suppose a new nature

to be communicated as an endowment to the man, this idea is sacrificed altogether.

I would earnestly entreat Dr. Pusey and his friends, to consider whether by this phrase they are not getting rid of a *mystery* for the sake of introducing a *mystification*; whether they are not departing from the text of Scripture, in those passages to which they most appeal, in order to steal a notion from their opponents, which of right belongs to them, and to the stage of life which they deal with; — (for the idea of a change of heart, where *heart* is taken for affections and desires, and when *change* is taken to be the turning these desires from a wrong object to which they have been conformed, to a right object to which they are meant to be conformed, is surely a legitimate idea, and one not at all at variance with the idea of Baptism as a covenant, but the fulfilment of its intent and the fruit of its promises; and change of *nature* in any other sense than this, no Evangelical who understands himself supposes to take place at conversion or any other period;)— whether they are not forcing themselves into a series of consequences which actually set at nought the truth they are so eager to defend. For, *first,* no persons are more anxious to assert the dignity and glory of the church than they, —to upset the notion that it is composed of a number of individual atoms, instead of being a Divine constitution into which men, from age to age, are brought; and yet, by representing Baptism as that which confers a portion of grace on each particular child, and not as that which brings him out of his selfish and individual con-dition, into the holy and perfect body, they do very much, as I think, to destroy the idea of the church, and to introduce a Genevan, individual-izing notion in place of it. *Secondly,* no men are more anxious than they to assert the truth, that the Holy Ghost actually dwells with each bap-tised person; and yet, by supposing the essence of Baptism to consist in a change of nature, they make something which happens at a particular instant or crisis to the child, and not the constant presence of a Friend, and Guide, and Teacher, to uphold the spirit in its battles with the flesh, to train it in the knowledge of itself and of God, to comfort it in its sorrows, to guide it into all truth and love,—the gift and blessing of Baptism.

Again, it is still more mortifying to find that men to whom, besides great learning and diligence, God has given a higher grace, the willingness, I mean, to make sacrifices that their poorer bre-thren, in this corrupt metropolis especially, may hear the Gospel, and enjoy Christian ordinances, should, by their theories, defeat the effects of their own bounty, and well nigh close the lips of the preachers whom they are so anxious to provide with churches. Yet this is actually the case; for they, looking at Baptism as an act done in an instant, and accomplishing its purpose in an in-stant, and not rather as the witness of an eternal truth, the sacrament of constant union, the as-surance of a continual living presence, are driven to this conclusion,—that the moment after it has been performed is a period of ideal purity and excellence, from which the future life even of a saint is a deflection, and which those who have wandered far into sin cannot hope to recover;—these must be content, by much prayer and fasting, to seek for God's mercy, which may perhaps, though there is no certain promise to uphold the flattering expectation, once again redeem them out of sin and hell.

Where is the minister of Christ in London, Birmingham, or Manchester, whom such a doctrine, heartily and inwardly entertained, would not drive to madness? He is sent to preach the Gospel. What Gospel? Of all the thousands whom he addresses, he cannot venture to believe that there are ten who, in Dr. Pusey's sense, retain their baptismal purity. All he can do, therefore, is to tell wretched creatures, who spend eighteen hours out of the twenty-four in close factories and bitter toil, corrupting and being corrupted, that if they spend the remaining six in prayer,—he need not add fasting,—they may possibly be saved. How can we insult God and torment man with such mockery? But who urge us to take that course? The very men to whom we,—mere journeymen,—appointed to live in the noise and hurry of the world, not in the quiet of colleges, looked for deliverance from the Calvinistic theology, by which we were pressed out of measure, so that we despaired even of life. When we were feeling the intense, the intolerable misery of being

G 5

obliged to treat these poor people as outcasts
from God's mercy, of whom one or two *might*
find their way to the waters of healing, if an angel
first went down and troubled them; when we
were tormented with the horrible contradiction of
having to say, in one breath, ' Believe;' in the
next, ' You cannot believe;' now, ' You ought to
look upon God as a gracious and loving Lord;'
then, ' We have no proofs that you are some of the
elect children whom he loves;' first, ' Christ's death
is the only means of salvation to you, believe in it
or perish;' by and bye, ' But we cannot have the
least certainty that he died for any of you;'—when,
I say, we were almost in despair, because we must
either speak those inconsistencies, or at least keep
them in our hearts, and infect all our preaching
with them; these kind doctors told us, or seemed
to our ignorant and longing minds to tell us, of a
Catholic theology which taught that our people
were still under the covenant of God's holy Baptism; that the love of God was brooding over
them; that the grace of Christ was given to them;
that the energy of the Spirit was with them, to
put them in possession of true righteousness.
Now all this comfort is taken from us; and if we
believe our instructors, we have a worse message
to deliver than before.   But, although we be
ἄνθρωποι ἀγράμματοι καὶ ἰδιῶται, only picking up
snatches of knowledge here and there, and thankful that a race of men has been provided, of
larger capacities and greater leisure, who may impart to us what little we are fitted to receive;

yet we also have the forms of the church, and the Word of God, and a holy commission, and the Holy Spirit, and so long as these are continued to us, we will not, in this solemn matter, give place to these doctors in subjection, no not for an hour. We will assert that the *covenant* of Baptism encompasses the publicans and harlots to whom we preach, let them have as little of baptismal purity as they may,—we will preach repentance to them on this ground, and on no other—that they have a Father, and that they may arise and go to him; that they have a Saviour, and that he will deliver them from all their enemies; that they have a Spirit given to them, and that he is willing and able to cleanse them from their sins, and to endow them with the blessings which they need, righteousness, and peace, and joy in the Holy Ghost. By God's help we will do this, though the Calvinistic party, and the Catholic party,—CATHOLIC *party!* here lies the contradiction, which is the seed of all others,—unite to condemn us; and we invite all who desire a moral and God-fearing population in the land, to look on and say whether our course or theirs is most honoured to produce that unspeakable blessing.*

In this case, as in the former, I am endeavouring, you see, to defend able, and accomplished, and excellent men against themselves, or rather against the accursed spirit of party, which has set them at war with themselves. I do not require a

* See note at the end of the letter.

ghost to tell me, that of all tasks this is the most
thankless.   If you will but take a good, kind
man's side, in opposition to his neighbours, he
will forgive you very considerable differences on
points of his actual belief; and will account you
his dear friend and fellow-labourer.   If you suggest a compromise between two warriors, though
you will not get either of them to love you, yet
the bystanders, who care nothing at all about the
question, will call you very fair, and liberal, and
will " swear a prayer," after their fashion, that if
all the world were such as you; every thing would
proceed so quietly.   But if you at once resign all
pretensions to the character of a good partizan,
and yet obtain none of that credit for softening
and diluting opinions *till they can do nobody any
harm*, which persons of another cast covet, who will
listen ? " *Vel duo vel nemo*," I hear you reply. But
I am not so despairing ; I know that there are
many in the church who are secretly crying out
against divisions, not because truth is a thing indifferent to them, but because it is more precious
to them than silver and gold, because no mention
shall be made of rubies in comparison with it ;
and if such should discover that they can speak
out, and yet not identify themselves with those
who wish for conciliation, because they have as
little faith in one doctrine as in another; that, in
fact, we must unite and condense the principles
which we each recognise, in order that we may
have something firm and real to oppose to those
who think there is nothing firm or real ;—above

all, if they shall understand that such full-orbed truths alone accord with the Church or the Scripture, or can satisfy the minds of those without our communion, who are seeking rest and not finding it, I am sanguine enough to believe, that their hopes and their numbers will increase, even as their discontent with every school and every leader increases; and, in truth, it is worth while (had we no better recompense) to want the sympathy of all fierce parties and all careless people, or to endure their contempt, for the sake of one hearty and affectionate greeting from a Christian of this order.

In this faith I am encouraged to repeat my conviction, that the two principles which I have been setting forth, when certain notions which interfere with their soundness and stability have been cleared away, will be found, not the *same*, (if they were, each could not contribute its quota to the truth,) but strictly harmonious and needful to each other. The High Churchman declares the *origin* or *ground* of our salvation to be in the Will of God; the Evangelical believes the *order and method* of our salvation to be by our being constituted and redeemed in Christ. The one says God hath chosen and adopted you to " be his sons;" the other, " God hath chosen and adopted you to be his sons in Christ." The one lays the foundation of a universal family; the other gives the foundation on which the faith and life of each member of the family is to rest, as he grows to man's estate. The one shows the perfect

freeness of God's grace ; the other that grace, in
its proper sense, can only appertain to a spiritual
creature. Take the first principle without the
second, and the church sinks into a *world,* as it
did under the Popedom; take the second principle
without the first, and the church sinks into a sect,
or a body of sects, as it has been inclined to do
since the Reformation. In one you have a vague
sense of *unity,* superseding personal faith in the
majority, leaving personal faith without its object
to the higher few ; converting the first into mere
animals, the last into mystics. In the other you
have a vague sense of personal *distinctness* dif-
fused through society, making the ignorant impatient of being taught how to think and how to
live, because every man has a right to think for
himself, and to live as he likes ; turning the more
reflective into a separate caste, full of proud
thoughts and dark reserve, with ' Stand by, I am
holier;' or ' Stand by, I am wiser than thou,'
expressed in every action, and movement, and
look. Safety in a crowd ; the notion of getting
safe into port, because the ship in which we are
freighted is sure to arrive there, without reflecting
that it is possible to die on the passage, is the
continual temptation of the first ; the feeling,
' There are but very few tickets of admission to
the bowers of Paradise, and I have one of them,' is
the desperate delusion of the second. The conscientious among the former are inly racked, because they but dimly see that He, who they
confess most readily, died for their sins, also rose

again for their justification. The conscientious
in the other class are not less tormented, because
they cannot find what warrant, or what power
they have to believe in this justification. And if
from these practical effects, we return to the principles, we perceive, as I have shown already, that
each, since it has been separated from its twin
stem, has become overgrown with a fungus, which
is feeding upon it and gradually destroying it.
Beautifully did the excellent and delightful poet of
Fairy Land shadow forth the causes and consequences of this separation, in his history of the
arts by which Archimage persuades the Red-cross
Knight to doubt the loyalty of his chaste and
fair mistress, and of all the miseries which each
suffered from the divorce ; and truly and joyfully
did he prophesy that a day would come, when
the one should be purged from the effects of
his adulterous alliances, the other delivered from
all her persecutions, and when their bridal should
be celebrated amidst the rejoicings of earth and
heaven.

But there is a third element implied in these
two, which must, I conceive, be formally and
clearly brought out, before they can be reconciled,
or we can have a satisfactory idea of Baptism.
This third element constitutes the system of Mr.
Budd. Like both the other parties, he and his
followers are exclusive. They speak disparagingly
and contemptuously of the High Churchmen, as
men ignorant of the Gospel, and enemies of the
truth, doing more injury, I think, to their own

characters, by these prejudiced statements, than
to those whom they attack. Their doctrine, as I
told you, is, that the promise of God to believing
parents, that their child shall be justified, sanctified and saved, is so positive, that all doubt on
the matter is sinful, and that their business is to
look upon their child as already in the condition
in which they are sure it will be hereafter.
After what I have said as to my belief in our right
to call a baptised person a child of God, because
he *is* one, I need not tell you that I am not satisfied with a notion which confers on him that high
honour, because he is intended to become one.
From the following passage in an Appendix to
a Sermon by Dr. Pye Smith, I imagine that the
Dissenters generally are not disposed to view
this doctrine in a much more favourable light
than that which is maintained by the High
Churchmen.

" What but the most extraordinary and next to in-
credible perversion of the argument from analogy, can
have induced a minister of Christ so holy, single-
minded, and faithful as Mr. Budd, to rest on a ground
of *assumption* not having the smallest degree of evidence, his conformity to the Church of England, and
his satisfaction with those parts of her Liturgy which
are the most excruciating to thoughtful persons,
whether in or out of her communion ?—His principle is
that " The National Church——is, not a community
" of natural men, but a communion of saints ;——*as-*
" *sumed to be* no others than men resting on the promise
" of eternal life in Christ Jesus, and entertaining com-

" mon hopes in virtue of the promise.——The child in
" our Church is accepted in virtue of the promise; re-
" ceives the seal and sign of baptism; and in virtue of
" the same promise is *assumed to be* a sound member of
" the Church."—*Christian Observer,* Feb. 1834, p, 91.
Compared with this, what are all the fictions of law,
which have till lately created trouble and expense in
our courts ? They were only smiled at as relics of feu-
dalism, absurdities but not deceptions : but who can
look without shuddering upon this AWFUL and MON-
STROUS FICTION, held forth to the millions of our population, of all characters, not excluding blasphemers, infidels, and the most licentious profligates, if they die
without having been excommunicated ?"—*Appendix to a
Sermon on the Necessity of Religion to the Well-being of a
Nation, by Dr. Pye Smith.*

Whether the parts of our service alluded to in
this extract, are " *excruciating* to thoughtful persons," or whether they are excruciating simply to
those who do not think, or who think perversely,
I may inquire hereafter. Thus far I fully agree
with Dr. Pye Smith, that if we have nothing better than a hope, however certain that hope may
be, to rest this language upon, it does involve a
fiction,—possibly he is not wrong in calling it, or
any theological fiction, awful and monstrous.

But, strongly as I feel this conviction, I believe
that Mr. Budd's view is only false, because he
has separated it from the other two which prevail
among his brethren, and that when introduced as
a supplement to these views, instead of a substitute for them, it becomes really most valuable

Our Baptism is in the name of the Father, the Son, and the Holy Ghost. The idea of an adopting Father is, I conceive, satisfactorily brought out by the High Churchman. He is unsatisfactory, as I think I have shown, when he speaks of our constitution in Christ, or of the gift of the Holy Ghost. The Evangelical view, rightly interpreted, explains one of the High Church omissions, but only imperfectly and implicitly recognizes the other. The idea of the Holy Spirit, personally and actually inhabiting, educating, informing the mind of the child, — of parents, schoolmasters, legislators, being his servants and fellow-workers in training the whole family, and each member of the family, to realize the privileges of their constitution, and to become acquainted with the name and will of Him who has established it, —is a grave and glorious truth, which it is an high honour to Mr. Budd that he has been permitted to perceive, and which we should be very thankful to him for having, even in an inadequate manner, illustrated.

I must plainly tell him, that I conceive there is an idea of sound ecclesiastical education embodied in the forms of our church and the institutions of our country, for which his "Hints on Nursery Education" seem to me a very poor substitute. Since that idea has been lost sight of, corrupt and worldly motives have been introduced into the system, which have impaired its efficacy, and given it an air of inconsistency, which you can never detect in the modern schemes that are

wholly based on such motives. But it still lives,
though hidden; and a true patriot will be far
more anxious to bring it to light, and shew
how parts of the scheme, which now seem in-
congruous, are reconciled and explained by it,
than to introduce anything of his own in its
place. Another great principle Mr. Budd seems
to have hinted at, which I trust may one day be
thoroughly explored and worked out;—it is, that
our modern idea of missionary enterprizes is not
in accordance with the plan of Providence, and the
language of Scripture; that it is by preaching
God's kingdom to the heathen, declaring that he
has redeemed man and entered into covenant
with him, and by receiving them into that covenant,—not by preaching notions and doctrines
which are only intelligible when they have been
admitted into it—that we best fulfil the commission,—" Go ye into all nations, and preach the
Gospel to every creature, baptizing them in the
name of the Father, the Son, and the Spirit,"—
and may best hope to be the instruments of saving
the world.

I have now set before you my idea of baptism,
portions of which are acknowledged by each of
the parties in our church,—the acknowledgement
of which in its completion, would, I believe, lead
to the reconciliation of all their differences. And
this brings me to a further remark, closely connected with the subject of our present discussion,
and no less connected with the most interesting
controversies on other subjects, now pending.

You have heard of a progressive Christianity,—a Christianity for the nineteenth century, superior to, and destined to supersede the Christianity of all previous centuries. The whole style of these letters will, I presume, acquit me of entertaining any such notion as this; but there is hardly any notion so absurd or dangerous that has not its foundation in an important truth. Whenever the notion is widely propagated, there is a signal for us to search after that, of which it is the corruption. I see it is gaining ground among some of your Friends, as well as elsewhere; and I wish to shew you what light the question into which I have been entering may throw upon it. The High-Churchmen appeal, in support of their view, to the fathers of the Christian church; these, they say, are the standards of all theology; to these we must mainly trust for the interpretation and elucidation of Scripture;—accordingly, to these Dr. Pusey appeals as his witnesses on Baptism. Now, though I do not say that there are not passages, which may lead a person who identifies the phrases, " change of nature," and " new birth," into the notion, that they support the doctrine which their supposed disciple has advocated; yet I believe, when we have once understood the difference between those words, and when we have learned how strongly the fathers advocated that doctrine of the connexion of the Word with man, which, if once received, makes the supposition unnecessary, that we shall find not more passages in the fathers, capable of this interpretation, than have been twisted to uphold transubstantiation. Dr. Pusey will allow most readily, that there are abundant passages in them, written with warm feelings and conscious singleness of aim, which a writer, in whom that notion had taken root, might without any dishonesty convert into a support of it. Yet he will allow that, taking the whole context of their writings, the interpretation would be unjust and unreasonable. My impression is, that the passages (which must after all be considered picked passages) in his own tracts, lead to this conclusion, and this only,—that the fathers had a very strong and abiding sense, that God had entered into covenant with men, and by entering into covenant with them, had made them holy; and that, except at times when the speculative understanding got the better of their sounder judgments and hearts, they did not look further.

They believed generally, that they were baptized in the name of the Father, the Son, and the Holy Ghost; that in some way or other, they were members of Christ, and did receive the Holy Spirit. But each of these truths was far less explicit and prominent in their minds, than that general feeling of being adopted by God into his family. Now this seems to me just as it should be;—this feeling I think is the one which God, who revealed himself to Abraham, through the relations of the family, before he revealed himself to Moses, through the relations of the nation, would com-

municate to His infant church. All simple, child-
like, affectionate piety would consist with this
apprehension, and be called forth by it.   It would
imply, as the revelation to Abraham did, all that
followed after, all that was reserved in the wisdom of God for a full and clear development
in future ages.   Heresies and oppositions would
arise, and then it would be God's pleasure and
purpose to bring his church to apprehend things
involved in its own existence and constitution,
already revealed in his word, but not yet distinctly perceived by his servants.   This truth,
that men are constituted in Christ, and that they
must exert a direct faith in Christ, if they would
enjoy the privilege of being children of God,—
that they must feel themselves not to be mere
members of a holy family, but distinct, living,
righteous creatures in Him,—this truth, it seems
to me, was intended to be brought into distinct
consciousness at a later period, and was brought
out at the Reformation.   Then, first, it began to
be clearly understood, that baptism is a sacrament
which applies to all stages of life, and not merely
an act instituting a man into a position from
which he falls afterwards; then it came out in a
new character, as the ground for the doctrine of
justification by faith to rest upon; then, those
notions of repentance, for which I grant that
Dr. Pusey *has* warrant in the writings of the
fathers, (and according to my shewing might
be expected to have warrant,) were proved to

be incompatible with the nature of Baptism; or, as Luther expressed it, in a passage I have already quoted,—that there are not two planks on which we get to heaven, baptism and repentance, for that baptism includes repentance. If I am right in this view, the doctrine of the Reformers is neither strictly the same with that of the fathers, nor yet contrary to it. It was a portion of their truth,—a portion in earlier times received implicitly, but not, properly speaking, understood; consequently, in practice sometimes overlooked then, as in later times it was habitually contradicted.

The Evangelical party sets up the doctrines of the Reformation against that of the fathers: we have seen, that in order to do so, they are obliged to mangle and pervert the doctrines of the Reformation. Nevertheless, they are so far right, I conceive, that the Reformers did see some things that their predecessors did not see; they are right, also, in believing that some of them fancied that what they saw was the whole truth, and superseded or comprehended all which had been believed in former times. But now men are driven by the materialism, and death, and darkness which they see around them, to sigh and cry after some new truth, some fresh revelation, to renew that which is decayed, and restore the fallen age. Hence, Irvingism, Millenarianism, prayer meetings for the out-pouring of the spirit, &c. And now, the doctrine of baptism comes in to meet

this condition of society also, to speak of a mighty
spiritual power given to the hearts of men, to be
renewed in them day by day, to govern all their
thoughts and studies, all the events, arrangements,
accidents of their life, to unite them with each
other, to make them the willing servants of God.

If the age of the fathers was the infancy, that of
the Reformation the boyhood, we need not fear to
call the time when this truth shall not be perceived
merely, but realized, the manhood of the church.
But then it must be a manhood which does not
set itself up, either against the boyhood or the
childhood, which acknowledges that all, which it
is permitted to perceive hovered in dreams about
the church's cradle, was actually contained in its
institutions, hinted at in its traditions, expressed
in its divine oracles.   Thus we give to experience
what is experience's due; we believe it is an instrument in the hands of God, for training his
church; but we believe that it merely leads us
into the consciousness of truths, which, in fact,
were our inheritance long before; and that the
chief lesson which it teaches is, that one age cannot exist without another, and that one of the
greatest steps to advancement and perfection, is to
seek again those truths which, when we first felt
that a progress was intended for us, we carelessly
cast away.

I have not shrunk from explaining to you what
I consider is the imperfection of each existing
sect or system in our Church, and even of the
views prevailing in each age of the Church, be-

cause, while meditating on these apparent discre-
pancies and contradictions, I have been led, more
than at any other time, to understand the nature
of Christ's kingdom; the necessity of institutions
to uphold it; the weakness and partiality of human judgments; the wonderful method in which
the Spirit of God has overruled that very weakness and partiality and made them the means of
bringing out mightily the portion of truth needed
in each period ; the connection of the truths
strongly realized by one set of men, with those as
strongly realized by another; the certainty that
truth *is*, whether we acknowledge it or no ; the
certainty that all who submit to the guidance of
God's Spirit, and do his will, shall apprehend it
in its integrity and fulness ; the impertinence of
any limb of Christ's body saying to any other
limb, ' I have no need of thee ;' the difference
between the charity which flies from truth as an
enemy, and that which is the twin sister of truth,
and in life or death cannot be parted from her.
In such sweet and melancholy tones the History
of the Church

> Speaks to the ear of faith ; and there are times,
> I doubt not, when to all it doth impart
> Authentic tidings of invisible things—
> Of ebb, and flow, and ever-during power,
> And central peace subsisting at the heart
> Of endless agitation.

What coherency it adds to this idea, to believe
that God has preserved a set of forms from age
to age, teaching persons to express in them more
than they themselves understood, and to preserve

H

that which their own notions would have led them to abandon, till a time arrived when circumstances ascertained their meaning, and proved their necessity, I shall have to explain in a future letter.   At present, without requiring your assent to any such opinion, I shall merely call your attention to the fact, that the forms of our church do recognize every portion of that idea of Baptism which I have been setting forth, and do not recognize one of those notions, by which I maintain that each portion of it has in turn been mystified and corrupted.

If you read our Baptismal Service, you will find the strongest and plainest assertion, that the baptised child is regenerate ; that it is a child of God. You will not find the phrase ' change of nature,' or any phrase which can, without violence, be construed into a synonime of it.   The High Church *idea* is distinctly brought out, that the child is taken into covenant with God, and that it is really and truly a spiritual creature, redeemed by Christ, and adopted into union with Himself. The High Church *attempt to explain* the mystery is in nowise sanctioned, and the need for it is entirely superseded, by the declaration, that the child's reception into the Ark of Christ's Church, *is* its deliverance from the evil of a fallen world.

The Evangelical *principle,* that we are only holy in Christ, and that all individual holiness is a contradiction, is fully asserted, and made the ground of the child's future life.   The Evangelical *notion*, that the Ark of Christ's Church means merely an outward congregation, endowed with certain outward privileges, is utterly repudiated by the express declaration that the child is made a member of Christ's mystical body.

The *idea* of Mr. Budd's party, of a promise which God, on his part, will most assuredly keep and perform, to guide the child into a knowledge of the glorious position into which it has been brought, and of the Father who has owned it, is recognized again and again. The *notion* of Mr. Budd, that the promise rests upon an assumption, and not upon an actual fact, or that it is contingent upon the faith of parents, is nowhere even suggested, and is set at nought by the whole principle of the service. The more you study it, the more you will understand what we mean when we say, that Baptism is a *sacrament*, grounded upon the atonement made for mankind by Christ, —therefore, of living force and application to every period of life, and not merely an *act* conferring a blessing at the moment, which future acts of the person receiving it may nullify and destroy. You may then study the rest of our services in this light; and you will see, that if those passages, which Dr. Pye Smith says are so excruciating to honest minds, were left out, every other passage in them would be unintelligible and unmeaning. If these passages be false in principle, every word that we speak, every act that we do as Churchmen, is false in principle. It is monstrous for any person to say, — 'there are a few lines in the Baptismal Service and in the Catechism, to which we object; if these were taken away, we would be very good Churchmen.' You might as well say, remove half the single line from the Turkish Confessional, — 'There is one God, and Mahomet is his prophet,' — and we could be very good Mussulmans. If men are not children of God, then they have no right to confess their sins to God as their Father; they have no right to believe that he pardons them their sins for Christ's sake. If they are not children of God, all their prayers, thanksgivings, adorations, confessions, are downright mockery.

I do not wish to drive good men to an extremity. I know they hold the truth in their hearts, even when with their understandings and lips they seem to contradict it. But, I must say that either on the Calvinistic hypothesis, that a few men only become children of God in consequence of some process which takes place in them in mature life, or upon the pseudo-Catholic doctrine, that men had this privilege once, but are continually apt to lose it, every part of our Liturgy, the whole manner of our worship, seems to me a contradiction. Yes, and no part of our forms is more a contradiction, than that Commination (pronounced by us every Ash Wednesday,) in which either of these parties might hope to find the confirmation of its views. Throughout that beautiful service, there is not one passage indicating that those who are so terribly warned, have not entered into the privileges of God's covenant, or have lost them. From first to last, it presumes that they have the privileges, and that having them, their sin is, that they do not use them, and live according to them,—their future judgment,—that ' light came into the world, and that they loved darkness rather than light, because their deeds were evil.'

Again, on any one of the partial views which I have set forth, our sponsorial system is quite unintelligible. Supposing Baptism to be an instantaneous act, producing a change of nature; supposing Baptism to be merely an admission into a body, possessing certain nominal privileges ; supposing Baptism to be merely a promise on the part of God, hereafter to confer a certain blessing, why does the sponsor, in the name of the child, renounce the devil and all his works, &c.? If the words contained, (as so many imagine, who are instructed by dissenting teachers, and never read the service,) a promise on the sponsor's part to *keep* the' child from the devil, &c., we might understand how his office would square with Dr. Pusey's theory,—he would be a guardian for the child's baptismal purity. If he merely said some formal words, befitting the formal representative of a formal corporation, admitting a new member, into the formal enjoyment of formal privileges, we might acknowledge that he was not a much more useless person than any other who took part in the unmeaning ceremony, which some modern Churchmen hold Baptism to be. If he

merely said, ' Hereafter, should the parents of this
child die, I hold myself the successor to their
functions,' his existence on Mr. Budd's system
might be reasonable.   But, as there is no printed
or manuscript authority for the dissenting emen-
dation of our service—as the words which the
sponsors use are not formal, but most actual and
mighty words—as the sponsor does not say, that
will be any thing by and bye to the child, but
puts himself in its place now, I do not see how
any of those parties can, without the greatest difficulty, interpret the Church's intention, or look
upon the whole mechanism of our system otherwise than as needless and clumsy.   On the other
hand, if you adopt my view, you will find it hard
to understand how the Church could have acted
differently, so as to express in a living act, the full
meaning and power of Baptism.   This child is
unconscious and ignorant, but I know that it is
not a mere natural thing.   It is, I am sure, a
person, though as yet it has none of the affections
and faculties of a person in exercise.   I put it,
therefore, into God's hands, humbly claiming for
it the privilege of humanity, the privilege of being
one with him who is the Lord of man, in whom
alone man can enjoy spiritual blessings.   I ask
this, and the sacramental act assures me that it is
granted.   But how?   The child is received into a
living and spiritual body.   God's covenant is not
with it individually, but with it as adopted to be
a member of Christ.   Of this, also, I must have a
witness.   What witness can I have?   A member

of that church, an adult member, one who is presumed to have claimed the blessings of the church for himself, comes forward, and in the child's name tenders the confession of that faith which is the bond of our church-fellowship; the declaration of that obedience, without which this fellowship is practically destroyed.   And now this child, admitted into the church of Christ, receives that Spirit which is given to the church and to us, so far as we are members of it.*   Take away the idea of Baptism, bring it within that low notion which the dissenters, or which the parties in our church, as parties, (*i.e.* as sects, *i.e.* as dissenters) have of it, and I confess that all the objections which have ever been taken to godfathers and godmothers are tenable; I can show that they have generally been raised by persons who actually did not know the very words of the forms they were attacking, and brought heavy charges against phrases of which they themselves were the authors,— but that is a trifle; they are right in saying that if Baptism mean what they suppose it to mean, there is no need of sponsors.

* For nothing is clearer, I conceive, from the language of Scripture, and the very idea of Christianity, than that we enjoy the presence of the Spirit, his teachings and illuminations, not as individuals, but as living portions of a living body. All enthusiastical, and all materialist notions, alternately succeeding each other, may be traced to the opposite doctrine; its theological root will be found, I believe, in that most practical heresy which destroyed the life of the Greek Church, and made it an easy prey to the Mussulman,—the doctrine, I mean, that the procession of the Spirit was from the Father only, not from the Father and the Son.

In the idea of sponsors is involved that of *Confirmation*. In baptism you treat the child as a spiritual creature, because you know that it is one. It has none of the signs or energies of a spiritual creature, as it has very few of the signs and energies of an animal creature. Nevertheless, you are certain of the fact, and you put it into that position in God's covenant, which is alone consistent with such a fact. You believe that it is now under the government of God's Spirit; every faculty and energy awakened in it, you believe is awakened by His power and operation; every thing that is not sin and death, you believe to be His gift. But there comes a time, when the child becomes *conscious* of these spiritual powers, when it not only feels and thinks, but begins to know that it feels and thinks. This is a wonderful crisis in education,—woe to your child if you do not mark it, woe to him if you too eagerly anticipate it. In the one case he is too likely to be always a child; in the other, all childish simplicity departs, he acquires a most precocious and dangerous knowledge of good and evil; he looks back hereafter to the child, not as the father of the man, but as his deadly enemy. Now the church seizes this time of consciousness,—this awful moment, when the mystery of our own personality first begins to scare and confound us,—when there is a dim perception of responsibilities, and a struggling of the sinful nature, to throw off the silken bonds of affection, because they seem to be turned into the iron chains of law,—when the hope of some connexion with an invisible Being, who can solve the doubts and quiet the tumults within us, is awakened by the recollection of the words of the catechism, of the morning and evening prayer, of the stories in God's Holy Word, all now beginning to lose something of their childish interest, and not yet having acquired a higher meaning,—then, I say, does the church meet us with her service of confirmation, tell us that these responsibilities are really ours, that these struggles of the sinful nature must be overcome, and that the duties may be discharged, the victory may be won; because the hope is no dream,—because the Spirit who took the charge of us in childhood, who has been himself educating us to behold the light which now seems to rush in upon us with such blinding power, will be with us,— not as heretofore the watchful nurse over thoughts yet unborn, hovering over the waters before the firm earth had yet been parted from them, before the period of form and distinction had arrived,—but henceforth the awful friend, and companion, and fellow-worker, the witness with our spirits that we are the sons of God. Such, I conceive, is the principle of this service, utterly inconsistent with the idea of some operation performed and finished in the act of baptism, with the notion of a mere outward admission into an outward society, of a mere promised blessing to a faithful parent; but perfectly consistent with the idea of a covenant, adopting the child into Christ's body, constituting it holy, endowing it from hour to hour with as

much spiritual life as it is capable of, and bringing
it into the conscious enjoyment of that spiritual
life afterwards.

After these remarks, I think it advisable to
extract a passage from a book which has lately
fallen into my hands, entitled " Secession from
the Church of England Defended," by J. C. Philpot; a tract which, it appears, has reached the
twelfth edition.

"Having finished his prayer, he takes the senseless
babe in his arms, and sprinkles a few drops of water on
its face, using at the same moment the solemn form—
" I baptize thee, &c." But this is not the worst. The
most painful part is still to come. The minister must
now kneel down, and solemnly thank God for having
"regenerated this infant with his Holy Spirit." At this
very moment he feels an inward conviction that no such
divine change has taken place. He is confident that as
the child was before it was sprinkled, so it is now. But
can he not then evade this solemn mockery, this awful
trifling, this deliberate lie? No. He cannot, he dare
not. The Church of England has tied him down with
a double chain, first, by compelling him "to give his
unfeigned assent and consent" to every syllable of the
Common Prayer Book, and secondly, by exacting from
him a promise, that he will "use this form and no
other." He is obliged therefore to repeat the thanksgiving for the regeneration of the child as it stands in
the Prayer Book, and he gulps it down as well as he
can. If the poor conscience-stricken minister could find
but one text of Scripture on which to rest the sole of his
weary foot during this service, how happy would he be!
If there were but one instance, but one precept, but one

intimation that it was Christ's institution that infants should be sprinkled, or but one promise that He would regenerate them thereby, how would his harassed conscience rejoice! But no. The Scriptures condemn it. God frowns upon it, and conscience falls in with the testimony of God, and writhes beneath the feelings of His displeasure.

" Who can describe the weight and burden of the baptismal service to a tender conscience, or what a child of God feels when he is thus compelled to mock Him to His face whom he desires to fear ?

" I shall take the liberty, then, of calling the ceremony which I have just described, ——— lie the first.

" The child, having thus in its long clothes made a beginning in hypocrisy and falsehood, must be trained up, as soon as reason dawns, in the same course. It is sent to a daily, or Sunday school in connection with the Establishment, and is there taught the Catechism And now comes lie the second. " Who gave you this name ?" Ans. " My godfathers and godmothers in my baptism, wherein I was made a member of Christ, the child of God, and an inheritor of the kingdom of heaven." What an awful profanation is this of those holy and blessed titles which the everliving God confers on his elect alone, that every ignorant child should be thus taught to call them his own ! God's own dear family, whom He has taught to fear His great name, dare not say that they are his children, members of Christ, and heirs of heaven for perhaps many, many years after they have been called by grace, and not until, after many groanings and bitter cries, Christ is revealed in them by the mighty power of God. But these ignorant little children learn from their Sunday-school teachers to claim these blessed titles as mechanically as they learn

their A, B, C; and are taught to repeat " Our Father,"
when a living soul cannot, and dare not call God
" Father," until he has received the Spirit of adoption,
and felt the love of God shed abroad in his heart."

I do not in the least complain of this language;
on many accounts I prefer it to that which I ex-
tracted a short time ago, from a sermon of Dr.
Pye Smith. As a matter of taste, I like the plain,
simple, Saxon word, " *lying*," better than the long
Latin, sentimental word, " *excruciating*", when
both obviously mean the same thing. Again, Dr.
Smith, as he has never used the service, cannot
tell whether our consciences are excruciated by
the use of it, or no. Mr. Philpot does know
that it was used for many years by one person,
who believed it to be a series of falsehoods. Again,
Dr. Smith's words are not tangible; they are of
that vague kind which inflict a very deep wound,
without giving the assailed person the power of
warding them off. Mr. Philpot's frank confession, that there are persons who have read this
service, and his declared belief that we all of us
do habitually read it with a consciousness of
deceit and hypocrisy in our hearts, gives every
clergyman an opportunity of saying that which
one clergyman says now, (repeating what he has
oftentimes spoken before, openly and in secret,
with a full assurance that One heard the words,
who, though he may reserve his most terrible
judgment of utter exclusion from his own presence for a future state, will yet sometimes even
here make those who commit any flagrant act of

sin a spectacle and a warning to all around them,) that he desires, should he ever be tempted to the horrible crime of uttering a word at the solemn season of baptism, which he does not believe, or doing an act to which he does not attach a meaning,—the tongue may be for ever silent which utters the blasphemy,—the hand may be withered which commits the sacrilege. Fourthly, Dr. Smith's words seem intended to suggest an excuse for us of this day, that we, never having considered the matter, having been trained up to hear these phrases from our infancy, fancy we *must* submit to them painful as they are. But this excuse will not avail Taylor, Hammond, Barrow, Bull, for they were constantly brought into contact with persons who objected to our services, and must have considered them. It will not avail Hooker, Herbert, Donne, for they were continually meditating upon each of these forms. It will not avail Davenant and Hall, for they mixed with the members of foreign churches, and to a great degree sympathized with them. It will not avail Usher, for he was in constant communication with English dissenters. It will not avail Leighton, for he was the son of a Puritan divine. Hence, every one of them must have been wilful and deliberate liars;—Mr. Philpot I am sure will not, Dr. Smith should not, refuse to bestow the name upon them. Lastly, Mr. Philpot's statements bring the question to the right issue. He perceives that it is just as inconsistent with sound Calvinistic doc-

trine to teach a child to say, " Our Father," as to
teach it that it is a child of God, a member of
Christ, and an heir of the kingdom of heaven.
This is true, this is honest language; and it gives
us an opportunity of saying a word to Christian
fathers and Christian mothers, which no desire to
defend ourselves from the most dreadful charge
which can be brought against the ministers of
God should have wrung from us, if we did not
feel that it was called for by the wants and
miseries of these times. We tell them then,
plainly, that because they have not taught their
children to say, " Our Father,"—because they
have brought them to hear many long prayers,
but have-never led them to feel that they had a
right to join in those prayers,—because they have
inculcated it upon them, that they had something
to do with Christ and that they must perish if
they did not understand their relation to Him, yet
have never told them that they had any relation to
Him,—because they have forced them to read
their Bibles, have told them at the same time that
they could not understand their Bibles without
the aid of the Holy Spirit, and have never told
them that this Holy Spirit was given to them,—or
if they have talked to them in a vague kind of way
about God being their Father, yet have mixed
these words with such contradictory statements
respecting their outcast condition, as have led
them to suppose that there is some other God
than the Father of our Lord Jesus Christ, that
the word Father does not mean Father, that a

man may have a Father, and yet not be a child,—in short have led them into such a maze of hopeless contradiction and perplexity,—have so disgusted them with the very name of Christianity, —have so confused them with telling them that their carnal hearts were fighting against the truth, when they knew in themselves that the better desires which strove after life, and holiness, and heaven, revolted against much which they heard, (and of course they could not distinguish which part was hateful to the flesh, and which to the Spirit);—therefore it has come to pass, that every *esprit fort* pounces upon the children of religious families as his most sure victims; that the ranks of political infidelity are recruited from these families; that from these proceed the most uncompromising servants of evil, because they feel like Julian, (as falsely indeed as he did,) that they have known, read, and condemned,—that they carry out into reckless, practical immorality, the principles which, in others less instructed, may sometimes consist with kindliness of nature and even purity of life. Are these things so? If they are, is it wonderful, should that be true which we affirm, that these religious parents have despised and forgotten the covenant of their God?

But the question, after all, is not, Are other men doing the very things which they hold us up to scorn? but, Have we a right to adopt that language which is used in our formularies, in that sense in which I have endeavoured to shew you that it was understood by the fathers and

Reformers, and in which it is implicitly recognized by all the parties in our church, recognized most when they are in the wisest and most holy state of mind,—I mean, when they most shew that they understand themselves, and are least disposed to quarrel with each other? Have we warrant in Scripture for speaking of baptized people, as children of God, members of Christ, and heirs of the kingdom of heaven? I said, in the beginning of my letter, that we were justified in it, by the scheme, the spirit, and the letter of Scripture; I will now shortly direct you to the proofs of my assertion.

We are told, "Abraham believed God, and it was counted unto him for righteousness," and the covenant of circumcision is said to have been the seal of the righteousness thus imputed to him. Here we have the distinct announcement of man's connection with God, and of his own righteousness, being the effect of faith or confidence in the righteousness of God; and we have St. Paul's authority, in the very passage in which he is confuting the Jews' pretensions to rest merely on the fact of their *having* a covenant, that they had a right to exercise precisely the same confidence that their forefathers exercised. His whole arguments are set at nought, if this be not admitted; for the charge, the condemnation that he passes upon the Jews, is this,—that, having this covenant and sign, they nevertheless did *not* trust in God, as Abraham trusted, before he had the covenant or the sign. Knowing, from the nature of the trust which

Abraham exercised, what the meaning of the covenant was, and it being as much theirs as it was his, they yet went about to establish their own righteousness, and would not take the blessing of that righteousness of God, which by this sacrament he so freely assured to them.

Here we have a full recognition by the apostle, of the principle, that the circumcised nation, as such, was as it is always described in Scripture, a righteous and a holy nation; and that the wickedness of the members of that nation consisted in this, that they would not avail themselves of their inestimable privilege,—that they would not act, as if they were righteous persons, by virtue of the covenant into which they had been brought with a righteous God. Now, if you consider the nature and object of circumcision, as they are developed in Holy Scripture, you will see that it was a perpetual witness that the nature of man, that to which he would be in subjection, if he were not brought into subjection to, and union with God,—was an evil and a cursed thing, something in which he could have no confidence, something which he must account as separate and cut off from himself, that he might enjoy personal union with his unseen Lord and Friend. Such was the Jewish dispensation. The mass of men are looked upon, as in that condition which *is* the *natural* condition of every man, to which man, by sin, has reduced himself:—one nation is called out, to be a witness for the *true* state of man, as raised above his flesh and united to God.

They are taught that this is the only condition in which they can be a *nation*, for that all national order, and life, and law are destroyed by those selfish lusts which lead a man to regard himself and his fellow men alike on a level with the brutes.

This truth God himself teaches to the chosen people; and every fact in their history, down to their captivity in Babylon, illustrates and expounds it. After that time, he ordains that other nations also, before the coming of Christ in the flesh, shall realize a portion of this truth; and, though ignorant of the true character of God, shall nevertheless believe that there are beings upholding them against the tendencies of their nature, and that the acknowledgment of such beings is the only bond of national life, the only security for the distinction between a civilized polity and a barbarous horde.

At length the Son of God comes in the flesh,— comes to fulfil all the promises made to the fathers, that the Lord of righteousness, whom they had honoured as the king of their nation, with whom they had had communion in their secret hearts, should one day manifest himself, and should be the founder of an universal and everlasting kingdom. His forerunner is heard in the wilderness, proclaiming that that kingdom is at hand; calling men by his words, not more than by his example, to turn from all the fleshly delights to which they had given up their spirits to their unseen King, confessing their wanderings from Him; that when

He should manifest himself to them they might know Him and receive Him. He came to bear witness of the light which lighteneth every man that cometh into the world; of him from whose fulness he and all the foregone prophets had received, and grace for grace. He came *baptizing with water*. I do not enter into the long question whether this was the ordinary mode of initiating Gentiles into the Jewish covenant. The scholars who maintain that opinion are, I conceive, quite as numerous and respectable as those who oppose it; and you may think it would be in favour of my argument to assume this point, for then the very act would say to every Jew, " you have a carnal nature as much as the Gentiles; your covenant of circumcision, if you have entered into its meaning, must have taught you that you have such a nature, it must have taught you that you are better than they, not in virtue of an hereditary privilege, but because you are admitted into a relationship with God ; because, by union with him, you are able to subdue your nature. Come, therefore, and take your standing upon this ground; claim union with God—confess how you have renounced that privilege — and receive this token, that he remits your past sins and receives you still as his people. And do this especially now, because a kingdom is about to be set up in which all men will be treated on the same footing, — in which all will be dealt with as spiritual creatures, united to a spiritual head, and expected as such to subdue their flesh, and to act as if they were in fellowship with a Righteous Being.'

If Gentiles were admitted by this rite into the Jewish covenant, I say this must have seemed to any reflective Jew to be the meaning of calling upon them, the circumcised people, to be baptized. But without that supposition John's own words are strong enough. " Think not to say within yourselves we have Abraham to our father; for I say unto you, that God is able of these stones to raise up children unto Abraham. And now, also, the axe is laid to the root of the tree, every tree therefore that bringeth not forth good fruit is hewn down and cast into the fire." So far I and your friends, shall probably be agreed; that Christ came as the Lord of men's spirits; that he came to deal with the inner man, the root of the man; and only with his carnal nature as shortly to be set aside and condemned; and that this was the grand distinction between his covenant and that which it superseded. But now comes the passage on which all the controversy between us turns. " I, indeed," saith John, " baptize you with water unto repentance, but one standeth in the midst of you who is mightier than I. He shall baptize you with the Holy Ghost and with fire." Hear — your friends exclaim, — how clear, how express these words are ! John, indeed, baptized with water, but when Christ comes, no more water ! Then begins a new kind of baptism, with

the spirit of holiness and the fire of affliction. Let
us see how far the rest of the history bears them
out in this interpretation.   Shortly after these
words had been spoken, Jesus himself comes to the
water, descends into it, and as he rises out of it, a ·
voice is heard proclaiming, " This is my beloved
son in whom I am well pleased ;" and the spirit is
seen descending like a dove and resting upon him.
Immediately afterwards, we are told, he was led by
the Spirit into the wilderness, to be tempted of the
devil.   He encounters the enemy of man in the
great human temptations of appetite, worldly
ambition and spiritual pride, and overcomes.
Straightway, we are told, he begins to announce
that the kingdom of God is at hand; and to
do acts proving him the Lord of the body and
spirit of man.   He sends forth his ministers to
proclaim the same truth and to exercise the same
powers.   He expounds the laws of his kingdom—
laws fulfilling the principle without abolishing the
words of the old dispensation—laws for the spirit
as they were laws for the flesh.   He unfolds the
nature of his invisible kingdom over the spirits of
men, through the forms of his outward kingdom
of nature; the processes in the one by the processes of the other.   He announces the steps to
its establishment, the resistance it would meet with,
the judgment on its enemies. All this time he
permits his disciples to neglect many things which
it befitted them as Jews to do, and to do many
things (when not contrary to express commandment,) which it befitted them as Jews to omit;

and even, mark you, to transgress the customs observed among John's disciples, as well as the Pharisees, for the purpose, as he tells us himself, of
proving that new wine could not be put into old
bottles; on purpose to prove that he was come to
establish a spiritual kingdom. And yet all this
time his disciples, acting under his express directions, baptize—baptize while they preach this new
kingdom.

At length the time comes, so often foretold :
never so distinctly as when the disciples had just
beheld his glory on the mount of transfiguration :
when the Son of God is mocked and delivered to
the Gentiles and crucified and slain. Hitherto he
has been doing perfect human acts, now he enters
upon a series of perfect human sufferings. He is
in agony, and dies, and is buried. He rises again
from the dead. He meets his disciples, saying,
" Peace be unto you ; as the Father hath sent me,
so send I you ;" breathes on them, saying, " Receive the Holy Ghost;" tells them that they are to
tarry at Jerusalem till they receive the promise
from the Father, and concludes with the magnificent words, " All power is given me in heaven
and on earth, go ye into all nations and preach
the gospel to every creature, baptizing them in
the name of the Father, and of the Son, and of the
Holy Ghost.".

He ascends on high ; the disciples do tarry at
Jerusalem, praying and fasting ; yet in the midst
of the solemn and unspeakable meditations of
that season, deeming it no unworthy or vulgar act to

arrange a point respecting the order of the future
church, to complete the apostolical college.   On
the day of Pentecost the promise is fulfilled; the
Spirit takes possession of their faculties of understanding and speech, and proves his presence, and
proves that he did come to establish a united and
universal church, the opposite of the Babel polity,
by making the apostles intelligible to men who
speak a number of different dialects.   But this
marvel is only the prelude to a calm plain discourse, in which the chief of the apostles declares,
that he whom the Jews had crucified was risen on
high, to be a Prince and Saviour; exhorts all who
heard him to acknowledge the glorified King;
announces baptism as the admission to his kingdom; and promises, to all who submit to it, that
they shall receive the Holy Ghost.

Thus was the kingdom of which the Baptist, and
Christ himself had long spoken as at hand, set up
amidst signs and wonders; and yet its great privilege, *that which distinguished it from the dispensation of John*, was connected with the ordinance of
baptism. Consider next the progress of this kingdom; how carefully for awhile, (after the principle
of universality had been so distinctly asserted by
the gift of tongues,) it was confined within the
limits of the Jewish nation, that the universal
kingdom might be seen to stand on the foundation
of prophets as well as of apostles; that the church
might seem to be not a new and gorgeous palace
suddenly raised by the wand of an enchanter,
but a temple which had been gradually rising with-

out noise of axe or hammer, ever since God said
" Let us make man in our own image ;"—how the
great apostle of the circumcision was himself selected to open the doors of this kingdom to the
Gentiles;—how when these doors had been opened
and the spirit himself had testified of the admission of Cornelius and his kindred, they were yet
baptized, as much as ever the Jews had been at
Pentecost ;—how, afterwards, (while St. Peter still
continued to be a pillar of the church at Jerusalem,) another apostle was raised up to be the
herald to the Gentiles, selected in a wonderful
manner out of the straitest sect of the Jews,—
converted from the belief that the glory of a Jew
was to possess a privilege which no others possessed, into the belief that it was his glory to be an heir
of the promise, " In thee and thy seed shall all the
families of the earth be blessed ;"—how this conversion was effected by a glorious manifestation
which identified the glorious King whom he looked
for, with the crucified man whom he despised—
identified both with the divine word, by whose
presence his conscience had been so often goaded,*
—proved that he who had so near and intimate a
a connection with Saul was united also to every
one of those whom Saul was persecuting ;—
how when he had received this faith, he was
yet told to arise and be baptized, and wash away
his sins ; how when it had thus pleased God to
reveal his son in him, as really and vitally, and

---

* ' It is hard for thee to kick against the pricks.'

not by a mere hereditary privilege, united to him,
—united to him as a man, and not as a Jew—he
was able to preach him among the Gentiles; how
he did preach him and establish churches, first, in
Asia, then in Europe; how all of these were
bound together by Baptism; lastly, how careful
he was to re-baptise into the Christian covenant
those who had only received the Baptism of
John.

When you have weighed these facts separately,
and in their connexion with each other, you will
be able, I think, to decide the question,—whether
the proofs from Scripture that Christ did establish
a spiritual covenant, as distinct from the carnal
covenant of circumcision, do at all interfere with
the assertion that he established water as the
permanent sign of the covenant. Certainly it
would *seem* that every part of the evidence which
proves one of these positions proves also the
other.

With respect to your notion, that the outward
Baptism was a temporary deference to Jewish
prejudices, it must, to be good for anything, take
this form. You must suppose the Apostles to
have said to the Jewish proselytes,—' We cannot
comply with your prejudices by *circumcising* the
Gentile converts,—that would bring them and us
again under the Law; but we will meet you half-
way. We will not wholly abolish ritual observances; but in place of circumcision we will
adopt that ordinance which you were wont to use
when you received the Gentiles into your pale.'

I

This, I say, is the only plausible form in which this notion can be put; for, to baptize a *Jew* was not to humour his prejudices, but to do them the greatest violence; it was, in fact, supplanting, or at least to a great degree superseding, the covenant which he considered so precious. How, then, stands the case? Did St. Paul, who you say baptized so very reluctantly, (and evidently for the sake of peace) only baptize Gentile converts? What says the text of which you are so fond?—" I thank my God that I baptized none of you save Crispus," &c. And who was Crispus? Turn to the Acts of the Apostles, and you will find that he was the *Chief Ruler of the Synagogue*. Strange blunder to be committed by a Hebrew of the Hebrews, brought up at the feet of Gamaliel, to fancy that he should conciliate his countrymen by compelling one of their principal men to undergo a ceremony which was to put aside circumcision! I think, therefore, that it is better in this text, as in others, to let St. Paul speak for himself than to ascribe an intention to him which does not seem very consistent with itself. He says, " I thank God,—........ *lest any should say that I baptised in my own name.*" Here was a good reason for rejoicing. He knew that he was in a town which was frequented by numbers of sophists of various schools, all contending for their own system, and notion, and sect. He would not be believed, if he could help it, to be the founder of a sect of Paulites or Paulicians. He fulfilled his commission, therefore,—he preached the kingdom of God; but he allowed the ministers whom he ordained to baptize, lest any should suppose that the church was a sect,—lest any should suppose that Baptism was anything less than an admission into the body of Christ. But perhaps you may say,— ' No ! this was not done by way of compromise or conciliation; it was necessary in the case of the Jew as a proof that the old covenant was set aside, and to the gentile as a proof that he turned from dumb idols; but it ought not to have been retained when the Jewish polity passed away—when God manifestly showed by his acts that a new age was begun.' Now I do not at all desire to explain away the immense, the transcendant importance of that great day of judgment, which was the signal that a new world had been created out of the wreck and ruin of the old. But before I can admit that an institution set up for the express purpose of witnessing to the establishment of a kingdom became unnecessary, in consequence of the event which proved it to be established, I must have either some express declaration to that effect from our Lord or his Apostles, or at least some hint that whereas the sign of the carnal dispensation remained till its extinction, the sign of the spiritual dispensation was to be abrogated, as soon as it had fairly commenced. At any rate I must have some evidence from reason that the abrogation ought, by the nature of the case, to have taken place, or some evidence from experience that, had it taken place, the spiritual dispensation would have been more clearly understood. That the history of your Society does not, in my opinion, afford this last kind of evidence, I have said already, and shall have occasion to say again.

I told you I should not moot this point till I had fully established the truth of your Friends' position that there is a spiritual kingdom in the world, and that all ordinances must be unchristian, if they substitute what is outward and formal for what is inward and spiritual.

For the same reason I have not as yet entered directly upon the question in which so many of your seceding Friends are interested,—whether the Baptism of infants is authorised by Scripture. Till the meaning of Baptism is ascertained, I do not see how it is possible to begin that controversy with any reasonable hope of a termination. I am rejoiced that the Independents and other sects of the dissenters can see their way clear, on their principles, to maintain an ordinance which I am sure it is greatly to their advantage not to lose; but I think it must require a cleverness and subtlety, which I do not possess, to hold their ground tolerably against ingenious men of the Anti-pœdobaptist party, and I feel a strong persuasion that the Swiss Reformers (Calvin especially who was so incomparable a logician) could not have been preserved, even by the strongest early prepossessions, from becoming Anabaptists, if the atrocities at Munster and in the Peasants' war had not made them unwilling to examine the arguments of their opponents fairly, and to consider how far it was possible, consistently with their other notions, to resist them.*   But supposing it be true that Christ came to establish that universal spiritual kingdom for which the Jewish kingdom was a preparation, — supposing the elder covenant led the Jews to perceive their union with an invisible head, and that upon the basis of that union, established and ratified by the death and resurrection of our incarnate Saviour, the covenant of Baptism stands, — supposing the utmost pains were taken to prove that one superseded the other, but that both had the same author and the same object, would it not seem strange that our Lord did not seize an occasion to say some such words as these, — " You remember that under the old dispensation children of eight days old were admitted into God's covenant.   But it shall not be so among you.   You might indeed argue with yourselves, — ' Our covenant is larger, freer, more universal, more evidently built upon grace than the one which preceded it.   It seems less to depend upon the acts of men, more obviously to be the principle and source of those acts ; surely, therefore, children are even more eligible to the gospel than they were to the legal sacrament.' You might think that as I had not in the days of

* Mr. Coleridge has expressed the same opinion ; but he has extended the remark, unwarrantably I think, to the Reformers generally.   I may perhaps be permitted to observe, that the Essay on Baptism, at the end of the " Aids to Reflection," strikes me as by far the least satisfactory portion of that admirable work, which I trust is becoming more and more precious to Christian students, and to which some confess, with humble thankfulness, that they owe even their ownselves.

your fathers been born, been an infant, been
a boy, the difficulty of supposing those conditions
of life holy, rested with *them ;* you might have
drawn the same inference from my not refusing
the infants when you wished me to refuse them,
from my saying, not that they did not belong to
my kingdom, but that they did; but all these
notions, plausible enough I allow, are not to
weigh with you.   I decree that the old laws of
God, in reference to his covenants, from this day
forth are repealed." Do we not, I ask, require
such a decree before we can act upon the presumption that a method which God has once
prescribed, He does not now approve? But if this
decree is not found in any canonical Scripture,—
if there is not even a tradition of its existence,—
should we not at least expect the inspired historian of the establishment of the church, though
he might not say in so many words,—' The
Apostles never adopted infants into the church,
according to Jewish precedent,' would at least be
most cautious to leave no loophole for the notion
that they did? Is he cautious? Why then did
he let fall those strange phrases about households,
which, though in themselves they prove nothing,
yet are most dangerously ambiguous when all the
presumptions are in favour of infant Baptism?
Why again does St. Paul, who touches on so
many Jewish notions and practices, — who spends
a whole Epistle in exposing the deadly principle
involved in forcing circumcision upon the Gentiles (on this ground especially that the new
covenant was the consummation of the old) why

does he never stay for an instant to hint that, though in all other points the Christian church was more comprehensive than the Jewish nation, in one particular point there was great danger in not considering it more exclusive? If our principle then be true,—if there be nothing in the nature of Baptism inconsistent with its being administered to infants,—we require a positive prohibition before we can depart from a principle,—before we can set aside as unnecessary and useless all the previous dealings of God with His creatures.

And now I must say a few words on the *Spirit of Scripture*. First, then, it is one of its essential characteristics, to refer the origin of every state in which man can be placed, to God, and to speak of every transgression as a departure from that state. Look through the law and the prophets, and say whether this feeling does not breathe through them all. You find nowhere a hint of man putting himself into any position except an evil and an anomalous one. I will be bold to say, there is not a passage in the whole of Scripture, in which a man is blamed for any thing but rejecting a position into which God, of his free love and grace, had brought him. So far, then, the idea of Baptism as a covenant in which man is put, a state conferred upon him, with which his acts may be either in accordance or discordance, harmonizes with what every Christian man feels to be the tone and mind of Scripture. But, again, the spirit of Scripture is eminently one of fellowship. See what havoc you are obliged to make of the most living parts of it

when you are determined to individualize it, to
make every passage bear upon your own experience. You have twelve prophets, all writing
upon national sufferings, sins, and judgments; you
have sixteen or seventeen epistles, all written to
bodies; only six letters to particular persons; and
the three longest of these to men, not as individuals, but as officers of the church. How impossible is it to enter into the spirit of Scripture, unless you will identify yourself with a body; unless you will look upon yourself as possessing the
highest spiritual privileges, only because you belong to that body, and not on account of any
favouritism shown to you, or any excellence belonging to you as an individual? On this ground
then, again, the idea of Baptism, as I have developed it, is especially in agreement with the
spirit of Scripture. Once more; the spirit of
Scripture is evidently a spirit of confidence, submission, and hope. Men are told to trust in
God; to confide in a Being who has manifested
that he cares for them. They are to submit to a
Being who has the power and government of all
the springs of life within them; they are to hope
for that blessing to which he has promised to
guide those who do not resist him; the blessing
of being acquainted with their best and dearest
friend. The idea of Baptism has these three
criteria of being a Scriptural doctrine : It bids
you confide in One who has taken you into union
with himself :—it tells you are constituted in a
righteous Being; that the flesh, and the world,
and the devil are seeking to separate you from

Him; that it is a narrow way in which you have
to walk: — it tells you that it is a sin not to hope
that this journey and this conflict shall have an
end; and that you shall enter into the fulness of
that communion, of which you have enjoyed only
dreams and glimpses on earth.   I could say much
upon this last subject; for I believe it will be
found, that a false view of the rewards which God
has provided for those who love him, is the secret
cause of men's objection to the views of Baptism
which I have been now expounding.   How it can
be dangerous to tell men that they are freely admitted into a kingdom of righteousness, and peace,
and joy in the Holy Ghost; that all spiritual
blessings are freely bestowed upon them; and
that these blessings are what every man really
wants, and without which he cannot be satisfied,
—those who invented the calumny can best explain.   But this subject I reserve for my next
letter.

   And now I may ask you, without fear, to examine the *letter* of Scripture, to look plainly and
steadily at the different *texts* in which Baptism is
spoken of. Commence, then, with the Gospels, and
see first to what shifts persons who deny the principles which I have been advocating, are driven, in
order to get rid of that phrase, ' *kingdom of heaven,*' which meets them in every chapter, almost
in every verse. Now they think they have escaped
the embarassment which it causes them, by calling it the ' Christian dispensation;' now it is
' Christ reigning in the heart of believers;' now
it is ' going to heaven.'   I do not deny that each

of these expressions has a meaning, and that all
their meanings are included in the words ' kingdom of heaven;' but I must say, that if persons
would recollect their own often repeated appeals
to the text of Scripture, and would steadily and
manfully grapple with this one phrase, they would
find how very little light their vague notions
throw upon it, and, on the contrary, how very
much light it would throw upon them. I think
you must, at least, grant, that I do not in this
instance depart from the letter. It is said that
Christ came to set up a kingdom, and I believe
he did set it up, and that this kingdom is that
restored or regenerate constitution in Christ ;
that constitution, according to the Spirit, and not
according to the flesh, which, by his incarnation
and atonement, he has asserted for mankind, and
into which we do, on that warrant, receive every
member of our species by Baptism.

In the next place, spend a few minutes (they
will suffice,) in meditating on those instances in
which the word regeneration, παλιγγενεσια, is used,
and see whether they accord better with this
meaning, or with that which the word bears in
the vocabulary of the religious world.   Next, I
would ask you attentively to read St. Paul's Epistles to particular churches ; calmly to inquire
whether the adoption of this principle does or
does not deliver you from the necessity of introducing some most awkward, and not over-honest
interpolations, and of doing outrage to what seems
to be the plain sense of innumerable passages.
Supposing, for instance, I meet with such words

as these : ' We are buried with him by Baptism
unto death; that, as Christ was raised from the
dead by the glory of the Father, we also should
walk in newness of life;'—is it not something
very like trifling with Scripture to be obliged to
say, — ' You must not understand that persons
are actually buried with Christ in Baptism, but
only that a believer has the privilege of becoming
more and more dead to the world every day, and
more and more alive unto Christ :' in other words,
that the allusion to Baptism was merely a gratui-
tous ornament of speech, introduced by the
Apostle without any reason or purpose.   Or
again, when it is said, shortly after, ' Count
yourselves dead indeed unto sin, but alive unto
God,' — are not some good people driven hard
upon Popery, in order to get rid of the letter,
when they say, ' That is to say, you know, *the
believer*, the justified holy man, is so to account himself dead.'   For if this be not the *de-
finition* of a believer; if a believer is not one who
accounts himself dead to sin and alive unto God,
what is he ?   Do you not see, that an inexplicable
something called *faith* is here thrust in between
man and his Lord, just as the ' works which were
to deserve grace of congruity,' were thrust in by
the Romanist ?   Again, is it not comfortable, when
St. Paul says in the Epistle to the Corinthians,
' All things are yours, whether life or death, or
things present or things to come, and you are
Christ's, and Christ is God's,'—to believe that he
meant what he said; and that he had not a secret mental reservation of this kind :— ' I do not

mean that all things belong to the disputatious,
high-minded, heady, sectarian, sensual part of
you; I do not mean that all these glorious privileges belong to that person who committed
crimes not to be named among Christians; I mean
only the true believers among you.'   Is it not
pleasanter to believe that St. Paul wrote in what
we call an honest, straight-forward style,—and
did not write less in that style, because he was
inspired by the Spirit of Truth,—and that he
really did mean, without exception, that all those
rights, and dignities, and glories appertained to
every one of them,—and that precisely the sin he
meant to charge upon the very worst of them,
was not taking the benefit of that which did belong to them? When, again, in the same Epistle,
we find him saying, as a reason against fornica-
cation, ' Know ye not that Jesus Christ dwelleth
in you? know ye not that your bodies are the
temples of the Holy Ghost ?'—is it better to
think that the Apostle did mean to address these
arguments to persons who were tempted to this
deadly sin, or had fallen into it,—is it better to
give some force to his reasoning and some meaning
to his words;— or to listen to the doctors and
doctresses of religious coteries, who are shocked
that we should apply these words to wicked people, and, consequently, in *their* exhortations, put
evil consequences, the danger to health or to reputation, or the horrors of hell, as substitutes for
the awful and astounding, yet most loving persua-
sions of the Apostle; which give the sinner such
an impression of his evil, as the very sight of the

lake that burneth could never strike into him ;
such a hope of deliverance as could not to be ex-
ceeded, if he heard his Lord say with his own
voice, ' Thy sins be forgiven thee ; Arise and
walk ?'

Again, when St. Paul plainly tells the Galatians
that it was a fall from grace to submit to circumcision, because it was returning again to the
law, and giving up the Gospel privileges of adoption and sonship ; is it better to suppose that he
meant to censure them,—all, every one,—for not
considering themselves as sons ; for not acting as
adopted children ; or that he considered it was
right in a few to think that they had those titles,
and a solemn duty in the rest, to feel that they
were not, at any rate as yet, theirs ? When, in the
Ephesians, he speaks without any distinction of
their being ' chosen in Christ before the foundation
of the world, that they might be holy, and without blame before him in love ;' — is it better to
suppose that he had a few picked persons in his
eye ; or that this declaration is connected with
what he says afterwards of a mystery, which in
other ages was not made known, as it is revealed
now to his holy apostles and prophets by the Spirit?
—his own commission being, ' To make *all men*
see what is the fellowship of this mystery, which
from the beginning of the world, hath been hid in
God, who created all things by Jesus Christ ;' and
that he is, in this magnificent Epistle, setting
forth a constitution in Christ, to which, because
it is for men, Gentiles as well as Jews were admitted, and into which it was the inconceivable

glory of these Ephesians that they were called;
which they might inherit, if they would not resist
the Holy Ghost? If you have any doubt which interpretation is most natural, most coherent, most
literal, ask yourself whether any honest Calvinistic minister with whom you are acquainted,
would sit down and write to his congregation in
the way in which St. Paul has written to the
Ephesians? Are you not morally certain that he
would introduce some such words as these: —
' But all that I say of these glorious privileges is
intended for those of you, my dear brethren, who
have undergone that saving, renovating change,
without which, you know well, there is no hope
or joy for any man. For the rest, — I say it with
tears, — you are outcasts from God; strangers to
the covenant of promise; the blessings I have
been speaking of are nothing to you. I solemnly
warn you not to delude yourselves by supposing
that you have any part or lot in the matter. God
forbid that I should shut up the gates of mercy
against you. I invite you, I beseech you to avail
yourselves of his mercy; but do not fancy for a
moment that you can claim union with Christ, or
remission of sins, or any other of the comforts
which God reserves for his dear children.' Is not
this the language which you would look for in such
a document as I have supposed? If these phrases
were not used, would not this minister accuse
himself, would not his neighbours accuse him of
want of faithfulness? Above all, if he ventured
upon the opposite language, if he addressed all as if
they were elect or saints; if he merely left it to

be inferred that some had no claim to these titles, would he not hear most hard words from others, and perhaps be inwardly tormented himself? And yet this *is* the habitual language of St. Paul. You may alter it, of course, to mean something else; but there it is, the very style which the preacher I have supposed, would feel, in his own case, to be so delusive and wrong. Are you then prepared to say—St. Paul,—he who withstood Peter at Antioch because he was to be blamed; he who endured persecutions from Jews, and Gentiles, and false brethren; who trembled at nothing *except* prevarication, *except* bearing false witness for God,—was a less scrupulous writer than the ministers and preachers of our day : or that he had a less feeling of responsibility and of the effect of what he wrote upon future ages; or that he was less taught of the Spirit? If not, where is the refuge but in the belief that he wrote not in one, but in all his Epistles, upon an entirely different scheme and principle from that in which they write. And what is this scheme and principle, but that which I have been attempting feebly to expound in this Letter?

If you pursue your studies to those Catholic Epistles wherein the Apostles of the Circumcision harmonise the truths developed in such clear and beautiful order in the writings of St. Paul; and explain their relation to the conduct of Christians, to their position in the world, to their communion with God, you will find, perhaps, still more startling illustrations of this great principle.

There is one passage in Scripture, the most

frequently quoted in this controversy, to which I
have scarcely alluded,—the conversation of our
Lord with Nicodemus; but I hope I may have
given you some assistance in studying it for
yourself. You will not now, I think, be surprised
to find the Baptism of Water and the Baptism
of the Spirit closely connected in this most spiritual discourse of our Lord;— you will not be
surprised to find both connected with our " seeing
the Kingdom of God;" — you will not be surprised to find the spiritual dispensation of the
Gospel connected with the conflicts in the heart
of a particular man. All *bears* upon the struggles between the flesh and Spirit in man, but
all is not *included* in those struggles. Here is the
turning point of the argument. These conflicts are
constantly taken notice of by your Friends; and
it is a notion that the doctrine of our church, in
one way or other, makes light of them, which
leads you, and in some degree the other dissenters, to regard us with so much aversion.
But I hope you may be by this time beginning
to perceive, that the doctrine involves no such
consequence ; that it not only recognises the distinction between the flesh and spirit of man in its
fullest power and meaning, but is actually based
upon that distinction. The difference between us
then is this : *We* say that, in the older dispensation, the struggles of men after light and knowledge, after union with this Divine Word, after
the knowledge of God, were exactly those which
your friends so vividly describe.

But we say, that since the new kingdom has

been set up in the world, men are no longer' to
be taught, that they are to seek God, if haply
they may feel after Him and find Him ; but they
are to be' told that God is seeking them ; .that
He has revealed himself to them in the person of
his Son ; and that He has made a covenant with
them, that they shall be to him children, and that
He will be to them a Father.   The emancipation
of man's spirit from the flesh, is therefore, we
coℵtend, to be spoken of as the effect, not as the
.cause of his being a child of God.   On the other
hand, not as the ultimate blessing intended for
men, but as the necessary step to his seeing the
kingdom of God ; to his entering into the apprehension of its truths and mysteries ; to his being
made its willing and cheerful subject.   And our
charge against those who reject this doctrine is
twofold,—that they lay a narrow and imperfect
foundation for men's salvation ; and that they
darken men's views as to the end and consummation of that salvation.   They do not bear witness
to the love of God, as the ground upon which all
redemption is built; they do not bear witness to
the knowledge of the love of God, as that fruition
to which redemption is leading.

This charge I consider in a great measure applicable to all sects and parties which have established any basis of communion, less comprehensive than that of a universal atonement, and a
universal covenant.   But it is more especially applicable to you, who have brought the question to
a test, Whether the outward sacrament of water
is or is not of importance to the purposes of God,

and to the salvation of man. For you have taken our own premises; you have spoken of a spiritual kingdom; you have asserted a light and salvation for all men; you have even maintained the truth, that it is by submitting to an operation from above, and not by the struggles and strivings of our own spirits, that those spirits become free from their shackles, and enter into life, and peace, and joy. And yet these very truths have, as I showed you in my last Letter, failed in bringing you peace of conscience; failed in keeping you at unity among yourselves; failed in leading you into a clear apprehension of the mysteries of the Gospel. What is the reason? My answer is, because God has appointed this water, as the witness and seal of that universal love to man; the seal of the universal fellowship established between man and man; the witness, that the power which raises man out of the death of sin, is of God and not of himself. Hitherto you have been enabled, by God's goodness, in spite of this deficiency, often to exhibit, as individuals, much reverence for God, much love to man, many high and noble spiritual aspirations. I do not think you know for how many of these you have been indebted to that very sacrament of which you have thought so lightly; for the rainbow of God's covenant spans the arch of heaven, and speaks to hundreds,— who only seem to regard it as a congregation of shadowy colours, soon to pass away,— of an earth which had sunk beneath the waters, and at the word of God was born anew. Nor while I admire and reverence the charity you have so

often shown to your fellow-men of every colour
and kind, can I help feeling that you have de-
frauded them of a witness more important than
warm clothing, or healthy prisons, or the right
to receive wages — the witness, I mean, that
God has sent his Son to enfranchise mankind;
that, as a Father, he had yearned over his
children, and sought them when they were lost;
that the Holy Dove is brooding continually
over them. For, do not imagine that any words
in which human art, or even Divine Wisdom,
speaks to man, carry these truths home with
such a power and witness to their hearts, as a
sign which it requires no learning to interpret;
which speaks alike to rich and poor, old and
young, in every nation and kindred under heaven.
Oh, surely, if your charity is so warm, and tender,
and universal, as on some occasions you have
shown it to be — the thought, how many sick and
lonely men and women, in obscure corners of the
the earth, apart from human teaching and human
fellowship, have remembered the name which
they received in childhood, and, too ignorant
to understand any thing else, have yet apprehended this truth, that a fellowship had been
established between them and the invisible world—
that a Father, Son, and Spirit were watching over
them in love, have believed this, and by this belief have entered into that repose of childlike confidence, to which the most learned theologian,
the most experienced Christian soldier, must be
brought, if he would share their joys—the reflection how many who had strayed into the

ways of evil—had forgotten every fatherly instruction, every word of peace and life that they
had ever listened to, may have been struck by
the recollection of that sign and that name, and
have returned to Him who was the guide of their
youth, saying, " Father, I have sinned;" not to
speak of the silent influence which it may have
had among Pagan nations in counteracting many a
Christian blasphemy,—such thoughts will lead you
to consider that the pride which tempted your
fathers to reject this ordinance, because, forsooth,
they had all the fruits and blessings of it in their
hearts, is a black and grievous stain upon their
philanthrophy. Nor dare I suppress my conviction,
that however for a time God may have averted the
calamity from you, the hour is rapidly approaching when you will feel, that, by this rejection,
they were injuring their own posterity even more
than they were testifying their want of sympathy
with the human race. A thousand indications
prove, that a crisis is approaching, when the question, whether there is a universal society or no, in
which men may claim fellowship with each other,
will be debated, not between schoolmen and
theologians, but by labourers and handicraftsmen
in every part of the world. Schemes of universal
government, fellowships cemented upon principles inconsistent with national society, subversive
of family life, are arising all around us. This
craving in men's hearts cannot be stifled, it must
be satisfied. The question is, how shall it be satisfied ? By polities based on universal selfishness,
carrying in themselves the elements of their own

destruction; or by a polity based on love, wherein all its members are bound together in one head. Such a polity your fathers tried to set up. Where is it? What is become of it? What satisfaction does it offer to the anxious hearts and spirits of men? At the very moment it is wanted, it is crumbling in pieces. It rested on human faith, with the loss of human faith it perishes. Such a polity, we say, is the universal church of the living God; the kingdom of heaven set up on earth; a kingdom which has lasted in despite of human ignorance, crime, unbelief; a kingdom which shall last until it has subdued them all under its feet. But to *see* this kingdom, to enter into its principles, to partake in its sorrows, to share its triumphs, to be able to discover it when it pleases God that kings should be its nursing fathers, and queens its nursing mothers; that it should be surrounded with power, and honour, and glory, claiming the whole earth and the fulness thereof for its Lord; to know it, too, when it is in abjectness and poverty; when its ordinances are despised, its existence questioned; when kings of the earth are sending presents one to another, because they think that the witness against their crimes is at an end,—this is the gift for which, above all others, we ought to long and pray. I cannot think that it is a gift which those will receive, who glorify their own graces and spiritual attainments—who will not take the blessings of God's kingdom as little children,—who will not uphold and prize the witness of God's free love.

Let us be sure, my dear friend, of the ends

which we propose to ourselves; then we may hope to understand the means by which we are to seek them. Whatever may have been the case in former days, he is a foolish politician and a bad calculator, who in this day seeks for honour and respectability, and the esteem of the world, by bearing witness for the name of God, and defending his ordinances. If you seek these ends, I own, without a moment's hesitation, that the argument which a celebrated dissenting minister addressed to his own flock, is applicable also to you : " If you did not join the church in its high and palmy state, will you join it now, when even its admirers and patrons are forsaking it ?" If, on the other hand, you desire to be witnesses for that spiritual and universal kingdom, of which your early friends delighted to speak, to spread it among men, to enter into the mysteries and truths upon which it is grounded, you cannot too quickly submit yourselves to God's laws, however simple or insignificant in human estimation, and thus resume the position which your fathers not in wilful obstinacy, but with much ignorance and precipitancy, abandoned.

Believe me,

Yours very faithfully.

* * * *

NOTE TO PAGE 99.

I RATHER fear that in the text of this Letter, I may have led the reader to think that I object to Dr. Pusey's theory of repentance chiefly because it presents the Gospel in so cheerless and hopeless an aspect to *men*. But this is not the view of his doctrine which is most distressing to myself and to very many whom, with reason, Dr. Pusey would be far more grieved to offend. The light in which it exhibits the character of God, as willing the death of the sinner, — as hardly persuaded to set him free (though the freedom he seeks is from Sin) — the utterly selfish character which it imparts to penitence and prayer, — the encouragement which it gives to the notion that we are not to seek for union with a Being of perfect purity and love, from whom by our impurity and lovelessness we have been separated, but by great efforts to alter the feelings and disposition of God towards us, — are far more shocking to our minds than the consequences which we believe must follow from the doctrine, though we do not deny that those consequences seem to us to be nowhere so accurately described as in the article on Predestination; —if generally received, " it would thrust men into desperation, or into wretchlessness of most unclean living, no less perilous than desperation." These being our feelings, it would be rank cowardice to be deterred by the most unfeigned respect and admiration for the recent reviver of this tenet, or by our belief that he and his fellow-labourers are intended to confer great blessings on the church, or by our conviction that their hearts are probably far freer than our own from all the evil which we think is involved in the notion, from expressing, at every fitting opportunity, our intense dislike to this part of their system.

If we wished for a strong practical protest against it,

we should seek it in the following beautiful lines from the " Christian Year:"—

> And wilt thou seek again
> Thy howling waste, thy charnel-house and chain,
>   And with the demons be,
> Rather than clasp thine own Deliverer's knee ?
>   Sure 'tis no heav'n-bred awe
> That bids thee from his healing touch withdraw,
> The world and He are struggling in thine heart,
> And in thy reckless mood thou bidd'st thy Lord depart.
>
>   He, merciful and mild,
> · As erst, beholding, loves his wayward child ;
>   When souls of highest birth
> Waste their impassion'd might on dreams of earth,
>   He opens Nature's book,
> And on his glorious Gospel bids them look,
> Till by such chords as rule the choirs above,
> Their lawless cries are tun'd to hymns of perfect love.

The lines on the first Sunday after Christmas are equally striking on the same subject—

> How shall we 'scape th' o'erwhelming Past ?
> Can spirits broken, joys o'ercast,
>   And eyes that never more may smile :—
> Can these th' avenging bolt delay,
> Or win us back one little day
> The bitterness of death to soften and beguile.
>
> Father and Lover of our souls !
> Though darkly round thine anger rolls,
>   Thy sunshine smiles beneath the gloom,
> Thou seek'st to warn us, not confound,
> Thy showers would pierce the harden'd ground,
> And win it to give out its brightness and perfume.
>
> Thou smil'st on us in wrath, and we,
> Even in remorse would smile on Thee ;
>   The tears that bathe our offer'd hearts,
> We would not have them stain'd and dim,
> But dropp'd from wings of seraphim,
> All glowing with the light accepted Love imparts.

The lines in the " Lyra Apostolica," (a volume of beautiful poetry lately published by Rivington) beginning,—" I prayed, I fasted," are also a clear and admirable assertion of the truth which I think Dr. Pusey's tract contradicts.

LETTERS TO A MEMBER

OF THE

SOCIETY OF FRIENDS.

BY

A CLERGYMAN OF THE CHURCH OF ENGLAND.

No. III.

ON BAPTISM AND THE LORD'S SUPPER.

LONDON:
W. DARTON AND SON, HOLBORN HILL.

ADVERTISEMENT.

THE Author of these letters had at one time intended to throw them into the form of dialogues, in which a Quaker, another dissenter and a churchman, should have been the interlocutors. There are many advantages he thinks, beside the obvious one of escaping the appearance of egotism and dictation, in this form of writing. In no other is it equally possible to make the treatment of a particular controversy the means of elucidating a method which shall be applicable to all controversies. In no other can you so easily do justice to the reasonings of an opponent without any affectation of liberality or indifference. In no other can you with so little effort exhibit truths which belong to all ages, in the drapery of that one with which God has intended you most to sympathize.

But there were some objections to this plan, which induced the writer, not without reluctance, to abandon it. The form of dialogue has been adopted by the greatest artists and philosophers of every age as the happiest medium for conveying their thoughts. One who has no pretension to rank himself in either of these classes, might on other grounds than those of mere modesty avoid the very appearance of such presumption. Without securing him the attention of speculative men it would lead men of action and business to suppose that he did not write for them. A dramatic form of writing is always connected in their minds with contrivance and authorship. They cannot conceive that it is intended in a plain and straight forward way to remove practical perplexities from their hearts, and guide them to practical conclusions. At all times much should be sacrificed, every thing perhaps but earnestness itself, for the sake of convincing men that we are in earnest. But it was especially a duty, to aim at producing this impression in a series of letters intended primarily for the use of a sect which counts simplicity the first of virtues, dealing with questions which at this very moment occupy and distract the hearts of hundreds of its members, and purposing to prove to them and to all others, that they must take a certain practical course, if they would be delivered from their theoretical difficulties.

For such a work as this the epistolary form with all its presumption and impertinence seemed more suitable and even more modest than that which upon some accounts the author would have preferred to it.

In writing the present letter the author has often wished that he had adhered to his original purpose. He could then, without awkwardness, have introduced one of the parties in the dialogue urging any objections to opinions advanced in the former tracts, although they had occurred only to the writer, or to some private friend. On the contrary, he has been obliged in this letter to put forward objections to his own positions without stating who suggested them, or by what arguments they have been enforced, He is fully aware that such a course is inconvenient; but it could not, in justice to himself or others, be avoided. He knew that he had been supposed grossly to misrepresent the opinions of some for whom he expressed and felt the greatest respect; and if there were the least chance of any other of his readers being led by his language to fancy them chargeable with doctrines which they had never professed, it was his duty to explain that language, even at the risk of repeating himself and appearing to answer a shadowy opponent.

With respect to the imputations upon his own principles, he is very thankful for them, as they have enabled him to give a more perfect view of that method which, as he said just now, he conceives is applicable to all controversies, than it might have been easy to exhibit while he was occupied with the details of a particular one. In this respect, his present letter may belong more to other sects and to churchmen than those that have preceded it; but he trusts also that the Quakers will perceive much more clearly, by means of it, how he conceives their disputes may be reconciled, why he refuses ever to speak of his church as a sect, and why he takes so much pains to persuade them that the church is an actual living body, not a fiction or a theory.

It will be observed that the author here has only entered on the subject of the Eucharist. He thought that the *history* of that sacrament would be the very best

illustration and support of the principles laid down in
the first part of this tract; but he could not overcome
a great unwillingness to enter upon the more deep
and mysterious parts of the subject, while he was under
the possible influence of any personal or controversial
feelings.   He trusts that he may have removed some of
the most serious obstacles to useful meditation upon this
topic.   If he should hereafter be enabled to give a
right direction to such meditation, the highest end he
proposed to himself in writing these letters will be
accomplished.

   March 6.

LETTERS

TO A

MEMBER OF THE SOCIETY OF FRIENDS.

No. III.

My Dear Friend,

I am most anxious that you should clearly understand my letter upon Baptism. It has, I am grieved to find, been most sadly mistaken. That opinions should have been imputed to me which I abhor, is some cause for personal annoyance,—that I should have been supposed to impute opinions to others which I know that they are as far from holding as I am, is a ground for serious sorrow. I have determined, therefore, in justice to myself and to them, before I enter on the subject of the Eucharist, to spend a few pages in explaining my sentiments on the other Sacrament.

I. I will notice a charge which affects the whole character of these letters. If it is believed, my purpose in undertaking them is frustrated, and every word that I have uttered, or shall utter, will create an impression exactly the reverse of that which I intended it to produce. I have been accused of a leaning to *Eclecticism*. I will explain to you, in a few words, what I conceive eclecticism to be. There are a number of different systems, schemes, notions of morals, metaphysics, and theology, prevalent in this and in former ages. Each one of these has its respective professors, disciples, and noviciates. Some of these are more occupied in attacking the views of their opponents, some in defending their own; but all discover so much of zeal, and ardour, and passion, that you may see they are contending for that which they find it very hard to sacrifice. After a while a man arises up of capacious powers of intellect, disliking the violence of all these sects, not sympathizing with the feeling of any of them, but yet convinced by reflection and observation, that each has something to say for itself;—each, he says, brings forward arguments which the other cannot answer,—the theory of each strikes him as maimed and imperfect. He conceives the magnificent notion of constructing a great theory, which shall contain the fragments of truth that are scattered in all these different opinions; he will make a system, all the portions of which shall fit rightly into each other, which shall be a fine harmonious whole. Such a man is an eclectic; such were those who corrupted Platonism, and endeavoured to amalgamate their notions of it with certain Judaical and Christian notions in the first ages after the Christian era,—such, in the present day, is the most learned and accomplished of French writers, M. Cousin.

Well, you will say, and does not this scheme meet your views? Is it not exactly what you are striving after? Supposing it could be realized, should not we have those full-orbed truths of which you spoke? Should not we have that charity and union which you seem to think possible? I answer at once, and without hesitation. Admitting this scheme to be possible, I should infinitely prefer any one of the doctrines, prevailing in any one of the sects, to that fine theory which would combine them. I say farther, that I believe in each one of those sects there would be more *truth* than in this great eclectic doctrine ;— I say once more, that I believe in each one of the exclusive sects there would be more real charity and love, than in the professors of this all-comprehending one. Are you startled at such assertions? do they seem to you inconsistent with the method and principle of my last letter? I am perfectly ready to justify the words I have spoken, and to maintain their agreement with every word that I have spoken before.

The object of the eclectic is to build up a great *theory*. Of the actual wants that have been experienced from age to age in the heart of man, or that are experienced by him now, he knows nothing ;—all the sighs, and tears, and longings, which way-faring men, which the ignorant, the

helpless, the sinful have actually realized,—all the
conflicts with foes without and foes within,—all
the toil, and pressure, and misery of the world,—
all, in short, that is real, all that is not mere
paper and print, are to him as dead letters.   The
living eye, the living voice, are nothing; he looks
only at his stop-watch.   This notion will fit into
that notion; this argument, by a little scraping
and paring, will associate very civilly and kindly
with   that   which   has   been   always   goading
and affronting it.   Famous   designers! exquisite workmen! " Bricks have they for stones,
and slime for mortar." With such materials they
may build their Babel easily enough,—they may
raise it to heaven if they will; but when it is
finished, what will it be worth;   Will the inhabitants speak one language? Will they not be far
more divided, far more unintelligible to each other
than they ever were before? For what is to ce-
ment them? The *system* may be perfect, but
what is that to them?   Their sympathies, wants,
sorrows, joys, faith, and hope have contributed
nothing to the edifice. It stands in its naked and
solitary stateliness, to be gazed at and wondered
at; but the living, working man feels that he has
nothing to do with it. The object has been to
exclude everything living, because *that* seemed to
be the cause of confusion and division.

    And yet, I am convinced, such Babels are
building, and will be built in our day; and that
men are running, and will run into them, because
they find that their own houses are too narrow

to dwell in,—that they are plastered with un-tempered mortar, and will not stand when the rains descend and the winds blow. And though my weak judgment would exclaim, ' Let them stay even in those houses, because there they will have some warmth, though it may be from sparks which themselves have kindled, — some light, though it may only make its way through cran-nies and crevices,—let them not go where all will be utter coldness and desolation; yet I see that this is not the will of God; I see that men will either fly to mere Babels of speculation, or will take refuge in that house composed of " living stones, in which there are indeed many man-sions ;" but not one cut off from the rest,—not one that does not communicate with every other, —not one that is not necessary to the order and coherency of the whole building.

Therefore it is my wish to show the mem-bers of different sects, which I see are falling, some more gradually, some more suddenly, to pieces, — *first*, that they will not long be able to stay where they are ; *secondly*, that when they fly, they must go where they will be able to retain everything that has been really good and vital in their old and exclusive faith, everything that has really tended to humble and purify their minds,—where they will have to part with no-thing but their pride, and self-will, and dislike of their brethren.

II. It was in pursuance of this purpose, that I addressed myself to the members of your Society.

I found it rent asunder by parties, one of which was ready to escape into another sect, out of mere disgust to certain principles which they had received from their parents and instructors, and which they felt did not satisfy certain wants that had been recently excited in their minds. This is not a time, it appeared to me, in which men can afford to part with one single strong living conviction; least of all is it a time, in which we can afford to throw aside that reverence with which the instructions of fathers, and of ancestors, have inspired us. Just in proportion as we lose either, it seemed to me, we are sure to hinder ourselves from attaining that higher life, that deeper awe, which connects us with the Holy and Incomprehensible God. The Sects, I saw, were willing to receive your fugitives,—willing to confirm them in all their prejudice against early Quakerism. This, I said, I will not do. As a man I disliked such a course, as a Churchman I detested it. On the contrary, I would show you, that those feelings and principles which I would not have you part with for the world, did indeed require facts and principles to sustain them, of which you had taken little account, and of which your seceding friends were now beginning to perceive the importance; but that neither the old principles, nor the new, nor both combined together into a theory, would satisfy the wants of your minds, or heal your divisions, or make you real assertors of truth to the world. There were great living ordinances appointed by God, in

which these truths and these facts were expressed, which bound together the doctrines
which you had neglected, with that Christian life
of which you had spoken so much ; — prevented
the first from degenerating into mere letter, the
latter from evaporating into a dream,—became
the appointed witnesses for the one, the regular
channels for conveying the other. These ordinances your fathers had discarded, fancying that
they were enemies to spirituality,—that they substituted a fictitious unity for a real one. The
time had come, I said, when experience refuted
this notion, when you were threatened with the
loss of all spirituality—the loss of all unity. It was
right for you, then, to inquire, how far we were
right in saying, that these ordinances were the
great preservers of both, — that all attempts to
build up a church upon a foundation, either of
dogmas or of feelings, or of both combined, had
been confounded by the demonstration of history,
and that by means of these, the universal church,
built upon the unity of three persons in the Godhead, and upon the reconciliation effected for
mankind by the death and resurrection of Jesus
Christ, has been upheld, in spite of the ignorance
and inconsistencies of its members, from its first
establishment on the day of Pentecost unto the
present hour.

III. It was my business, therefore, to bring before you these different ordinances,—to show you
what meaning we attached to them,—to prove that
our meaning was justified by the language of

Scripture,—to show that they did offer you exactly that of which you had need. All right method required that I should begin with the ordinance of Baptism. But here an obstacle immediately presented itself. I was to set before you the view which we took of the Sacrament of Baptism. But who are *we ?* If that pronoun was merely a pompous way of expressing the sentiments of the author of the tract, it did not avail much for the object which I was seeking to promote. If, on the other hand, it meant any particular section of the church, I was still deciding upon my own judgment for the views of that section, in opposition to those asserted by every other. I did not blink this difficulty; I showed you that I had not the slightest wish to evade it. I contended, that though to my feelings the fact of such difference was most painful, yet to my argument it was profitable. And this in two ways, —*first,* if a church is so liable to be torn by the oppositions of its particular members, surely its stability does not rest in the faith and wisdom of these members; *secondly,* if ordinances be, as it was my wish to convince you that they are, the reconciliation of opinions which, while they are held merely as opinions, are necessarily opposed, it was to be expected that when men began to theorise and systematise concerning ordinances, each would but apprehend one portion of the truth of which *they* embodied the whole. Thus this obstacle, which, superficially looked at, seemed insurmountable, when fairly examined becomes a

confirmation of our past conclusion, and an encouragement in our future course. But what direction shall that course now take? Now, perhaps,
though we had shunned that road hitherto, we
must run into the eclectic method, and strive to
fashion a great theory out of the discordant elements furnished by different parties. Or was it
not rather true that this was precisely the moment at which we could not, without the most
flagrant inconsistency, adopt any such scheme,—
precisely the moment at which we had no temptation to adopt it, because another and much
more obvious one presented itself? If the idea
of the ordinance had been, according to our hypothesis, destroyed by the attempt to theorise
upon it, how dare we, proceeding upon that hypothesis, invent a theory broader or narrower
respecting it? If the idea of the ordinance had
been, according to our hypothesis, destroyed by
the attempt to theorise upon it, and yet, by the
same hypothesis, some strong and vital feeling of
its nature and meaning had been kept alive by
the providence of God—working through the ordinance itself, in each of our parties, what need
had we to *invent*, when it was much easier and
simpler work to *distinguish;* to note where speculation had intruded upon the really strong and
energetic faith of each class,—had concealed and
cramped it,—had set it in apparent oppugnancy
to that with which it was meant to have the most
fraternal harmony.

Thus you see how very small a work I as-

signed to myself; I merely undertook to show
the earnest lovers of truth in each party what
portions of their creed were really so near to their
hearts, that they could not, without tearing every
fibre asunder, rend it away; what portions were
merely the products of their carnal understanding,
and not only were not necessary to the other, but
impaired their life and efficacy. I knew this to
be a work of *faith*. I did not expect at once and
suddenly to make my case good to the most
honest and single-minded man. I expected that
some of the most honest and single-minded, if not
previously practised in such inquiries, would at
first resist the evidence most stoutly, because they
would be the most fearful of parting with anything really precious which they had held. But
with them I was sure the principle would work
in time. This fermentation, indeed, I might in a
hopeful mood regard as a sign of its working.
With those who did not care for truth, and were
not single-minded, I did not care to argue. They
have their own teachers. Ἄφες τοὺς νεκροὺς θάψαι
τοὺς ἑαυτῶν νεκρούς. So far I was not *departing*
from the principle,—the anti-eclectical, Catholic
principle, which I had followed in my discussions
with you. But, happily, in this part of my subject, in the arguments I had to carry on with the
members of my own communion, I had even less
to trust to any perceptions or powers of my own,
than in the other case. Here I could not only
appeal to experience and feeling, I could appeal
to permanent forms, recognised by all the dis-

putants. I could say,—' Is it not true, not only
that your *feelings* respecting this ordinance are
clearer, simpler, deeper, when your theories respecting it are cleared away, but that these *forms*
can be interpreted more literally and exactly,
with fewer interpolations, omissions, mental re-
servations, when that clearance has been effected ?'
Do not these forms embody the principle, the
feeling of each of you, without the notion where-
with you have incumbered it ?

IV. Supposing I made this point good, I was
then in condition to turn round to you and say,
' Now, then, these divisions of opinion among us,
do not, you see, in the least affect my argument,
or present the least obstacle to your finding, in
our church, all that you cannot find elsewhere.
On the contrary, you have heard the discourse
which has been going on between us. I wished
that you should hear it. I did not ask you, as
strangers, to withdraw. We did not carry on our
dialogue in *asides*. You have heard it all, and
you see with what new force I am able to say,
' This is what WE *mean* by Baptism; is it not
what YOU *want* ?' To this task I therefore addressed myself; and, while performing it, I found
that I was able to do more than I promised, more
than you could have demanded. I was able to
give a still stronger emphasis to the word *We,*
than it could have derived from the virtual consent of existing parties, and from the positive testimony of forms, to which they all appeal. We
were able, at least, to make a tolerable guess, not

unsupported by positive evidence, that if we con-
sulted the opinions of past ages, they, too, would
be found witnesses, both for the propriety of our
method and the rectitude of our conclusion. The
course of the argument I must shortly explain, because it is here that I have been most misunder-
stood myself, and am supposed to have dealt most
unfairly with others.

V. Baptism being, in the forms of our church,
connected with regeneration, it was important to
understand the sense of that word. The majority
of the religious world, we found, affixed *this*
sense of it; they supposed that at a certain period
of a man's life, his nature or heart is changed, or
that a new life, or a new nature, or a new principle is infused into him. The controversy between the parties we found, turned mainly on this
question. ' To what period shall this change, or
this infusion, which all in some sense admit, be
referred?' The Evangelical party contend very
stoutly, that such a change must take place in a
conscious subject; that the heart or affections are
the seat of it; that these naturally take a wrong
direction; and that the period at which they are
converted into the new direction, is the period of
regeneration. When, therefore, they found this
word in the church service, connected with the ordinance of Baptism, they said,—' Here it is used
in a different sense; we do not say it is a wrong
sense; we know that there is authority for it;
but it is not the great important sense; here it
means only *admission into the visible church*. Now

it has been usual, in arguing against this hypothesis, either to deny the reality of these conversions, or to maintain that they are exceptions to a
law, rather than instances of it.   I did not take
either course; neither would have accorded with
my principle of defending the living feeling of
every party against its notions; neither would
have exactly squared with my convictions.   I
took these histories of conversions as real, and I
gathered from them this important conclusion,
that in all those cases which bore the strongest internal evidence of genuineness and sincerity, there
was a distinct acknowledgment that the converted
man entered into the enjoyment of a state which
it was his sin and misery not to have claimed previously.   He then takes up the privileges of a
child of God and a member of Christ; and he
blames and condemns himself for having so long
refused these privileges.   If this be so, what, I
asked, becomes of the Evangelical assertion, that
the words of the Catechism, affirming baptised
children to be members of Christ, and children of
God,—*can* only mean something nominal, because those who have been baptised, often (to
say *always*, would be false, but it would make
no difference to my case) do not begin to lead
a holy life till they have reached a mature age?
Why may not the words assert that very truth,
which the converted man himself testifies, that
this was his *state*, and that his *life* was evil, because he did not believe it to be his state?

But I had another argument. The Evange-

L

lical party appeals to the Reformers of the sixteenth century as the standards of their divinity,
but as especially sound upon the doctrine of justification by faith. Well then, what say the Reformers on this point? Why, they distinctly call
upon men to believe in Christ on the ground of
their baptism. They rest their practical arguments for a man taking up his position as a justified man, upon the fact that he was established
and constituted in Christ by baptism, and that
he has no right to doubt of the reality of that
constitution. What was the just inference from
these facts? That the regenerate *life* of which the
Evangelical speaks, presumes a regenerated *state*,
with which it is in accordance; that if a man's
life be good, it is because he believes that this is
his state, and acts as if it were so, renouncing himself, claiming union with Christ, submitting to
the Holy Ghost; that if his life be evil, it is because he disdains that state, refuses to consider it
his, acts upon the supposition that he has not
been redeemed, justified, and admitted into God's
family; that if his life be changed, it is because
he relinquishes his unbelief, and takes up the
freedom which he ought to have possessed long
before. Thus, we affirmed, that these writers had
done their feelings and their truth mighty injustice, by that very denial which set them at war
with their brethren.

We found another set of persons in the church,
whose tastes, education, habit of mind, were altogether different from those we had been hitherto

examining,—far more learned, far less mixing in
the world, and, to say the least, as zealous, devoted, self-sacrificing. These persons had adopted
the Fathers, as the Evangelicals had adopted
the Reformers for their standards of divinity.
Taking the work in which the sentiments of this
school had been most clearly and profoundly expressed, I found that the author started with *assuming* the Evangelical notion of regeneration as
the true one. Let me be understood. He com-
mences his tracts with arguing the question precisely in the manner I put it just now :—Does
regeneration take place in mature life, as some
affirm, or does it take place at Baptism? I
said therefore, you may remember, that any view
of regeneration, but that implied in the words
' change of nature,' had evidently appeared to
this writer inadequate. I did not mean that the
words, ' change of nature,' were used by him. I
merely meant, (as my readers will, I trust, have
understood from the pages which preceded,) that
he attached no notion to regeneration, but that
which the Evangelicals attached to it when they
spoke of it as a change of nature, a change of
heart, a new life, or a new nature. Still less did
I intend, by this remark, to intimate that this
learned divine attached no value to *Baptism* but
that which is expressed in these words. I knew
well that he had spoken again and again of our
being graffed into Christ; of our receiving the
Holy Ghost; nay, I said, in the strongest terms,
that no persons were more anxious to assert those

truths than the gentleman in question, and those who thought with him. My complaint of him was simply this,—that by introducing the notion of a new nature or an infused life into the question, he weakened the rest of his principles; he destroyed the idea of regeneration as an actual constitution in Christ, with which the baptised person might or might not be in agreement, but which belonged to him, and could not cease to belong to him, though he might reject all its blessings; he enfeebled our Lord's analogy of the *new birth,* which seemed, (according to his conversation with Nicodemus, and according to the name φωτισθεις, which the primitive church gave to the baptised person), to intimate not an infusion of any thing, but a passing out of the darkness of the flesh into union with the living Lord, or else, as Luther expresses it in one of his sermons, a destruction of the Old Adam Nativity, and the acquiring of Christ's Holy Nativity; he had led many persons to substitute a notion, half physical half spiritual, of an infused life for the actual gift of the Holy Spirit,—and thus, lastly, he had brought back the doctrine, that the baptismal act rather confers a natural purity upon the subject of it, than unites him to a Being who is purity, and drove us to the conclusion that this purity might be lost in some other way than by loss of faith in that Being, and could not, in ordinary cases, and according to ordinary principles, be reclaimed by the renewal of that faith.

These were my objections to the *theory* of the

powerful and deeply interesting work to which I
alluded; objections not grounded upon inferences
of my own from the statements contained in it,
but upon the direct assertions of the writer, in that
part of it which developed the doctrine of *Repentance*. On the one hand, the theory seemed to
me to affront that view of Baptism so strongly
taken by Luther, which made it the ground of repentance and faith; on the other hand, it seemed
liable to all the same danger as the theory adopted
by the pseudo-Lutherans of later times,—which
leaves us utterly at a loss in what language to address our fellow-sinners, whether as the adopted
children of God, who have wandered from their
Father's house, and may arise and return thither;
or as children of wrath, exiles from his presence
and his love. For, whether the privilege of adoption had never been given them, or being given
had been lost, our way of considering them must
be the same; or rather, we were bound to look
upon them in the last case, as more excluded from
all the blessings and invitations of the Gospel
than in the former.

In expressing my dissent from this theory of a
new or infused life or nature at Baptism, I distinctly complained of the *inconsistency* in which it
involved its supporters, by weakening those truths
respecting the adoption of the child into Christ's
body, and the gift of the Holy Ghost, which " *no
persons were more anxious than they to assert.*"
With inexpressible astonishment, therefore, I have
heard that I libellously charged these writers

with meaning to impugn these doctrines; and
have read extracts taken from the work, on which
I commented, for the purpose of convincing me
how unjust I had been.   Once for all, I never
made such a charge.   I must have been not a
calumniator merely, but a madman to have made
it.   I should not merely have contradicted the
plain evidence of a book, which is in every one's
hands, but I should have flatly contradicted myself.   I did know perfectly well that throughout,
the " Scriptural views of holy Baptism," a graffing
into Christ is spoken of as an incident, the leading incident of regeneration ; nay, that there are
passages in which the author seems to speak of
it as regeneration itself.   My regret was, that
he did not always so speak of it ; that he had
brought in a notion having no warrant in Scripture or in the language of our forms, which interfered with that simple and glorious idea; a
notion which had nothing in it real or heart-
warming ; a notion which he himself forgot,
when he rose into earnest, living appeals and exhortations, and yet a notion which infected all his
habits of thought, and compelled him to the most
startling practical conclusions.

But in endeavouring to get rid of this inconvenient notion, I was very fearful of two results,—
one was, of impugning that grand truth, of which
it seemed to be the weak representative, that the
Holy Ghost actually and formally, in that solemn covenant, takes the baptised person under
his own training and government, and promises

to guide him, if he will submit to be guided, into all knowledge and all love;—the other was, that it is the Will of God, apart from all faith, as well as all acts in man, 'which constitutes us righteous persons. The first doctrine seemed to me so all-important, that I expressed my delight and satisfaction that it had been presented with great power to a particular writer,* who in all his other views of Baptism, seemed to me thoretical and obscure. I felt that it was so much the very truth of which we in this age stand in need, as the counteraction to our materialism, and our intellectual self-glorification, that I did not wonder it had been adopted with all the accompanying notions of its propounder, by many earnest seekers after truth. Nevertheless I contended, that when once the High Church principle and the Evangelical principle had been stripped of their accidental outgrowths, and had been restored to practical and living power, this would harmonise with them; and would be found to stand firm, without the ' assumptions' and ' fictions' that had been appended to it. The other great principle,—the first in theological order, though in act and working inseparable from the other two, — that the will of God is the only source of our righteousness and salvation; this great principle, I said, seemed to me to be asserted with such power, clearness, and sweetness by those who are imbued with patristic feelings

* Mr. Budd.

and learning, as I could not find in the very best writings of the Reformed, or the modern school. These last had spoken finely of the blessings of our union with Christ, to be apprehended by faith; and some of them of the illuminations, teachings, and comfort as of the In-dwelling Spirit. But they were too entirely occupied with what is technically called ' personal religion,' to say much upon a subject, however deep, and glorious, and needful, as the ground of all meditations and all life, which had not an apparent practical signification. Or if they were driven, by the necessities of their minds, to such inquiries, you heartily wished they had never ventured on them. For in their hands they became dry and hungry speculations on the mere sovereign power of God, introduced to explain, and that by most wretched arguments, drawn from vulgar analogies of human character and procedure, why some are not saved,—a point which we are *not* told that the *angels* desire to look into,—rather than to discover the first fountain and well-head whence all the streams of mercy and life have flowed forth upon mankind.

The spirit and feeling of Dr. Pusey's tracts,—which I am sure will be admired by every man who loves what is pure and Christian, and which, (though for reasons of no importance to you or my other readers, I did not speak largely of them in my last tract), were one of my reasons for disliking his theory, because it seemed to me so utterly at variance with them, — this exquisite spirit and feeling had their birth, I thought, in his deep and simple apprehension of our Heavenly Father's gracious will and power to save his lost creatures, and endow them with all spiritual blessings in Christ Jesus.

With extreme pain,—pain not occasioned merely by the uncomfortable feeling that no words, be they expressed ever so guardedly, are safe from the most monstrous misconception, if those which I uttered could bear the one that has been put upon them,— but also by the more distressing thought still, that any persons, themselves of candid and generous minds, could suppose me capable of uttering a foul and wilful calumny, I learn that I am supposed to have accused Dr. Pusey of regarding God as our Father in some heathenish sense, and not as our Father in Christ. In the solemnest manner in which it possible to say the words,—I declare, that the most distant thought, or dream of such a charge, never entered my mind. I was stating wherein I thought the High Church party strong, not wherein I thought them weak, when I said that the idea of an adopting Father was that which they seemed to have brought out and presented with the greatest clearness to my mind. What! if a teacher in Christianity says to me,—You may learn more respecting the doctrine of justification than you can of the doctrine of the Trinity from Luther, does he call Luther an Arian? If he says you must read Athanasius on that Catholic truth; of course you must not look to him for the refu-

tation of heresies which had not arisen in his day
—does he therefore say Athanasius implicitly recognised these heresies ? And yet such inferences
are not one whit more unreasonable than those
which have been drawn from my words.

In fact, if this principle of interpretation is followed out to its consequences, some of the most
recognised common-places of divinity must be set
at nought. A man shall no more dare to say,
there are different gifts, but the same Lord,—different operations, but the same spirit,—one is
called to illustrate this portion of truth another
that,—all such sentences, of which our text-books
are full, must be exploded,—they bring construc-
tive heresy upon all the teachers of the church ;
and if any one, following the example of a pious
and powerful writer of our day,* shall apply them
to Scripture, and maintain that St. Paul and the
Apostles of the circumcision followed two distinct
lines of thought, converging to the same point,—
I know not how he will escape the charge of imputing to the inspired writers a direct denial of
some important article of that faith which they
were commissioned to deliver to the saints.

Believing that this principle of distinct gifts and
vocations, of which the gentleman to whom I have
referred has made so bold a use, is a fundamental
part of the idea of a church, as set forth by St.
Paul in his First Epistle to the Corinthians, I

* See a Sermon on St. Philip's and St. James's Day, at page 202
of the 2d volume of Parochial Sermons, by J. H. Newman, Fellow
of Oriel College.

ventured next to contend, that the schools of theology to which our existing sects respectively profess allegiance, would probably be better understood and appreciated, if they also were taken as illustrations of it. If we found certain devoted students of the Fathers, much imbued with certain habits of feeling, which they could not have derived from their own age, it was a fair presumption that these habits of feeling,—it was probable also that some indications of the theory which had fastened itself to those habits of feeling,—would be discoverable in their writings; though it would be quite likely, and according to ordinary analogy, that the latter should be more prominent in the disciples, the former in the teachers. In like manner, if other persons of our day had conceived a very vehement admiration of the Reformers, the best part of the habit and temper of thought which these divines exhibited, might be looked for in the books which they loved, together with the germs of any inconvenient notions and expressions, by which the growth of these good habits had afterwards been choked and stunted. Both these inferences, so natural and unavoidable from our premises, I did not, in my last letter, however, rest upon any other evidence, than an appeal to the passages quoted from the Fathers in Dr. Pusey's own tracts, and certain extracts which I made from Luther's Sermons. Yet it has been said, that in these remarks, I was on the one hand pretending to a learning which I did not possess, and had positively disclaimed; on the

other, that I was again substituting a theory for
facts. I deny both charges flatly. There was no
assumption of knowledge in what I said,—there
was nothing like a theory. To make a few familiar extracts from a well known book, which,
through a translation, is within the reach of every
English student, did not, I suppose, argue much
pedantry. To say that the passages I met with
in Dr. Pusey's work, did not bear out his conclusions, was asserting no more than that I had
read a book, which came out in sixpenny numbers in the year 1835, and was published in St.
Paul's Church-yard. Nor does there seem much
theorising in such observations, unless it be
considered a theory in a little child, who looks
at the countenance of a nurse or parent, to
say, 'that expression is cross, or that is kind.'
I should think every body reading a book with
his eyes open, formed some notion as to the
feelings which the book expressed. It may be
theorising to do so,—not to do it is all one with
being asleep. If, however, I had gone much
further than I went in my last tract, and I *do*
mean in *this* tract to carry the application of the
principle a little further,—if I had ventured to
state what a meditative study of ecclesiastical history led to me think was the relation of the
different ages of the church to each other, I still
contend that I should have been doing nothing
that savoured of arrogance or quackery. I should
not have intruded ipon the function of those who
devote themselves laboriously and exclusively to

the study of any one of these ages; for, amidst
the many incalculable blessings which they may
confer, the one which, we are certain from all experience they will not confer upon us, is that of
enabling us to understand what is the general
scope and spirit of the books, which they have considered atomically,—what is their connection with
the workings of thought and society in other
ages, which they have not considered at all. Nor
will my humble attempts to assist the ecclesiastical student, in discovering what kind of benefit
he is likely to receive from reading the Fathers
or the Reformers, or how much he has need
of that reading, make him at all less inclined to
value the labours of those who bring them
within his reach.   While so many are endeavouring to discourage us from all study of
antiquity, threatening us with every kind of
mischief and confusion if we engage in it,—I
conceive the promoters of that study need not
count as a very troublesome enemy a person who
seeks, in however poor a manner, to excite an appetite for it, and to show that it will turn out to
be food, not poison.   I shall have more to say
on this point before I conclude my letter; in fact,
it will be my object, in all the latter part of it,
to show how this doctrine respecting the character of different periods explains the history of
the Eucharist.   My observations will, I believe,
remove some preparatory difficulties from your
path, and enable us to enter, hereafter, upon the

M

full consideration of the subject. But I must first
remove some further objections to my former
tract, which, if they are of any validity against
that, must still more strongly affect all that are
to follow it.

VI. I shall not refer to that part of my last letter
which treated of our forms, and of the argument
from Scripture; for to these I have not heard
any objections. Assuming them, I will sum up
what I conceive to be the difference between the
reconciling method, which is adopted by the
eclectical school, and that which I have adopted.
*The Eclectical harmonist endeavours to exhaust all
sectarian notions of the feeling which is mixed up
with them, that he may amalgamate them into a
great theory, of which he is the author. The Christian harmonist endeavours to discover the latent
feeling, for the sake of which the sectarian values
his exclusive notion, to show him how that feeling
has suffered from its intellectual satellite,—how it
has been kept from fellowship with other feelings,
with which it must be united, if it would attain
its proper strength and proportion, — how it is
united with all those feelings in the confessions,
forms, and ordinances of the Catholic Church,—
and how these forms and ordinances, while they
preserve in clearness and integrity the faith, hope,
and joy of every way-faring man, and expound
to him the connection between his own heart and
the written word, do also lay the best and only
foundation for a system of dogmatic theology, which
shall exhibit the method of God's revelations, with-*

*out converting them into a theory, and shall enable
the professional student and minister of the word,
to preserve the spiritual life of his brethren, both
from the pollutions of the senses, and the inventions of the intellect.*

VII. But to tell the truth, I believe this explanation, however it may relieve me from the charge
of eclecticism, will rather aggravate than diminish
my guilt in the eyes of those who preferred it.
They would have thought me far more excusable
for endeavouring to construct a great and all-
comprehending theory, with which the feelings
and wants of men should have nothing to do,
than for entering into those feelings and wants,
and pretending to connect them with so solemn a
question as that of belonging to the Catholic
Church. 'Feelings! wants!' they will exclaim,
'what concern have we with those? What does it
signify to us that certain self-willed men in certain
sects are experiencing certain doubts and anxieties and perplexities? There is one plain course
for the Christian minister who really does apprehend the importance of a church and its ordinances. He must say to these men, — God has
instituted a great scheme for the salvation of
mankind. He has appointed a certain method by
which you may enter into that scheme. If you
refuse it, you do so at your peril; if you submit
to it, you will receive the blessings of it.'

Now I fully believe that it is not expedient
for every member of the church to be busying
himself at all times about those who are not

within its fold. I do not in the least want to buy
golden opinions of you and other dissenters,
by pretending that I think it is a more glorious
vocation to fetch any of you back into the bosom
of the church than to watch over its regular
members. On the contrary, I will frankly confess that I conceive that one is the appointed
task of those on whom God has bestowed his
richest and noblest gifts; the latter only the
business of certain men not well-drilled, nor
suitable for, any great employments, — men of no
mark or likelihood in the general camp, whom,
by certain processes of education, known perhaps
chiefly to themselves, He has rendered more
fit than their betters for these foraging excur-
sions, and has taught, by many signs not par-
ticularly gratifying to their fleshly pride, that
they should be only too thankful to be permitted in this or any way to serve such a master. I should therefore, I hope, feel no kind of
displeasure that those who are, as I believe,
serving Christ in another and much higher
sphere, should think very scornfully of my random labours; and if their sphere of operations
chanced to lift them very much out of the pur-
suits and proceedings of this age, and to throw
them back into the feelings and temper of a
former one, I should not be surprised if their
natural notions of contempt took even the form
of indignation, — if they declared that a person
pursuing such an entirely different line from their
own could not possibly be promoting, even in

the most humble and insignificant degree, the same ends; that one burrowing amidst the anxieties and disquietudes of that period of restless excitement and speculation into which it is their misfortune to have been born, could not possibly be keeping in view any really noble design; that pretending to gather in a way so strange and peculiar, it must be the effect if not the purpose of his labours to scatter. All this, I say, I should have expected, and instead of complaining I should have rejoiced that there is one very pleasant exercise permitted to those who are not called to the noble enjoyment of loving those who hate them; that of admiring those who despise them, — "Contemnant si velint, scribant modo." Their scorn will be very endurable if they give us good editions of the Fathers.

But when this scorn assumes a grave and argumentative form, when we are told ex-cathedra, that it is positively wrong to take any other course for convincing men that there is a Catholic Church, and that it is the haven intended for every man, but that one which they have laid down for themselves, we must have the liberty of inquiring if not the reasons at least the authority for such a dictum. They will not, of course, be quite so illogical or so dishonest as to escape into some declamatory sentence such as this, — ' What, then, you deny the authority of the church? *then* we have nothing to say to you,' — because they knew perfectly well that we should retort instantly, — ' Have you the authority of

the church for saying that this is the only line of
argument which it is lawful to use? and because
they knew as certainly that to this question they
would not have one word or syllable to answer.

On the contrary, the commonest charges against
those whom they delight to honour, curiously
resemble that one which is brought against the
plan of these Letters. It was a grievous offence
in the eyes of St. Paul's enemies that he would
become all things to all men, and that he *could*
do this, — could enter into all the habits of mind
which belonged to the Roman politician, the
Greek metaphysician, and the Hebrew ritualist,—
without abandoning one jot of his principles, or
knowing anything but Jesus Christ and him
crucified. It has been a charge repeated by
Milner and his school *usque ad nauseam*, that the
Fathers would labour to connect great Christian
truths with the old systems of philosophy. It has
been a sneer, in which Englishmen have not been
ashamed to indulge, against Gregory and our
Augustine, that they did not outrage all the best
and devoutest feelings of the heathens to whom
they brought the glad tidings of Christ, but tried
to compel them into his service. So that, unfor-
tunately for our accusers, if Catholic antiquity is
to decide the question, we stand upon rather
higher ground than they do. We do not find
these old churchmen trampling upon all the
thoughts and feelings of the world around them,
— we do not find them counting all the cravings
and longings of men after life and light, things of

no moment, which the preacher of the Gospel
was to look upon his heavenly commission as
superseding and setting at nought;—such notions
did not belong to these holy men. And whatever guise of simplicity they may put on, and
however they may be seemingly put forth as a
counteraction to philosophy and vain deceit, I
believe that if they be well sifted they will be
found to contain a marvellously large infusion of
that pride and self-glorification and contempt
which are the worst characteristics of philosophy,
falsely so called.   And let their authors magnify Christianity as they will, if they do not see
and feel that Christianity in its highest and
simplest form is the satisfaction of all the real and
permanent desires that the heart of man hath
ever known, or ever shall know, I think they
have not even begun to apply right measures in
estimating its greatness and dignity.   As for
simplicity, I do not want a nobler specimen of it
than that ancient man at the first Nicene Council,
who, bearing on his body the marks of his Master's Cross, said to a philosopher who came to set
on foot a controversy, " Hear me, Sir ! I believe
in God the Father Almighty maker of heaven
and earth," and so rehearsed the articles of the
Apostles' Creed, counting them better than much
disputation.   And yet this confessor went upon
precisely the principle which I contend for.
He produced that which he knew the philosopher
wanted, and that which he knew would satisfy
his wants.

There are specimens of the other course, I
know, specimens in abundance; but they must
be got *mutatis mutandis* from Geneva and from
the sects. *They* say to each other,—' Your opinions are at variance with the Bible, therefore
renounce them.' The persons of whom I speak
would say,—' Your opinions are at variance with
the opinions of the church for 1800 years, therefore renounce them.' Both statements may be
true,—both arguments *sound* most reasonable.
But what effects have they produced? I told you
in my first letter,—I told you that they had produced hollow, unsatisfactory converts, deniers and
scoffers, haters of the old creed, but not believers
in the new; men in whom truth seems every day
more a dream, and love more an impossibility.
There is no charm in the words, ' Submission to
the church,' more than in the words ' submission
to the Bible,' to prevent such a result. And this
experience has shown clearly enough, and will
show, I fancy, to those who are not yet convinced,
more abundantly hereafter. Many a man who
has run the gauntlet of the sects, who feels all
that was once strong or living within him, destroyed by a life of change and excitement, who
is conscious of a premature senility in heart and
mind, will gladly betake himself at last to this
phrase, — submission to the church; intending
by it an acquiescence in the want of all inward
convictions and earnest hopes; because to rest in
that which was settled ages ago, is the humbleness required of those who are the servants of

Christ. But is this the kind of submission which the good and pious men with whom I am arguing require? I am sure it is not. I am sure they know what these proselytes are worth at the out-set, what they will be worth at the end of their career; and I could almost venture to prophecy, that some day or other they will discover, that those who have been led by a very different course than this to submit to the church, and delight in her ordinances,—who have been brought to them after years of painfulness, as the termination of practical doubts which nothing else could solve, — as the fulfilment of hopes which nothing else could satisfy, will be found not less humble, (for how much have they had of that which does humble, the experience of their own ignorance and wretchedness,) than those who have been " rocked and dandled" into Churchmen; not less tenderly careful of the ark of God than those who never discovered its sacredness, till they thought, like Hophni and Phinehas, that it would have a charm if they carried it forth with them to battle.

I do not wish you to think, my dear Sir, that it is for your sake principally, or for the sake of your friends, that I fight so earnestly against the notion of the church being merely a great power, commanding obedience, rather than a store-house of blessings for the satisfaction of all wants. I am bound, indeed, to feel much sym-pathy for you, because I know that, instead of its being an indication of teachableness in the member of a sect to yield himself easily and at once to

the church, it is often a proof of just the opposite
feeling. It often shows that he has not cared for
that ordinance of the family, which, as I believe,
God intends to be the preparation for, and induction into the higher ordinances of the church.
It is to me very shocking language which some
members of our church use, when they say, — ' I
have no hopes of you, you defy the opinion of so
many generations ;' for it shows that they have not
considered what a sacredness has been stamped
by God upon the authority of parents and early
teachers, — one from which all feelings of reverence to past ages must grow; certainly what does
not spring from this root will be a bastard reverence, and to destroy the root seems to me the
readiest way to destroy the flower. All such arguments, therefore, when addressed to you, though
you will appreciate them hereafter, must needs
seem vicious to you now ; whereas, if you could
but feel that all which you have learned from
youth upwards must perish, unless it be sustained
by church ordinances, and shall attain its full development by means of them,—that very feeling,
that holy feeling, which in the other case coun-
teracts our endeavours, becomes their strenuous
ally. But yet I would not have you suppose,
that I mainly object to this idea of the church, on
account of the mischievous effects which it must
produce upon you. I object to it, because I consider it greatly robs the church of the glory which
it has pleased its Divine Author to put upon it.
Let them exalt its *powers* as they will, I will not

quarrel with them, if they do not make *power* the first, and noblest, and greatest thing; if they do not lead men into a forgetfulness of the truth that love is the essence of the church, power only her accident and attribute; if only they do not lead us to feel that we must crouch to her as a terrible task-mistress, not be raised by her out of the intolerable tyranny of the world, into the manly and joyful freedom, which is her great, holy, and living possession. This tendency seems to me to be gaining ground among persons whom, on other accounts, I am much disposed to respect, and more than any other indication which they have yet exhibited, has inspired good men with trembling and displeasure. For it would not be a light thing if this disposition extended no deeper; it could not be a light thing if in any one instance power were represented as greater and more awful than holiness and love. But such a notion never prevails on a low ground, without ascending to the very highest; if it be forgotten that Jerusalem, the city of the Great King, is pure gold, like unto clear glass,—the perfectest love in the purest light,—it will be forgotten that the throne itself has a rainbow round about it like unto an emerald. No man who speaks of the power of the church more than of her beauty and loveliness, but will speak of the power of the Creator more than of his beauty and loveliness. And then we can no longer prove how perfectly the crucified man is the image of the invisible God; the attempt is scouted as rationalism; nay worse, if we bring a doctrine to the test of its presenting the character of God, as Christ presented it, we are called *profane*. Now, persons who do know what rationalism in its evil sense is, and who do look with unspeakable horror upon profaneness, and at the same time know that there is no evil so terrible into which they may not fall,— are likely enough to be for a time quite overpowered by such charges as these. Men of honest hearts have need, in these days, of strong nerves also; as many times through fear of committing sin, of which greater men than themselves, with solemn aspect, have warned them, they will be withheld from taking the only course to arrest that danger which they fear. And so, I believe, it is in this instance. We are told, that if we appeal to men, as Mr. Erskine has done in his book on the Internal Evidences of Christianity, on the perfect suitableness of the Incarnation to all the desires which God has excited in their minds,—this is rationalism. Our answer is plain and direct: It seems to you rationalism, because it is the very cure of rationalism. Infidel rationalism says,—We have an apprehension of a Divine Being within us, and that apprehension is the substitute for a Revelation. The Christian answers: You have such an apprehension, and therefore you need a Revelation; and if you will be honest with yourselves, you will find that it is this revelation of God in Christ, which your inner man is seeking after. Deny the assertion

of rationalism, and you deny a fact,—a fact which
we believe, and Churchmen down to the age of
Locke have also believed, to be involved in all
Scripture. Put aside the fact of rationalism, and
you leave it in all its infidel power, a mighty anti-
Christian principle; acknowledge its truth, and
show, that without a revelation, and your revelation, the truth becomes a lie, and you have taken
out its sting, you have made it a minister of
the sanctuary. So again they say, If you affirm
a particular doctrine, (respecting repentance, for
instance), to be inconsistent with the revealed
character of God, you are profane; all you have to
do is to ascertain whether such and such is his plan
and decree; you are presumptuous, and almost
blasphemous if you look beyond this. Here,
we reply in like manner,—Our course is not a
profane one, it is the only deliverance from profaneness. We do not say so, because some of the
highest men in the English Church held this
opinion; we do not say so, because it was the
doctrine of Smith, and More, and Whichcot, and
Worthington, and Cudworth, and Norris, and
Leighton; all of whom consider the character of
God as the centre of divinity; using it as a
test whereby the nature of all opinions was to be
tried; accounting every wrong apprehension of it
as the source of profaneness, urging the continual
contemplation of the ineffable charity, and the
perfect, absolute love, as the only way to holiness.
We do not rest upon human judgments, although to be profane with such men were no very

hard sentence; but we have better witness than theirs. To be very jealous for the name of the Lord of Hosts; to hate every false god, because he had not the signs of truth, and love, and purity, was the characteristic of every saint in the Old Testament; to declare that name, in its fulness and simplicity, after the darkness had passed, and the true light had shined, was reserved as the most glorious privilege for the most aged and perfect saint of the New. And what strange language is this, to tell us that God hath provided a way of salvation, and that we are to walk in it, in the hopes of at last attaining eternal life; but that we are not in anywise to inquire respecting his character, when he himself gives us to understand that salvation is the deliverance from the sin, of which the cause at once and the penalty, is ignorance of him, and that this is eternal life to know him, and Jesus Christ whom he has sent.

It was absolutely necessary that I should have discussed all those points, but especially this last, before I entered upon the subject of the Eucharist. Were it true that men must be commanded to submit to the church, before they are told any thing of its meaning and its principle, it would be utterly improper in me to address you upon the Sacraments at all. And this much I freely concede, that if I proposed to *explain* this Sacrament in the ordinary sense which we give to the word ' explain,' I should be undertaking a very dangerous as well as very foolish task. It is my very earnest desire not to do this; but, in the *first* place, to make you feel how and why this Sacrament is above explanation; and, *secondly*, how and why the heart of man loves it and longs after it, and cannot be satisfied without it, although it be above explanation. Now this paradox, for a paradox it is, and must be to the carnal heart, I propose to prove to you by the simple evidence of history. I am not about to produce any new facts, — those which I shall notice are familiar to every ordinary reader,—neither shall I, out of these facts, form any theory; I shall merely endeavour so to set them before you, that they will explain themselves. As we proceed, you will see how the principles which I have been discussing in this letter, help to make the facts intelligible, and how the facts in turn illustrate the principles. Believing, as I do most firmly, and as I hope to convince you, that I am about to enter upon a deep, and holy, and awful subject, I must needs desire to be preserved from making any careless step, — to be endued with a reverent spirit,—never to forget that I am speaking of a mystery, and yet never to forget that there is now no veil over the face of God's ministers; that the awfulness and dignity of our station consists in our being invited, with open face, to behold his glory, that we may be changed into his image; and that the more deep and awful our impressions of the mystery are, the less we shall affect any needless concealment, the more we shall be taught to use all plainness of speech.

This idea of a kingdom or state, though clearly recognised by your friends, as it must in some way be recognised by all men, (for the notion of a new and Christian life, without the acknowledgment of some state, with which that life is in agreement, is, whatever persons may fancy, too great a contradiction, to be practically admitted into any system,) is not, however, the subject on which they dwell with most interest and affection. They have seen, most rightly, that the condescension of God, was not merely something for the contemplation and wonder of angels, but that it had a mighty object in reference to men. The Creator stoops to the creature, that he may raise up the creature to fellowship with the Creator. The Holy One enters into all the miseries and sorrows incident to the unholy and fallen race which He had formed, that He may lift them to the contemplation and participation of his own essential holiness, and purity, and glory. This process has occupied a much larger share of your attention than the other; and, the connection of the two is precisely the subject on which your writers are most obscure and unsatisfactory. I hinted in my last letter, that in their description of the struggles and conflicts through which man comes to realize the glory which is intended for him, they led us back to the period of an earlier dispensation, and bore little witness to that mighty interference of the Father and Lord of Man, to *seek* that which was lost; without which, it seemed to me, that the other truth, important

as it is, loses its proper foundation and its great
comfort. Nevertheless, the accounts in the writings of your friends, of their struggles after
light—of their baffled hopes and bitter disappoint-
ments—of their discoveries that they must submit
to a power above them, in order to rise above the
opposition of the carnal nature—their repeated
assertion of the necessity of self-sacrifice in order
to victory—of the Cross as the way to the crown,
—seem to me so profoundly interesting and *real*,
that I cannot read the criticisms and censures of
your modern Seceding Friends upon them, without some uncomfortable, and, I fear, some uncharitable feelings. In time I am able to suppress
all such emotions, by reflecting that these critics,
though they may be attacking that which, in itself, is very good, are conscious of a deficiency in
such statements, which is to them of the most
practical importance. Putting myself in their position, I feel that I could be as harsh and as bitter
as they are. My wish, therefore, is not to complain of them, but to show them how they may
gain a position, which will enable them to feel exactly what the truth of these views is; feel why
they have been unable to give peace and satisfaction to their consciences; feel how they may be
able to reconcile these positions with those which
they have newly embraced, and henceforth hold
them more strongly than they were held by those
who first asserted them; yet in perfect and living
harmony with all that they have seemed to contradict. The Sacrament of Baptism, considered

N 3

as that whereby God brings men into the regenerate *state*, which Christ vindicated for men when
he took their nature and reconciled them to God;
was that which upheld one of the principles of
your founders, and connected it with the general
method of God's plans. The Sacrament of the
Lord's Supper, considered as the means whereby
God communicates and preserves to men that regenerate *life* which he claimed for them when he
ascended on high, is that, I believe, which can
alone support and vitalize those of which I have
just been speaking.

It is a fact, of which I wonder that your early
writers, Barclay and Penn especially, who were
cultivated men, and had read ecclesiastical history, did not take more notice, that the progress
of thought and feeling upon theology, and, I
might add, upon morals, and even upon natural
science, is inseparably connected with views of
this Sacrament. It might surely have led them
to pause and think, whether these elements could
be really such insignificant and beggarly things as
they fancied, when they found that they have
been the centres round which the theories and
the practices which have most affected the church
for good and for evil, have revolved, almost from
its foundation to their own day. It must, I think,
have struck you, that the history of the church,
I had nearly said of mankind since the coming of
Christ, would be almost involved in a history of
the two Sacraments. But I do not introduce this
point here, for the sake of drawing any inference

from it; I merely intend it as a preface to a few
remarks on the different leading schemes. respecting this Sacrament, and the circumstances
which were connected with the rise and popu-
larity of each.   In the course of these observations, I hope to show you, as in the case of Baptism, that each partial view, even when it has
seemed to exaggerate the importance of this institution, has in fact degraded it ; that the idea
which reconciles them, is at once larger and
simpler than any of the three ; that this view is not
now for the first time discovered, but has existed for
centuries in living forms ; that there could be no
clear view of the rite, which did not recognise the
sacramental principle of it; and that the principle becomes vague, powerless, and even contradictory, when it is not.embodied in the rite.

The idea of Baptism which I supposed the early
church to entertain, was this,—That a gracious
and merciful Father has sent down his Son from
heaven, to seek after creatures who had wandered
from Him, to bring them back, and to adopt
them as members of his own family.   This one
feeling of an adopting Father lay underneath all
their thoughts and expressions.   The church was
a great family.   The relationship of each member
of it to its Head, was a peculiar relationship indeed ; but yet different in dignity rather than in
kind from the corresponding earthly relationships.
The earthly bonds made the heavenly ones intelligible,—the heavenly bonds glorified the earthly.
This simple principle may have been expanded

into a number of forms, but you will scarcely
ever find it giving place to any other.   The child-
like affectionateness of their piety has this origin ;
the heresies which they combated were felt as heresies, because they trenched upon this principle.
When they became philosophers, and studied the
remains of Greek or Hebrew wisdom, you would
expect to find a perplexity in their minds ; you
would expect to find the comfortable truth of a
brother and friend of their hearts, half explaining,
half refusing to mingle with the awful idea of a
living Word and Monitor.   In like manner, you
would expect to find their speculations on nature
full of interest, full of confusion.   All things
around them presenting images and types of the
life which was in them,—a world seeming to contain those feelings which were really cast upon it
from within,—every thing admired,—something
felt, nothing understood.   No wonder that the
indications of such a state of mind should lead
some men to look upon this as the golden age of
Christianity, to sigh and cry for its return, and to
think no sacrifice too costly in order to procure it.
Without agreeing in their opinions or their wishes,
I can admire much more than the particular features of this or any age, that Divine Wisdom
which endowed men with qualities exactly fitted
to make them the safest guardians of those institutions by which he intended the being and life of
his church to be sustained through all times, as
well as of the formal confessions of those truths
which these institutions livingly expounded.

You will not, I think, be at any loss to understand how that institution which is the subject of my present letter, must have presented itself to minds fashioned in this mould.   A Father has adopted us into his family. He will surely sustain and feed us. But what nourishment do we want? Such as will preserve us in this new life,—such as will keep us united to our Father and our brethren,—such as will enable us to act out our relations.   They know that He that came down from heaven to reconcile their Father to them,—He who took the flesh of them all,—identified himself with all the sufferings of humanity,—offered up his body and poured out his blood as a sacrifice, did, on the night that he was betrayed, take bread and bless it, saying, " Take, eat, this is my body;" that He took the cup, and gave it to them all, saying, " This is my blood, which is shed for you and for many, for the remission of sins."   They have no doubt that Christ came to establish a kingdom, of which his Apostles were founders.   They have, further, no doubt that they are admitted by Baptism into it, and are inheritors of its blessings.   They have no doubt that Christ, by taking the body of man, united men to each other; that by offering it up to God, he united them to God.   They have no doubt that he had glorified the body which he took, and that this glorified body is the permanent bond between them and the Creator.   They have no doubt that God means to feed them as his children.   They have no doubt that what they want is to realize the connection between God and themselves. They have no doubt that, when he gives them the bread to eat and the wine to drink, he satisfies this want. He says of the bread, " This is my body;" and they receive it as such. He says of the wine, " This is my blood;" and they receive it as such. The thing itself is a profound wonder to them; but that he should use these elements is not wonderful to them, that is exactly what they would have expected and desired. They did not ask themselves, — they could not have imagined if they had,—how he could have dealt with them in any other way.

The prevailing idea in the minds of these early Christians, was, you perceive, that of the condescension of God to the weakness and evil of men. Hence the feeling of its being a Eucharist. The feeling of thanksgiving takes precedence of every other. With this, however, are necessarily mingled other and more painful thoughts,—the child has wandered from his Father,—the member of the family has forgotten the bonds which unite him to his brethren. Confession becomes another element of the service. There must be pardon before there can be rejoicing. The bread and wine assure the communicant that it is granted; he feels himself restored [to the privileges which he had wantonly sacrificed; he fears, but rejoices, because he is forgiven. And why is he forgiven; and what is the foundation of his confidence? He is taken out of himself; he is carried up into fellowship with a higher nature; he enters into the

enjoyment of that glorious humanity which is in
Christ. What this means he knows not, he cannot explain; but it is connected with eating this
bread and drinking this wine; his whole heart,
and mind, and spirit are at times *transubstan-
tiated.*

These living feelings rose above the level of
their general apprehensions, and consequently
expressed themselves in obscure language. On
the other hand, that apprehension, especially
when they tried to explain it to others, led them
into some inconsistencies. They believed that
Christ, by his death and sacrifice on the Cross,
had fully reconciled them to God; and that in
Baptism they had received his pledge that their
sins were not imputed to them, and that they had
a new and holy nativity in Christ. This was the
very ground of their thanksgiving; and yet they
felt that they did actually fall into sin, and that
those sins hung about them, and that they did
not enjoy any of the fruits and blessings of this
reconciliation, unless they were partakers of this
other Sacrament. Hence their minds would be
tempted into the notion, that practically, the sacrifice of Christ was not complete; that something else had to be done, in order to accomplish the reconciliation; that unless he were
in some manner offered and presented again, his
death was to them as though it were not. This
puzzle, I say, would intrude into their minds, not
being capable, as yet, of a clear solution; would
give rise to many awkward expressions, in which

the critics of another age, looking back into their writings with a determination to detect flaws,— with no capacity for detaching himself from the feelings of his own time,—with very little know-ledge of the actual difficulties of his own mind, or no courage to face them,—may represent as dark or crude, betraying ignorance of the Gospel, and which may lead men of a far better temper, who read in a spirit of admiration and love, and not of criticism, to acknowledge that the light which those good and wise men for the most part honestly followed, was struggling through some earth-born mists, and that these mists after-wards settled for a while into thick and porten-tous clouds.

Again, they felt, that the body and blood of Christ was the bond between heaven and earth; the invisible had stooped to the visible; the Im-mortal had put on mortality. So far all was clear and delightful contemplation; but when they looked upwards,—when they thought of this pure and holy Being in his ascended glory, and themselves still in sinful flesh, unclean, and dwel-ling among people of unclean lips,—they were at times baffled and confounded. Some link be-tween them and him seemed to be needful; and those glorified spirits who had been fed with his flesh and blood, as they were, who had felt not only earthly infirmities like him, but had ac-tually committed earthly sins,—these seemed to supply the link. At those great feasts all heaven and earth seemed to partake, but with feelings

and joys how different! Might not their brethren,
who had gone before, have a more perfect experience of their present feelings, than it was right
or safe to attribute to their glorified Head? Such
thoughts, I say, not perhaps distinctly stated to
themselves, would occasionally rise in the hearts
of men who felt how God had stooped to his creatures; but did not feel so strongly how he was
seeking to raise them to the contemplation and
enjoyment of himself. From these causes it came
to pass, that the difference of the two Sacraments
was not always well ascertained; that infants, in the
early ages, were occasionally admitted to one as well
as the other. The mere notion of condescension,
the mere feeling of a gift and blessing, so much
pervaded their minds, that they scarcely considered
that the very notion of food implies a receiver of
a certain capacity and appetite. The very opposite of the feeling which prevails in our day was
their temptation. *We* refer everything to consciousness; they almost nothing. The intellectual
condition of the recipient is that which we dwell
upon exclusively; the disposition and power of
the Bestower was with them all in all. But there
was one great blessing upon this state of mind,
which, like its positive defects, was afterwards
converted into a curse. That which is the commonest element for the sustenance of man,—that
which is the greatest inspirer of his animal energies and life,—having been consecrated into the
symbols of a high mystery, everything else in
nature assumed a sacred and sacramental cha-

o

racter; everything spoke to them of a Being who
had stooped to take their nature upon him;
every common thing seemed to have been touched
by the Divine Enchanter, and converted into
gold. There was no notion of defining the number of such signs and sacraments, far less of
raising any of them to an equality with those to
which they all owed their beauty and graciousness. Still it would be likely, that the most important crises and institutions of human life,
should seem to be endowed with a peculiar glory,
—above all, the sacred institution of marriage,
throughout the Bible the symbol of the union of
Christ and his members, established, as they believed, for the very end of shadowing it forth,—
would almost, of course, be regarded as a mystery, and in some sort as a key to all others.

Such, it seems to me, is a tolerably correct,
though a very inadequate sketch of the feelings
with which this Sacrament was considered in the
early ages, and of the relation which it bore
to the other feelings of men. But there came a
crisis in the history of the church, which made it
necessary that men should understand something
more of themselves than they had hitherto done;
that they should have a power of distinction as well
as simple faith; that they should not only give
thanks to him who showered blessings upon them,
but should know in what way they become inheritors of these blessings. The rise of the Pelagian
heresy creates this necessity. A Welsh Monk
abuses the simple notions of the elder church, to

support the notion that our nature has in it something which is receptive of Divine grace, and only
wants its co-operation to bring forth good fruits.
It is clear, that all the practices and principles of
the Fathers, are implicitly at war with this doctrine. The very idea of mortification, not to say
the principle of a new birth, are in deadly opposition to it. But it is one thing to mean the
truth; it is another to be able to distinguish it
from falsehood, and make the grounds of the distinction intelligible to others. I cannot see that
this gift was intended for the earlier Fathers, or
that they would not have been less equal to the
tasks that were appointed them, if they had possessed it. They would, I conceive, have been less
able to maintain, upon the authority of Scripture
and tradition, those great truths respecting the
nature of God, without which the baptismal covenant was a nullity, and, as I shall endeavour to
show hereafter, all the longings of the human
spirit an unsatisfied dream, if they had been
better moral philosophers, or more exercised with
internal conflicts. The wonderful manner in
which Augustin was led to take up the study of
the old philosophers, — not as something to illustrate Christianity,—but as the satisfaction of
wants excited in him before he embraced it; and
the way in which these studies were connected
with the actual facts of his life, with the discovery
of the carnal and depraved nature, and, at last
with a joyful belief of a redemption out of that
nature,—gave him such perception of the distinc-

tion between the person and the nature in man—
between that which lays hold of the grace offered,
and only can receive it, and that which must be
rejected and cut off, because it is not subject to
the law of God, neither indeed can be,—such as
I do not suppose any foregone Father enjoyed—
such as, at the same time, enabled him, while he
resisted an existing heresy, to justify the writings of his predecessors, to establish a permanent
link between theology and moral philosophy, to
show what it is in man that receives that which
God imparts,—what it is in him that can eat the
flesh of the Son of Man, and drink his blood.

Augustin appears to me a philosopher or student of humanity, raised up for a particular purpose, in an age which was intended to be chiefly
one of mere divines, occupied with those subjects
which have reference primarily to the nature of
God, and but secondarily to the condition of
man. I make this remark, by way of protest
against those who depreciate a noble champion of
truth, as well as against those who exalt him
above his brethren. One class of writers cannot
speak of the Bishop of Hippo, without insinu-
ating that he wanted the simplicity of the other
Fathers, or had a lower notion of the perfection
attainable by man, or introduced puzzling and unnecessary questions; while writers who heap lau-
dations upon him, can scarcely spare a few cold
sentences of qualified approbation for the brave and
self-denying Athanasius, the narrative of whose
heroical deeds makes even the page of Gibbon to

glow. If the former will tell me what the theology of the Fathers would have been worth, had
not the opposition between flesh and spirit, grace
and nature, been asserted by Augustine; if the
latter will show me, what the distinctions of Augustine would have availed, if the Catholic idea of
a Father, Son, and Spirit had been lost,—I will
yield to either of their narrow and partial judgments. But perceiving that it was the purpose of
God in this first age, to bring out the one set of
truths, and yet, by a particular instance, to de-
monstrate that they could have no life or meaning
without another class, not yet so clearly apprehended ; perceiving, that if there had been no
Augustine, the great doctrines concerning *God*
would not have been linked in the history of the
church, to those which primarily concern *man ;*
and, that if all had been Augustines, Arianism,
in the simple form which it began to take in the
reign of Constantine, and Arianism in the more
developed and practical form which Mahomet
gave to it three hundred years later, must have
destroyed Christianity altogether ;—I would rather wonder at the wisdom of the Head of the
Church, in distributing gifts to it so exactly
suited to its necessities, than idolize or disparage
any of the servants and witnesses whom he has
from time to time raised up within it.

You may think that I am digressing from my
subject; but I warned you, that the doctrine of
the Eucharist is worked into the whole tissue of
ecclesiastical history. Unless you understand the

o 3

general vocation of the Fathers, you will not, I
believe, understand what side of this doctrine necessarily occupied their minds, to the weakening,
though not to the exclusion of the opposite one.
Unless you understand the particular vocation of
Augustine, you will not understand why the neglected side became afterwards more prominent;
what perplexities ensued from the confusion of
the two; what loss to Christianity, when, in
certain countries, one wholly supplanted the
other.   No one can fail to perceive, that with the
beginning of European society, when the nations
that overran the Roman Empire had been converted to Christianity, a new chapter in the providential history of the world commenced,—a new
era in speculation and feeling.   When those who
had heretofore been a set of tribes, distinguished
indeed by various peculiar features, but all confounded in the Universal Empire, under the
fostering influence of Christianity, and of those
ideas of order and justice which Rome had been
the means of communicating to them, began to
assume the position of distinct, organized nations;—it was reasonable to expect, from the
whole analogy of the Divine proceedings, that
habits of mind different from those which had
characterized the subjects of the great Italian
despotism, would be cultivated within them.   The
great questions which now began to be stirred in
men's minds, were questions respecting our own
human nature, — what it is; how we are connected with the world around us; with our fel-

low-men, and with God? Men seemed now called
to commence their upward journey again; and,
as they had been taught in the first age after the
promulgation of Christianity, by what methods
God had sought after his creatures; they were
now to inquire what there is in the creature which
desires, and is capable of receiving communications from God. This new kind of inquiry, and
the attempts to reconcile it with those of the former age, without a clear perception of the difference of the objects proposed in each case, constitute, it seems to me, what is called the *Scholastic
Philosophy*. It connected itself with the human
philosophy of Aristotle, as the earlier theology of
the Fathers had connected itself with the more
transcendent and superhuman philosophy of Plato.
But this is an accidental circumstance, with which
we are not here concerned. Without taking more
than this casual notice of it, we may explain how
this philosophy bore upon the religious feelings of
the period in which it was pursued, and especially
upon the doctrine of the Sacraments.

But, meanwhile, a great alteration had gradually
taken place in the external position and the polity
of the church, to which we must advert. Your
Friends, and the other dissenters, speak of the age
of Constantine as that in which the church corrupted herself by entering into alliances with the
state. I shall have another opportunity of examining this opinion, and considering its reasonableness. Thus much (and this is all I need
say at present), I willingly concede to you, that

the feeling of Christ having a kingdom upon
earth, over which he actually presided, setting
visible servants or princes over his people —
but not the less truly and personally directing
every operation of the government, may not have
existed in the same clearness and purity after
that event as before it.   But I will qualify this
assertion with two others :—One is, that the submission of the overgrown Roman Empire to
Christ, and the new life which that putrid carcase
received from the union, was one of the greatest
illustrations of the fact, that Christ's kingdom is
not a mere name, but a reality, which could have
been given to that age, or to the honest thinker of
any subsequent age ; the second is, that no inference as to the intention of God respecting the
connexion of his church with the kingdoms of the
earth, can be drawn from the accidents of its
connexion with a superannuated military empire,
carrying about within it the seeds of predes-
tined destruction, and only kept alive till the
new nations of the west were ready to inherit the
blessings, which it was the appointed means
of transmitting to them. If you would see clearly
that the idea of Christianity as a kingdom, and
not merely as a set of doctrines, had not been lost
in consequence of the act of Constantine, you
should trace the history of its reception by the
Germanic nations. You will find that those who
speculated about it, (the Gothic people in the
south, I mean, which embraced Arianism), could
not become regular nations, or escape the Isla-

mite invaders; that, on the contrary, it harmo-
nised admirably with the previous respect for
marriage, and with the principles of order among
the German tribes, and soon converted them into
settled political societies.   I contend, that this
idea of Christ being the King of kings and
Lord of lords ; that by him kings reign and
princes decreed justice, was not only not destroyed by the union of the church with the Roman state, but that it was never more strongly
asserted than in the forms of our own Saxon
constitution.

But there did come a time, after the great vic-
tories of Charlemagne, when the princes of the
earth, those even who proclaimed themselves the
Soldiers of Christ, violently invaded the principle.
From the moment that the new Roman empire
arose, it was evident that a kind of universal
kingdom, inconsistent with the distinct freedom
of each nation on the one hand, inconsistent with
the *true* universal kingdom of Christ on the other,
was beginning to manifest itself; and this anti-
Christian principle reached its height when the
monarchs of Germany began to dispose of in-
vestitures at their pleasure, subjecting the church
to their state convenience.

It was then that a man arose, of a brave and
noble spirit, pious and self-denying, to assert, as
he meant and thought, the supremacy of Christ.
Alas ! in the very act of lifting himself to maintain
his Master's rule over statesmen and politicians,
Hildebrand himself became one of them ; him-

self struck a more dreadful blow at the idea of
Christ's kingdom, than even the potentates whom
he defied.   For it was reserved for him, for this
good, and well-intentioned, and powerful man, to
assert the doctrine that Christ had appointed a
Vicar on earth ; in other words, that he was not
a real and present king ; that his ministers are
not princes holding immediately under him, but
holding of him, through a visible and mortal substitute.   I am not here speaking of the invasion
of the principle of Episcopacy, implied in the assumption of this paramount power in one bishop,
—that is a subject for future investigation.   At
present I am only discussing the vicarious doctrine, which was not indeed now first broached,
(how could so very natural a notion have been
then first broached ?) but which first assumed a
positive formal shape under the pontificate of
Gregory the Seventh, just a thousand years after
the destruction of the Jewish polity.   But how
does this point concern our present subject ?
Most closely.   The idea of an actual communion
established between heaven and earth, in the incarnate Mediator, was now practically set aside—
not resisted by the violence of self-willed statesmen, but denied *in* the church.   Now, the Sacrament of the Lord's Supper, if we have interpreted
past history rightly, stands on this idea.   When
it was gone, it was impossible that the simple
feeling of a direct communication of life from
God to man, of man being directly fed with
manna from heaven, could endure.   But was,

therefore, the *want* of such a communication,
less? No; it was, in one sense, greater than ever.
For men, as we have seen, were now entering
upon that stage, in which questions concerning
themselves, their own wants, their own connexion
with God, became the first and most prominent
in their minds. The feeling, God ' talketh with
man as with a friend,' had ceased; the feeling,
' I heard his voice walking in the garden in the
cool of the day, and I knew that I was naked,
and I hid myself,' was never so realized before.
The schoolmen, the intellectual expositors of the
feelings of the age, speculated, therefore, with
earnest and feverish and longing desire for wisdom to explain the nature of that bond which they
knew had been contracted between man and his
Lord, and of which they, more than even those
who had so simply and so lovingly recognised it,
perceived the necessity. They had the works of
the Fathers, of the Latin Fathers, at least, to
study and reflect upon; they had the forms and
institutions of the church still preserved, in which
to read the meaning of the Fathers; they had the
Scriptures, teaching them of sacrifices once appointed as means of a sinner's approach to God;
they had the Popedom standing in the way, as a
barrier against the belief that the actual incarnation of the Son of God was that which justified
the language of the Fathers, expounded the meaning of the forms and connected the Sacrifices of
the Old Testament with the Sacraments of the
New. How naturally, out of these elements, did

the doctrine of Transubstantiation arise. The body and blood of Christ are not perceived to be indeed the bonds between earth and heaven, between man and his Lord; therefore the bread and wine lost their actual, sacramental meaning. But the sense of their dignity, the want of the connexion implied in it, have not departed. Hence they are invested with a natural, sensible virtue; they are treated as at once natural and supernatural, dead and living, sensible and spiritual. Man is not lifted by them to heaven, but heaven is lowered to the conceptions and notions of man. And he is punished in that wherein he sinned. The intellect put itself in a position which it had no right to assume; the intellect was degraded by its own inventions; it created the contradiction which was its torment.

But the carnal heart was punished equally with the proud understanding. It sought peace in the sin which it loved; and the faster it pursued the faster the vision fled. It found comfort in the thought of a blessing brought so near, that it could catch it without being raised out of the slough into which it had sunk; but it never could realize the blessing. It rejoiced that instead of the manna it had quails; but while they were yet in the mouth the anger of God came upon it.

And now, then, all those points wherein the Fathers had shown that they loved God better than they understood men, became to their successors, distressed with these new problems concerning themselves, positive sources of confusion

and mischief. Man, not now chiefly busy with
the thought how heaven has sought reconciliation with him, but how he may seek reconciliation with heaven, inevitably falls back upon
the ideas of the older covenant; supposes the
offering up of the body of Christ at the Eucharist
the great work, and the offering up of Christ himself on the Cross, a comparatively unmeaning
thing; trusts in all the means whereby he had
been told to seek to realize the blessings of the
covenant as means of purchasing them, and continually invents schemes for himself, not good
for either purpose, in order to accomplish both.
Again, feeling the want of constant teachings and
illuminations from above, but not feeling that he
is constituted in Christ, and that these teachings
and illuminations are the continued endowment
promised to him, he supposes the union to be
established and created at those times, and by
those acts which Christ hath appointed for the
witnesses of it, and for imparting the blessings of
it. Again, seeking after fellowship with a Being
from whom he feels himself hopelessly estranged,
the idea of tiers of saints and angels, through
whom he is to ascend into the presence of his
Lord, becomes part of his habitual faith. Lastly,
it is a consequence of the same state of mind,
that men exalted the events and conditions of
their own lives, which, in the former age, had
been glorified by the two Sacraments, to a level
with them; and began accurately to define how
many of these conditions are deserving of this

P

mysterious honour. Thus, on the one hand, the
Sacraments were degraded still further by earthly
illustrations and interpretations; and the robe of
divinity which is meant to be spread over all
human life and all nature, was formally confined
to certain portions of each, the rest being left
cold and naked.

This degradation, then, was brought on partly
by a *political* cause, which is expressed in the
word POPERY, used in its strict signification;
partly by that *moral* cause, the unwillingness of
men to retain God in their knowledge; yet in
part, too, it was the consequence of their passing
through those subterraneous caverns of feeling and
self-inquiry, which, however gloomy and cheerless, it may be necessary that the race, as well as
each member of it, should enter, before it can
emerge, with unhurt vision, into the light of day,
and the different dim recesses of which are explored, and their echoes reverberated, in the philosophy of the schoolmen. The Reformation can
only be rightly considered in relation to each of
these causes. It must be looked upon as the
winding up of those inquiries which had distressed humanity so long, by the discovery of their
connection with the truths revealed to, and possessed by men in a former age; a conviction
which those men could not understand, at least
not at all to the same extent. The idea of a complete sacrifice for sin had been asserted long ago;
but then it was the sin of the *world*; the actual
sins of particular men; the sins of which they

were *conscious ;*—these seemed to fall under a different law, to be not provided for in that redemption. Now the great truth was asserted, that Christ made a full satisfaction, not only for the original guilt, but also the actual sins of men ; and that when a man turns round to God, and believes in his great atonement, he becomes personally delivered from the burden of committed and conscious evil, as he was at Baptism delivered from the curse upon the race, and admitted to a new, and glorious, and divine nativity. This, we said, it is probable that the first age of the church did not perceive ; passages may be quoted to prove that it did not ; or rather to prove that it was a faith of the heart merely, not of the understanding. Here was the great assertion of the Reformation, the key to all the rest,—that a sinner, actually and consciously a sinner, is set free from his sins, and becomes practically a new creature when he takes his stand upon his redemption and constitution in Christ. All righteousness and holiness, it was proclaimed, are in him ; man is holy and righteous only in virtue of his union with him ; unholy and unrighteous only by virtue of separation from him. He is redeemed and justified. By faith in Christ he may claim that redemption, and livingly enjoy it. Hence they were led to assert so strongly the doctrine of Baptism, as I showed in my last letter that they did.

Furthermore, the doctrine of an immediate communion with Christ was necessarily to a great degree restored. All notion, at any rate, of intervening mediators between man and the Great Mediator, was indignantly swept away. Thus the obstacles which the understanding had opposed to the attainment of moral life and illumination were removed; and when this purpose had been effected, the political obstacle could not long remain. The acknowledgment of a Vicar of Christ was felt by the monarchs of different states to be a hindrance to their lawful authority and their immediate responsibility to Christ. The same acknowledgment was felt by the individual Christian to interfere with his direct allegiance to his own Lord and Saviour; and these two feelings overthrew, in the Teutonic nations, this long usurpation, while they weakened, I apprehend, some great principles of spiritual order and coherency, which had interwoven themselves with that usurpation, though they were in nowise connected with it, and might have been used as some of the most powerful opposers of it.

Any one who considers the history of this period must see, that a thought had arisen in men's minds, which must either have been satisfied as the Reformation satisfied it, or must have broken out into the most hardy infidelity and defiance of authority. The feeling, ' I am not one of a mass, I am a distinct person, I will not be accounted merely a portion of a great Christendom,'—had been ripening throughout Europe. If this feeling had not been connected with other and more awful thoughts in the mind of Luther, I grant you that it could never have produced the effects which it did produce; but it would have produced other and far more appalling effects,—it must have led to a dissolution of society. In his mind it was accompanied with the consciousness of awful responsibilities and repeated transgressions, of an irreversible law, approving of the one, condemning the other. In his mind it led to the inquiry,—'Have I any deliverance from this curse, any power of acquitting myself of these demands?' In his mind it issued in the delightful consideration,—'Christ hath justified me from the curse of the law, being made a curse for me. Now I am not under the law, but under grace; for the law of the Spirit of life, which is in Christ, hath made me free from the law of sin and death.' These were the words which were heard from one end of Europe to the other; which found an echo in many a heart; which were welcomed by them as the very words which they had been waiting and longing to hear. They did not create the rebellious excitement of that period; they prevented it from breaking down every ancient fence and landmark. They showed men that, however much they may have been kept in ignorance of their true condition, however much held in bondage, it was not by self-willed acts, or by casting off the yoke of Christ, that they could hope to obtain freedom. His words and the forms of the church testified of that freedom; faith, and not infidelity, was their refuge. And thus, I must contend, against those who charge Luther with being a minister of sedition and division; that but for him, sedition and division would have been universal; that he was the means, in God's hands, of preventing the destruction of the church; and that to the truth which he preached it was owing, that instead of a wide-spreading anarchy, several of the nations of Christendom became more than they had ever been before, distinct and orderly polities,—acknowledging their kings as the servants of Christ, not as the mere chieftains of the Aristocracy, and the subjects of a foreign jurisdiction.

But although the conscience of man could only be delivered from the terrible yoke which had been imposed upon it, by the doctrine of justification, which Luther preached; and although, if it had not been delivered in this way, it would have sought a deceitful and wretched freedom in another, yet I must also remind you, as I did in my first letter, that the conscience is essentially that which causes each man to feel that he is a distinct person; it does not lead us to feel that we have a fellowship one with another. It is most important to understand this position; for there is none, I am convinced, which persons in the present day are so apt to deny. " What," they say, " do you mean that a purified conscience is not the best and only condition of moral existence and Christian communion?" Certainly! Just as I allow that each brother and sister in a family should be amiable, and honest, and generous, in order that they may live happily together. But I do also most strongly deny, that the amia-

bleness, or honesty, or generosity of sister or brother, is that which makes them related to each
other, or to their parents. And I do most strongly
aver, that if this notion shall intrude into their
minds, and if, on the strength of it, they shall
affirm, that the fact of sisterhood and brotherhood
stands on the qualities of the respective persons
bearing that relation,—they will as much destroy
all the principles of the family feeling which God
has established, as if they were each the most depraved of human creatures.   In like manner I
affirm, that though the continued existence of the
Christian Church would have been impossible,
without that truth respecting the conscience which
the Reformation introduced; yet that this truth,
when made itself the foundation of the church,
destroys that idea of Christ having a kingdom
upon earth, which, I showed you that the Papal
notion darkened and kept out of sight.

You will find, that the view which the Reformers took of the doctrine of the Eucharist, is
the great key to these remarks, and to their views
on all other subjects.   But before I treat upon
this point, to which all my previous observations
have been tending, I must call your attention to
some of the divisions which sprung up among
them, and proved that their principle, true and
mighty as it was, is a principle of distinction, not
of unity.

You will perceive, I think, that the character,
habits, and spiritual discipline of men, must have
greatly affected—not their belief in the doctrine

of the Reformation—but their way of regarding it.
A plain, business-like man, vexed with strong internal conflicts, driven to faith rather by the necessities of his heart than by the convictions of
his intellect, would occupy himself comparatively
little with the nature of the act by which he ap-
propriated the blessings which he needed; he
would seize them, and tell others to do the like.
Nor would he in general be distracted with the
question, How came it to pass that some did claim
those blessings, and others rejected them? As a
man he would be indisposed to a question which
drew him away from the object of faith, to
thoughts about its origin; as a preacher of the
Gospel, he would dislike, by exciting such doubts
in his hearers, to weaken his own assertion of the
blessing having been claimed, and being within
every man's reach.

On the other hand, a man of an intellectual
turn, much exercised in logic, not very social in
the habits of his mind,—conscious rather of internal evil than subject to great external temptation,—would speculate somewhat upon the character of faith, the organ by which it is exercised,
the power by which it is communicated; but
more on the ultimate reasons which determined
some men to follow their nature, and some to become obedient to the grace of God. He would
say to himself,—' It is especially the vocation of
Protestants to discuss these questions. That men
are justified by faith, and not by any outward act,
is our grand assertion. Outward acts any man

may perform; but faith is a gift. Evidently only a few possess it; whence, then, does it come to them? We shall have the doctrine of faith given as the reward of works; all the mischiefs which resulted from the belief of grace of congruity intruding themselves again, if we do not settle this question. Let us then at once lay it down, that it is the absolute sovereignty of God, choosing and decreeing that such and such shall believe and be saved, which originated faith in a man, and preserves it in him to the end.' Such you will see is the " natural history " of the Calvinistic system; so easily and directly deduced from Protestantism, and yet which never could have produced one of the mighty effects which Luther's preaching produced upon the character of the world.

Once more: you can conceive a person vigorous and practical like Luther,—but far less exercised than he with inward conflicts, — inspired with great indignation, like Calvin, against the Romish system, and desiring to destroy it root and branch, but without his deep habits of reflection and logical acuteness; to such a one another side of Protestantism will present itself most prominently. ' The real strength of the Reformation,' he will say to himself, ' has been manifested, not in its proclaiming this doctrine or that, but in the authority and emphasis which it has given to the written Word of God. To hide this from the multitude was at once the subtlest of Papal villanies, and that which made every other possible. If, then, we will maintain the new faith, away with forms and pressures past,—away with traditions and set prayers, — away with everything that has interfered with the reverence which is due to this sacred and divine deposit. And do you not see how the crafty enemy of souls has contrived to weaken this great witness against his plots by exalting the power and mystery of sacraments. See you not how the Word of Life has been disparaged under pretence of another life communicated through these ordinances.' Such, I conceive, are the thoughts which passed in the mind of *Zuinglius,* and determined the character of *his* theology.

It will strike you at once that these three sides of Protestantism were all acknowledged by each of the champions to whom I have alluded. No language that Calvin employed respecting his peculiar tenets, could be stronger than that in which Luther occasionally asserted them. No phrases respecting the authority of Scripture ever escaped the lips of Zuinglius which may not have been expounded with far greater clearness by Calvin, and enunciated with far greater power by Luther. Nevertheless, those who agree with the principle of this letter will acknowledge at once that the feeling with which these different parties were regarded by the Helvetic and the German reformers may have been most different, and that this difference may have far more livingly affected their theology than even a much more marked theoretic disagreement.

And it is, as I have hinted more than once, in

their doctrine regarding the Lord's Supper, that you find this difference practically realised. The fact is most striking. All notional differences might have been settled; armistices might not only have been made, but the terms of them observed, if only, as the disputants themselves fancied, doctrines and opinions which could be couched in language had been the matters at stake. But there was something deeper at work. Luther felt, that his idea of Christianity was different, essentially different, from that of Calvin or of Zuinglius, let their terms be as much assimilated as they might; and each party felt that there was an expression for their idea, which was more complete, more substantial, and yet more subtle than any words could offer. Yes! in that moment of intellectual power and prowess, when words were believed to be so mighty, and when they *were* so mighty, because the life was yet in them, — even then was this homage rendered to ordinances by those whose habits of mind would have disposed them most to think lightly of them. They were OBLIGED to make their notions of these ordinances the central points of their system; they were obliged to recognise *these* as the bonds of union among themselves; these, alas! as the barriers—(not the ordinances, but the notions of the ordinances,) to all reconciliation with each other.

The Zuinglian notion of this Sacrament reduces it, you are aware, into a mere memorial feast, to celebrate the offering which Christ made upon

the Cross for the sins of the world. This notion
expresses precisely the feeling of Protestantism,
considered simply as the exaltation of the Scripture records. The idea of a series of past transactions, the statement of which constitutes church
doctrine, and the belief of which frees the conscience
of the individual worshipper, is that which, in the
Zuinglian system, supersedes every other. You
must not suppose me to say, that it wrought this
effect in the heart of its author or his first disciples. With them the very notion of a mere
memorial feast, connected itself with most living
thoughts of a finished sacrifice. But if we trace
down this notion through the ages that followed,
you will see its appointed fruit in the system
of the Polish Socinians, and in all the systems of
modern days, which, beginning with the exclusive exaltation, and almost deification of Scripture,
have gone on to the exaltation and deification of
those faculties by which the letter of Scripture
is examined, have ended in the rudest treatment
and grossest violation of their first idol; and, as
I believe, in the no less shameful degradation of
its successor. But this doctrine of the Sacrament
was at first supplanted in the Reformed Church
by the *Calvinistic.* The Zuinglian doctrine
trenched upon that belief of a real union between
Christ and his members in the Sacramental act
and service, which might have been greatly weakened, but had not hitherto been formally denied
in the church. This belief the Reformed Church,
better instructed by Calvin, again adopted.

The habits of that teacher's mind disposed him much more readily to feel, that without an habitual intercourse between the soul and its Lord, it can have no energy or life,—and why should he question that this feast was the appointed means of sustaining that union? It was not then a mere memorial feast, it was something much higher and more mysterious. But then, proceeded this divine, it is a mystery cognisable only by the faithful; no others can have admission to the feast. The more you exalt it, the more strict should you be in excluding mere professors from it. Here was a doctrine expressing the Genevan system. The conscious election of *individuals* becomes the foundation of the *church*. It consists of a set of persons redeemed from the fall, and admitted to certain high privileges not appertaining to mankind. The incarnation is not the central truth of Christianity, the ground of the Gospel, the establishment of a kingdom which had been preparing from the foundation of the world,—but *merely* a remedy against the consequences of the fall. I shall not develope the effects of this system,—we may, however, trace them in our next letter,—I shall simply tell you why I suppose it could not be embraced by Luther, and by what feeling he was driven into a third doctrine, different from either of these.

You have heard what he thought of Baptism, how he put it forward, as the ground of men's confidence in their own personal justification. Thus he presumed a union already established, as the ground of all faith; and if so, how inevitably it followed, that the Sacrament which expressed this union, and through which its blessings are conveyed, should not seem to derive all its virtue from the faith of the receiver? But how could this be? His mind dwells upon the difficulty. He enters into the feeling which led the old church to believe, that there must be some power, some virtue in the elements themselves. But he cannot go the full length of the school doctrine. He had felt its danger and bondage. He feels that he has a truth within him, which the ultra Protestants are disposed to reject, and which he cannot express. He reflects sometimes in despondency, sometimes in anger, — neither, most surely, the fittest moods for entertaining such a mystery. At length the confusion of his mind finds utterance in the doctrine of consubstantiation.

· If you say, Here was that Aaron, whose serpent rod had swallowed the serpents of so many magicians, in grief because his Lord tarried too long in the mount, casting his own jewels, and those of the people,—still longing for the flesh-pots,—into the fire, and bringing forth a molten calf,— I will not quarrel with the words; for though I confess it does not diminish my veneration for this wonderful man, that he was willing to offer up any sacrifice for the sake of his faith, yet I do not believe that the sacrifice which he did offer was a holy or acceptable one. To say the truth, I believe it was laid upon the altar

of that very carnal understanding, which appeared
to be itself the victim.

And this is the very lesson which I have wished
you to derive from these melancholy records. Being
aware how strong the prejudices of your Friends
are against this sacrament, and how much they
have been augmented by an opinion that one
notion respecting them has succeeded another,
and that each in turn has been found equally
baseless, I have been anxious to show you exactly what truth there is in that surmise, and how
it affects the real question at issue between us.
I have set before you five views of the Eucharist, — the simple doctrine of the early church,
the guardians of Christ's deposit; the form which
that doctrine assumed when men had lost sight
of their connection with God, and yet had experienced more than ever their need of it; then
three moulds into which the feelings of men cast
themselves at a period, when the principles of
spiritual union had been in some degree lost, —
when the peace and purification of the conscience were the only objects of spiritual solicitude, and when the understanding was most active
and restless to bring everything under its own
laws and conditions. It remains for me to show
you that the strongest argument for the reality
and glory of this sacrament is derived from these
attempts and these failures; that the spirit of
man sighs after something higher than mere
quietness of conscience, and will not be satisfied
till it be attained; that the understanding is out-

raged unless we acknowledge truths and mysteries which surpass it; that the faith which was
delivered to the church in its infancy, is that
which can alone sustain the wants which it has
experienced in its maturity; that with the preservation of this sacrament is connected the preservation of communion with each other as well
as of all personal life; lastly, that amidst all the
perplexities and contradictions which the restless
spirit of man has created for itself, God has not
left himself without witness, but has preserved in
living forms that idea of this sacrament which
contents the humble and contrite worshipper, is
a bond of kindred and fellowship between men of
all ages, converts doctrines into reality, and carries
us forward to that glory which it hath not entered
into the heart of man to conceive, but which nevertheless God has prepared for them that love
him.   This will be the subject of my next
letter.

   Believe me,

    Yours very faithfully.

           * * * *

NOTE.

Since writing the passages in the text relating to Dr. Pusey, I have read a letter addressed by the Rev. J. H. Newman to the editor of the Christian Observer. In this letter the author declares, for himself and Dr. Pusey, that they object to the view of Regeneration generally adopted in the religious world, as feeble and inadequate. He had, it appears, been attacked by the editor of the Christian Observer, for maintaining, that Regeneration is a privilege specially belonging to the New Covenant, which could not by any accurate divine, be attributed to an Israelite. The reviewer had been pleased to consider this a most startling and dangerous assertion, involving the doctrine, that Voltaire had a spiritual character which did not belong to Abraham. Mr. Newman replies, first, that every privilege which his opponent, or any of the party to which he belongs, claims for Abraham, would be claimed for him by Dr. Pusey. That he only differs from them in refusing to consider sanctification and regeneration as the same, and to treat those who *receive* the promises which the Patriarchs of the elder dispensation *expected* as on a level with them. Secondly—That he sees nothing monstrous in the notion that Voltaire may have inherited higher blessings than belonged to any Jewish Saint — his sin being that he fell from those blessings. It will be perceived, that these sentiments are exactly those which I have

advocated in this, and my former letter. I have maintained that men are admitted into a regenerate constitution at, Baptism, into which, before the incarnation of
Christ, it was impossible they could enter, and I have
asserted as Mr. Newman does, that the sin of men under
the new dispensation is, that they refuse this inestimable
privilege. But the question is, has this doctrine been
strengthened or enfeebled by Dr. Pusey's language respecting a "new or infused," or Mr. Newman's respecting an "angel nature?" I contend that it has been
greatly weakened : I contend that by these phrases,
they have brought themselves into apparent conflict with
the assertions of the Evangelical party, when they need
only have brought themselves into conflict with their
negations. The Evangelicals say, " A new life is given
at conversion;" meaning that when persons turn to
God from sin, they become inheritors of a new life in
Christ,—they become justified and sanctified men as
Abraham was.—Dr. Pusey, says, "No, *this* new life is
given at Baptism." Why need he say so ? Why might
he not say,—Men are then brought into a glorious
constitution in Christ ; (I will not say an angel constitution, because I think it something much higher, seeing
that " Verily HE took not upon him the nature of angels,
but the seed of Abraham,") they are made the members
of Christ, children of God and heirs of everlasting life ;
they are made inheritors of life and glory ; and when
they are afterwards brought to acknowledge their relation to Christ, and when they are at length brought to
the full glory of God ; it is but the entering livingly
into that very state which was theirs long before ; and
of which the Spirit then undertook to give them the
possession.

Put the doctrine so ; and the period at which the con-

scious and sanctified life begins has its honour; and the
period at which the glorified life begins has its honour;
and neither is in the least inconsistent with the idea of
baptism being the induction into all Christian felicity.
Put the doctrine in the other way; and the mere period
of baptism is set up against all the other periods of human life; the child is supposed to be holier than the
man conscious of pardon and sanctification; better than
the saint who beholds the glory of God and is changed
into his image; the notion of a gift or impregnation
displaces the idea of all blessings being in Christ, and
being possessed by virtue of union with him; the fallen
baptised man is supposed to be lost and all but irrecover-
able; the dying Christian is supposed to be an imperfect
imitation of the baby. I ask again which doctrine gives
you the greater sense of the glory of baptism?

LETTERS TO A MEMBER

OF THE

SOCIETY OF FRIENDS.

BY

A CLERGYMAN OF THE CHURCH OF ENGLAND.

~~~~~~~~~~~~

No. IV.

ON THE LORD'S SUPPER.

~~~~~~~~~~~~

LONDON:

W. DARTON AND SON, HOLBORN HILL.

ADVERTISEMENT.

IT is intended that these Letters shall form three vo-
lumes, to be published under this title, " The Kingdom
of Christ ; or Hints on the Principles, Ordinances, and
Constitution of the Catholic Church In Letters to a
Member of the Society of Friends."

A Preface, explaining the Author's general design,
and the connection of the future Letters with those already published, will be bound up with the first volume,
which is now complete, and given to the purchasers of
the separate numbers.

April 1.

LETTERS

MEMBER OF THE SOCIETY OF FRIENDS.

No. IV.

My Dear Friend,

In my last letter I endeavoured to show you how
the other feelings and opinions of men in different
ages, have been connected with their feelings and
opinions respecting the Lord's Supper. There
was, I said, a period in the history of the church,
when all blessings were considered in reference to
the giver rather than to the receiver of them. In
this period ordinances were regarded with deep
reverence and delight, as the appointed channels
through which the mercy of God flowed forth
upon mankind. To preserve them exactly as
they had been delivered, was the great diligence
required of those who were the appointed stewards
of God's blessings,—humbly to partake of them,
with an assurance of their mighty and mysterious

efficacy, was the great qualification desired in the disciples. There came another period, in which men began to think much of their own nature, and to realize their own wants. Many clouds, raised by sin and ignorance, intercepted the views of Him from whom all good things come; but those very clouds led men to experience, more than they had ever done, their inward necessities. They began to be conscious creatures,—conscious of powers, of wants, most of all, of evil. Sin had presented itself to man, first admitted into the family of Christ, as the wandering of a child from its parent, to be wept for and forgiven, unless by repeated disobedience the privileges of the family had been forfeited,—it presented itself now in the awful form of transgression against a positive irreversible *law*. Each man felt himself standing in the presence of a Judge; and the question began to be, by what means his anger could be propitiated, his favour restored? Ordinances now assumed a new aspect,—they were instruments for averting threatened peril and calamity, rather than thanksgivings for actual deliverance, and communications of present life. The understanding devised notions about them, to please the sin-accused conscience; but the one recoiled from its own inventions, the other found no peace in them.

The world reached another stage in its history. The delusions which the understanding had practised on itself were discovered; the conscience became more restless every day, under the impo-

sitions to which it had sought for comfort. If the
noisy cries of the first had been listened to, all
ancient belief would have passed from the earth;
but the small voice of the second made itself
heard above these cries, and asserted that very
belief as its only protection. When it had
achieved its deliverance, all the other faculties
felt a new life; and haughty sceptics were sul-
lenly compelled to acknowledge, that faith had
broken the bonds under which they had only
groaned. And now the ordinances began again
to be regarded as precious witnesses of men's
freedom, and as mighty upholders of it. But this
was the only, or almost the only light in which
they were regarded; the pacification of the conscience was now the sum of theology; what mi-
nistered to this end could not be too highly
honoured; what seemed to have no concern with
it, was unheeded. How much, then, or how
little of the old system and constitution of the
church, served this great purpose, was the question which the Reformers debated, and on which
they came to different conclusions, according as
they were drawn by temper or by circumstances,
or divine discipline employing both, to meditate
more on the object of faith, on its origin, or on
the outward revelation, which was the great witness of it. The conscience of Luther craved
for a continual and abiding assurance of the
power and presence of his Lord to be the ground
of his faith, not to be dependent upon it,—the
Sacrament of the Lord's Supper he believed to

be the appointed means of obtaining that assurance; he interpreted it according to his wants;
and believed that the body and blood of Christ
were consubstantiated with the elements. The
conscience of Calvin craved for a continual attesta-
tion of the union, which, as he believed, his Lord
had established with his soul when he chose it,
out of death and ruin, to life and happiness; the
same Sacrament he acknowledged as that attes-
tation, and the value of it depended in his notion, not upon the dignity of the elements, but
upon their being administered only to those who
had a right to claim fellowship in the mystery.
The conscience of Zwingle craved some formal
and repeated act, to remind it that the redemption of which the book of God gave him information had been indeed completed. He believed the
Sacrament to be the act ordained for that end;
and he regarded it simply as a feast to comme-
morate a past transaction.

Such was the position of the Reformed bodies
on the Continent. Their theology had this
central idea,—that God had entered into relations
with men, in order to deliver them from the guilt,
and power, and consequences of sin; He may
have had other deep and mysterious objects, but
all was, in their minds, subordinate to this object.
With this peculiarity another was combined,
which was, however, less characteristic of them
than of their age. Accurate and formal definitions began more and more to be considered the
proper method for conveying theological truths.

We have seen what a mighty power there was in men's hearts, counteracting this conviction of the intellect. We have seen how they were forced to give greater glory to ordinances than to all the other parts of their system. Both in their controversies with the Papists and with each other, the doctrine of the Eucharist became more and more the turning point. But the Papists, equally with themselves, were now beginning to form systems of divinity, which practically superseded the old creeds of the church, and gave, as I believe, an entirely new form and complexion to Christianity. Let me explain myself.

The Baptismal commission is in this form : " Go ye into all nations, and preach the Gospel to every creature, baptising them in the name of the Father, and the Son, and the Holy Ghost." This commission, as I endeavoured to show in my second letter, is, in Scripture language, the foundation or setting up of a kingdom upon earth. All who were baptised were received into that kingdom. It was a spiritual kingdom; its laws, its influences, its rewards, affected man as a spiritual being; addressed themselves to the inner man, not to the mere creature of sense. But it was in every sense of the word a real kingdom; there was no metaphor in the word; it was that in the highest and most perfect sense which every kingdom aspired to be. Its existence had been foreshown, its necessity implied, in every foregone kingdom, that had been constituted upon right principles; to make it an abortion in the womb to strangle it in the moment of birth, to prevent it from attaining maturity, had been the strenuous and unceasing effort of every kingdom that had been built on a false principle, or had abandoned the true.   It followed, then, that it just as much behoved the ministers and officers of this kingdom to assert that *Name* which lay at its foundation, as it behoves the ministers of any other kingdom to declare the name of the sovereign to whom allegiance is due.   The nature, indeed, of the declaration, and the measures which enforce respect to it, would differ, as a kingdom appealing to the spirit of man, differs from one appealing to his fears of an outward disaster, or his hopes of an outward blessing.   But in each case the subject would be taught as a fact, that he was under such and such a government ; the only difference would be, that in the invisible government, the exposition of the fact, would necessarily be more careful ; and it would be such an exposition as addressed itself to the faculties and feelings which were competent to take cognisance of it.   Such is the description of our APOSTLES' CREED, the simplest declaration of the Name into which the child is baptised ; an exposition of acts by which God, in the person of his Son, hath entered into all the stages and conditions of humanity and hath finally glorified it ; and of the mysterious operations, which by his Spirit he is carrying on in his whole church and in its members, till he brings it to the same glory with its Head. Nothing can be simpler than the construction of this creed; it grieves me to have substituted even such a formal notion as I have given of it for its living words; words which seem to be very deeds. In this creed the child learns only what bountiful acts have been done, and are still doing for itself and its family; it is not led to contemplate the nature of the relation of the persons bearing this awful name to each other. Nor might the church, perhaps, have ventured even to speak of this mystery, if her way into it had not been clearly marked out by Providence. But the notion is proclaimed, that this relation is only a figure drawn from human relationships; in other words, the whole idea of the incarnation,—the foundation of the church's being,—is overturned. In her Nicene Council, she prepares a new act of allegiance, setting forth the truth and reality of that transcendant relationship as the foundation of all that we own upon earth.

A still deeper and more awful abyss of thought lay unexplored, and the church might have trembled to enter upon it. But the notion of an absolute Unity, superseding and excluding all distinctions in the Godhead, is cast forth upon the world,—the mockery of real Unity—a gulph of nothingness. In the third creed, or rather in the canticle called Athanasian, the idea of real Unity, as compatible with distinctions, and existing on no other condition than that of an equality of persons in a Trinity, the law of whose subordination is seen only in the incarnation, is brought out with a subtilty, which no one should say is needless, who has not meditated well on that to which it is an answer.

Thus, in these ancient creeds, the idea of a kingdom or family, of which this Name was the bond, was never for a moment lost sight of. Hence this Sacrament, by which the union between the members of the kingdom, and its unseen head, was asserted and realized, still continued to be the foundation of the church. There was nothing in its dogmas which robbed them of this dignity; they were still the great pledges of the fellowship between heaven and earth, of which the creeds were the verbal acknowledgment. The case became very different when the belief of this kingdom was lost in the manner I spoke of in my last letter. Then the church began more and more to assume the appearance of a body connected together like an ancient sect, by certain notions and opinions. The question was, who had a right to dogmatize in it? An infallible dogmatism seemed to be needful, else how could men be safe in the opinions which they accepted, or which they rejected? All such pretensions became inevitable, when once the habit had been formed of looking upon Christianity as a set of opinions, a habit sure to arise in such an intellectual age as that of the schoolmen. Yet for a time the extravagant pretensions of the Pope, the dogmatist of Christendom, to be the ruler over the nations, still kept alive the old notion,—still compelled men to feel that there was a Christian kingdom, or at least a mockery of it on the earth.

But when the Papal power had been put down in some of the nations of Europe, and had been scarcely less endangered by the insolent patronage of its supporters in the others, this idea of a kingdom became less and less palpable, both to the Reformers and to their opponents. The former had all the delight of feeling that they could speculate, without any authority to prescribe the course of their thoughts; the latter had no way of asserting their tottering power, but by laying down charts of doctrine, and denouncing all who departed from them. Thus by the Council of Trent, and the Creed of Pope Pius, the Romish Church virtually superseded those old creeds, which it professed to consider the standards of all doctrine; and the Reformers, who had begun with asserting the power of those creeds, and using them astheir text-books, gradually began to look upon their own confessions as containing all that these creeds contained, far more logically wrought out, and augmented by many important positions, of which the early church seemed to have taken no cognizance.

I dwell upon these points, because they are closely connected with all those objections which the early Quakers raised to the tone of religious thought and feeling in their day, and which have been a stumbling-block to their successors ever since. I grant you at once, that for four centuries before the Reformation, a tendency to make Christianity a system of notions, had gradually been gaining more and more ground in the church,

and that ever since the Reformation, the tendency
has been becoming so strong in the minds of
all men, that it is the hardest thing possible not
to fall into it, nay, even to avoid it, by seeking
the opposite, and, I believe, equally dangerous
extreme, of dispensing with theological definitions and dogmas altogether. That our modern
liberals do not escape the infection, I am very
sure ;—with all their tolerance, I know not where
we can meet with such determined and savage
dogmatists as they are. Nor do I think that
your Friends, with all their zeal against this tendency, have escaped it. But I believe that a great
providential scheme, for averting its evil consequences, has been at work during all the ages
that have been most prone to it; and that experience is now teaching us, what need we have of
that scheme, and how we may avail ourselves of
its blessings. As I proceed to develope it, you
will find that I have not forgotten the main subject of this letter; but that I am taking the best
method of fulfilling the promises which I made respecting it in my last.

Every one is aware, that the circumstances of
the English Reformation were very peculiar.
Even those who do not on the whole consider
that it took a worse direction here than abroad,
are nevertheless often disposed to complain, that
while the persons who chiefly influenced its movements there, were sage and holy theologians, to
whom a few Electors might be patrons or allies,
self-willed monarchs and politicians here moved

the secret wires, and directed the secret working
of the spiritual machine. A little more reflection
would have induced Englishmen at least to re-
strain these unthankful murmurs. By processes
of discipline, most worthy the study of every man
who reads history as the gradual development of
the plans of God, our nation had been trained to
uuderstand principles rather by their working in
institutions, than by an abstract or doctrinal stan-
dard. We had not been without our teachers
and schoolmen; we might claim some of the
greatest. But higher moral truths than it was
given to them to perceive, were gradually eluci-
dated in the history of our Monarchy and of our
Parliaments, in the silent progress of our legisla-
tion, in the establishment and progress of our
Courts of Law and Equity. The student of morals
and theology is startled by discovering what profound principles, of which he has in vain sought
a verbal expression, have been exhibited with
wonderful clearness, in the order and formation of bodies, which appear as if they had
only a civil and secular purpose. I throw out
these hints, which may suggest to you many valuable lines of thought hereafter, that I may lead
you to one particular reflection now:—It is, that
the apparent subordination of doctrine to politics,
in our Reformation, was not only a manifest token
that a divine hand was at work in it, shaping the
ends in despite of men's rough hewing; but also
was a reason why the Reformation assumed a less
purely intellectual, and a more spiritual character

here than abroad. I will add one observation, which may seem still more startling, that in consequence of this difference, the Reformed bodies abroad have been unable to preserve their existence amidst the changes of opinions and society, except by either standing entirely aloof from these changes, or slavishly submitting to them; that the English Church, on the other hand, has been supported through all these changes ; and is now, at the moment of her greatest apparent humiliation, able to interpret the wants of human society, to minister to them, and to direct its future progress, as no other body ever hath done.

I will explain what I conceive to have been the difference of the process in the two cases. Our Reformers had read and speculated about the points which were in controversy abroad; but the first practical movement concerned not the right to sell indulgences, the doctrine of penance, the doctrine of transubstantiation, but the *Pope's supremacy*. That question, which, in the minds of the continental Reformers, was merely consequent upon a number of others, became in our case primary. Nor was it the question, has the Pope a right to dogmatise for Christendom,—but it was the question, has the Pope any right, in a particular nation, over its own appointed king, which mainly occupied their attention. " That is to say," some one who worships the name Personal Religion, to the infinite danger of the thing, will exclaim,—" That is to say, politics were the first thing in their minds, and religion only the se-

cond." 'For my own part I do not care for words,
—have it so if you will. If I can show that the
glory of God, and the spiritual happiness of men,
were more promoted by what you call politics,
than by what you call religion, I am satisfied.
But you must remember, that the same difficulties
were in the minds and hearts of Englishmen,
which were in the minds and hearts of Germans
and Helvetians. There was the same burden
upon the conscience of the one as the other.
There was the same longing for deliverance in the
one as in the other. The debate is concerning
the mode in which it pleased God to lead men
to seek for deliverance, and as to the final issue of
the two methods. Now, I say that in England
we were not permitted to form systems of divinity
and confessions, to supplant what had been accumulating by means of the writings of schoolmen, the decrees of councils, the bulls of Popes.
By a series of acts, some violent, some accidental,
(where by accidental, I mean to describe those
events unsought for, and unprovided by man,
which are the effect, however, of previous deter-
minations of his will, and mark how God, through
that will, or in despite of it, is overlooking and
arranging every step), we were brought into
direct opposition to the rest of Christendom.
We were obliged to consider the nature of our
position. Were our king and nation indeed cast
adrift upon the world? Had we no sympathy
with all that went before us? Were we now to
commence a new history? But how could this

be? Our king, who had thus raised himself to this new dignity, was the heir of a line of monarchs, claiming a title, through both his parents, from the first Plantagenet, nay through him, from kings who reigned before the Norman invasion;—the very person whose acts and authority seemed to be bringing us into a new predicament, was the practical assertor of all that was established and ancient. Thus the minds of our Reformers, partaking in the influences of their age, experiencing all its anxieties and its tumults,—in some respects occupying a position more peculiar than that of all their brethren on the Continent,—were nevertheless predisposed, by habits long wrought into their minds and hearts, and strengthened, rather than uprooted by these new events, to see if they could not find something to connect them with their fathers, not how far it was possible to withdraw from them.

But again, whatever there had been in the personal character of the monarch to engage the heart or the fancy of his subjects,—whatever of refined accomplishments or chivalrous bearing, had been obliterated by deep and offensive crimes, with which all were well acquainted. There was nothing, then, in the new pretender to Papal authority, which could possibly lead an inquiring age to invest him with any individual spiritual qualities. The Universal Bishop might inspire a reverence in those who lived at a great distance from the actual seat of his power, who only heard by distant report of his luxuries or his profligacy.

No artifice could persuade men, who were beginning to doubt whether Christ could have any substitute or vicar upon earth,—that Henry was that substitute. A pretension so utterly novel, so far more extravagant than that which it superseded, could never have forced itself upon the minds of any set of men in the sixteenth century; far less upon the minds of men whose new feelings, as much as their old prejudices, led them in an opposite direction. The monarch presented himself to them as great, not by reason of any personal gifts or endowments, though these they might believe he would possess, so far as he humbly sought them in virtue of his appointed office; but as the representative of a line which had from age to age given the nation a feeling of its unity, and enabled the men of one generation to claim brotherhood and kindred with those who had passed from the earth. But then, by what right had these kings reigned? Who had conferred upon them their authority? What had upheld the feeling of their successive claim upon the obedience of their subjects, even amidst any interruptions in the regular order of their inheritance? They looked upon the forms of our old constitution,—they considered the oath by which the monarch bound himself at his coronation,—and they found that there was an eternal, immortal, invisible King, to whom each in turn did homage, from whom each in turn confessed that he received his dominion,—in whose indefeasible right,—the right of all these his perishing and

mortal servants, subsisted. So far as His great
and universal dominion was acknowledged, kings
reigned and princes decreed judgment in safety.
When it was forgotten, no human contrivances,
no earthly conventions, no fleets and armies could
sustain it.

Thus the Reformers of England were led, by
their peculiar discipline, into that discovery
of the truth of Christ's universal kingdom,
which had been received with simple faith in
the early ages; had resisted the efforts of the
Roman Emperors to destroy it; had been the
secret groundwork of the constitutions established
upon the ruin of their dominion; had been practically denied by those Popes who pretended most
vehemently to assert it; and was now in danger of
being forgotten altogether in the notion of Christianity as a system of dogmas or opinions. If
this be so, you will not think, perhaps, that we
have so much cause to lament that Henry the
Eighth should have been at times so vacillating,
at times so arbitrary, respecting transubstantiation,—that our Reformers should have been held
back for a whole reign after the Reformation from
the publication of formal systems and confessions,
and should have been led to embody all that
they knew, in books for the institution of Christian men, and should themselves have been kept
hesitating and uncertain about many points, on
which their continental brethren were very confident. You will not think, that it may necessarily have been a curse to us, that when the Re-

formation began to proceed, as it is said, with great rapidity in the reign of Edward,—that is, when the notions of the foreign churches began to gain great sway, and old forms and habits to be somewhat recklessly cast aside, God should have arrested its seeming advancement by the death of that young prince, and should have thrown us back into what might strike human eyes as a worse condition than the one from which we had been raised.   Nor will you think it so great a marvel, as it must needs seem to those who look upon our Reformation as the most contemptible of all, — our Reformers as the least brave and the least instructed, — that, on the one hand, a much hotter persecution should have been raised against the Anglican Church than against any of those on the Continent which had made it their main object to depart as widely as possible from Rome; or, on the other hand, that no country should have produced witnesses so resolute and unflinching.   From which last circumstance, it should seem, I think, that the political aspect of our Reformation was not so unfavourable, as many deem, to the vital and practical Christianity of those who took part in it.   And perhaps, with a little reflection, we might discover that what experience proves to have been the fact, reason would have prepared us to anticipate; for if the discovery and acknowledgment of a personal Friend and Deliverer, who had died for the sins of men, and risen for their justification, in whom only they could have pardon, and peace,

and righteousness,—if it was this which the sin-
burdened conscience of men required, then the
more directly, and actually, and livingly this
person was presented to them, the more did
they win the needful blessing ; and if the idea of
such a person, actually living and reigning, upholding the earth and the pillars thereof, when all
things but for him would have been out of their
course,—dawned upon them through the institutions of their own land, and the circumstances of
the age in which they appeared ; interpreting not
only the past ways of God, but also his Word,
which speaks to men of and through national
forms and institutions, their hearts would be
likely, one would think, to get a surer grasp of
him whom they required, and who was thus revealed to them, than if they had been trained to
consider him, first under the conditions and forms
of the schools, and only afterwards as connected
with the real doings of his creatures. The pious
and thankful mind ought, I should imagine, rather to notice how finely such an education was
contrived to deliver those who were blest with it,
at once from any dreaming phantoms of a merely
spiritual life, and from that hard and cruel dogmatism, which is just as far removed from every
thing sound, and hearty, and substantial.

And now you may begin to understand how all
these differences of feeling would affect the views
of the Lord's Supper entertained by our Reformers, and their Continental brethren. I use
this word *views* reluctantly, and merely to avoid

circumlocution ; for my great wish is to show you,
that the Anglican Church was led, not by reason
of any peculiar excellence or glory in the members
or teachers of it, but by a course of providential
discipline, to put worship and sacraments before
views, to make those acts which directly connect
man with God the prominent part of their system, — that which was meant to embody the
very form and meaning of Christianity,—and those
verbal distinctions which are necessary to keep
the understanding of men from error and confusion, as its accessary and subordinate part.   Believing the church to be a kingdom, which each
nation, from the time of its conversion to Christianity had become bound to acknowledge, bound,
I mean, for the sake of its own stability and existence; they started at once with the assumption
that every English child was to be received into
this kingdom by Baptism, and was to be treated
as a member of it.   It was as much admitted by
this rite into Christ's heavenly kingdom of the
church, as it was by birth into Christ's earthly
kingdom of the nation.   It was not cognizant of
the privileges belonging to either state, no, not
even of the lower, but still mighty privilege,
of being the member of a family,—but to each of
these blessings were its teachers, confiding in
God's promises and help, to awaken its inward
eye, as the outward opened upon the face of its
parents,—upon the hills and vallies of its native
land,—upon its towns and castles, which testified
that it was a land which the Lord God had cared

for,—upon its churches, which spoke of its connection with the mysterious and the invisible. The silent education under the eye of its parents, God's ordinance for calling forth the *affections*, — the stern sway of schoolmasters, his ordinance for awakening the *conscience*,—were alike an induction into the full enjoyment of those higher ordinances assumed in both, which showed that the awfulness of disobedience is never so great as when it is committed against a perfectly loving Father. Baptism lay at the commencement of this great scheme of spiritual education; the Divine declaration of the state of the creature before God, and of its relation to its fellow men, teaching the teacher with what an awful subject he has to deal, what mighty power he has at his command, for what a glorious end he is continually to be working; holding forth to the learner an unfailing hope of ever increasing life, and peace, and knowledge, of which even in his pupilage he enjoys the foretaste, of which only by the sacrifice of self-will he may obtain the fruition. Child, and boy, and man are alike instructed that they have an interest in this kingdom; that all the acts of their life can only be interpreted in relation to it; can be justly performed only while they keep it in remembrance. They are surrounded by it each morning when they awake; they are to rise and give thanks that it is theirs by every title of conquest and inheritance; to confess how little they have cared for its privileges; to plead the assurance which experience has taught them, that they shall fall from all its glories, unless they be upheld with fresh strength that day to receive the promised supply of pardon, encouragement, experience, wisdom, confidence, enjoyment. This kingdom compasses them in as they lie down at night, to bear witness of another day of continued unstartling miracles; of bodily and spiritual nourishment supplied, as much from heaven as if they saw the white flakes on the ground, and went out for the first time to ask what is it, and to inspire the prayer of hope and fear, that the Presence which has been with them through the day, the Angel of the Covenant, who has permitted the cloud to shelter them from the sun's heat, may be a light round about them in the night season. Every act reminds them that they are brought into this kingdom of righteousness, and peace, and love. A marriage cannot be celelebrated unless the King be present, to turn the water of an earthly ordinance into the wine of a spiritual mystery; he must be with them on their sick beds; he must go with them to death and the grave, in which he has been before them. Such was the idea of our Reformers, and in expressing this idea, they found they had no occasion to invent, they had only to purify. A kingdom they believed had been set up in the world ages before. Its subjects had been taught to express their wants, their thanksgivings, their hopes in every crisis of sorrow and joy,—in these men had found solace, and hope, and inspiration, excitements to their devotion when they were slug-

gish; sympathy in it which encouraged, not
cramped, their own aspirations when they were
cheerful; these reminded them that Christ was
the same yesterday, to-day, and for ever; and
that there was a golden cord of feelings binding
generation to generation.   Surely, to invent some
cold, and correct, and scholastic formulas of de-
votional propriety, — surely, to leave it to the
chance of individual feeling creating an expression for its own solitary and selfish wants, would
not have been so good a way of providing life for
that age, strength for those that were to come, as
to remove from the ancient forms whatever impu-
rities had crept into them, through the notions and
fashions of particular periods, and to give them a
permanence which should counteract more effectually than any other measure could, the effect of
similar corruptions hereafter, (sure to steal in by
means of improvised prayers), upon the mind and
theology of the nation.   But that which crowned
all these services and acts, as the service of Baptism lay at the foundation of them all, and that
without which all the rest are unintelligible, is
the service of Communion.   The prevalence and
dignity which our Reformers gave to this word,
above all that had been heretofore used to desig-
nate the Lord's Supper, though not to the disparagement of any one of them, is a help in interpreting the nature of our services, and, as I conceive, the whole idea of Christianity, which seems
to me unspeakably precious.   It at once lifts the
mind to this one sublime and awful thought, that

Communion with God in the largest and fullest
sense of that word, is not an instrument of attaining some higher end, but is itself the end to
which he is leading his creatures, and after which
his creatures, in all kingdoms, and nations, and
languages,—by all their schemes of religion, by
all their studies of philosophy, by art, by science,
by politics, by watching, by weeping, by struggling, by submitting, by wisdom, by folly, in the
camp and in the closet, in poverty and in riches,
in honour and in shame, in health and in sickness, are secretly longing and crying, and without which they cannot be satisfied. For all are
labouring after good or happiness of some kind or
other, and all testify by their acts, if not by their
words, that this good must be in some sense or
other out of themselves ; and all testify that this
good must some way or other be connected with
themselves, and that they must become capable
of participating in it. Wherefore there is not a
solid pursuit or a vain dream, recorded in the
history of man, or felt by him now, or that shall
be experienced hereafter, but points to this one
object, and tells him he must achieve that, in order
that he may attain any of the subordinate objects
which he also desires, and must labour after.

You will perceive, I think, *you* ought most especially to perceive, that there is something in
this idea far surpassing that mere aim after a satisfaction of the conscience, which seemed to me
almost the limit of the expression and notions of
the Continental Reformers. Do not mistake me,

as if I said Luther, and Calvin, and Zwingle did
not experience that want, which I say all men
experience,—did not experience it more strongly
than other men, because they were better than
most other men. I mean no such thing. I mean
merely that the notion of a deliverance of the conscience had such possession of their minds, that
they looked upon communion with God, and
upon every other blessing, rather as a condition
for attaining this privilege, than as itself the
highest and the most perfect end, to which that,
and every other must be subordinate. And so necessarily, I conceive, by the ordinance of God
himself, was this the peculiar and characteristic
feeling of that age, that I am not the least concerned to make out, nay, I should be sorry to believe, that our own Reformers were not almost as
much possessed by it, as any of their German or
Helvetic brethren. What I contend for is, not that
they rose altogether above the state of mind of
the time in which they lived, which would be a
very irrational notion ; for how should they have
interpreted the wants and feelings of an age with
which their own minds had no sympathy or correspondence ? but that having been led by a providential discipline, not to embody merely their
own feelings in the Liturgy which they compiled,
but to use language which had expressed the
mind of other ages, they were carried unawares
into another region ; and when they seemed to
vulgar, and even to some not vulgar eyes,—even
at times to themselves,—to be not advancing so

briskly in the career of improvement as their
knowledge warranted, were really withheld from
the sin of chaining down the church to the maxims of one particular period, and thus not merely
divorcing it from the past, but making it an inca-
pable and ignorant teacher for the future.

If you will consider what I said in my last
letter respecting the sacramental doctrine of the
early ages, you will see how, without imputing more
knowledge to those ages than I did then, or, the
least disparaging that light which I supposed the
Church to receive by gradual experience respecting the wants of its members, I may yet
suppose, that the forms which were preserved in
those periods, were the best fitted to prepare us
for the full apprehension and enjoyment of the
glorious Revelation of God. We described them
as considering everything, — a communication
from a Father to his adopted family. Every
blessing originating with Himself; Himself se-
lecting the channels through which it should
flow; Himself securing its transmission to those
creatures by whom they were needed. Further
than this, we supposed them, sometimes to inquire
—not much to apprehend; what these wondrous
and supernatural blessings are; how they fit the
constitution of those to whom they are sent; what
organs have been provided for their reception;
these were not parts of the faith delivered to the
saints; but it was a knowledge to which the Author of every good and perfect gift intended, by
various processes, to bring his children, that they

8

might know him better, and adore him more.
Thus much, however, was a part of the faith given
once for all, and never to be augmented or de-
tracted from—that there was one Being from
whom all blessings proceeded—one Mediator in
whom all blessings are contained, and through
whom all must come—one Spirit, by whom alone
they can be communicated to the church and to
all its members. That knowledge so high and
wonderful should give birth to more simple and
child-like overflowings of confidence, supplica-
tion, and love, than were likely to burst forth from
the soul after it had begun to pore over its own
nature, and qualities and operations, I think a reasonable man will be disposed to admit. But if
you have gone along with what I said just now,
you will admit something more; you will see that
the very same language which expressed in one age
a mere sense of the condescension of God, looking
down upon his creatures, pitying their infirmities
and supplying their wants, may be the most
suitable to him who has discovered that the enjoyment of fellowship with God, is the very blessing which his heart most craves after, and is the
centre round which all others must revolve ; that
the very same Mediator, in whom the Father can
alone, well-pleased, behold his creatures, must be
He through whom the creatures can alone behold their Father; that the Spirit which comes
down to dwell among men, must be the only Being who can open the eyes of the creatures, to
look upon that Lord and Friend of their hearts,

in whom they may at length behold the awful and ineffable Godhead.

I have spoken of language,—but you will see also that all the principles contained in the earlier apprehended truth, wonderfully connect themselves with the later; that all the forms which embody the one, are suitable for the other. Through human hands,—the hands of men,—consecrated and set apart for this office, says the old church, does it please our heavenly Father to give us this sustenance. Men, weak, fallible men, not in virtue of any holiness appertaining to them, though holiness *is* their privilege, and without it every thing they do is a monstrous contradiction, —but in virtue of a separation formally ordained and outwardly signified to the world, have the glory of transmitting to you this amazing gift. Two common elements,—one, the necessary food which sustains the frame of all men, the other, that which most invigorates their life,—are the outward instruments through which it pleases the Author of your bodily as well as spiritual constitution,—the Inspirer of your spiritual as well as your bodily life,—to distribute the amazing boon. The early church, contemplating the deep condescension of the act, scarcely conceiving the possibility of any other instruments, thankfully receives those which it believes to be appointed. The Christian of a later age, contemplating the magnitude of the blessing, after which he feels that he and all other men are aspiring—reading the history of the baffled hopes, and profound igno-

rance, and miserable failures of the men who have
striven to reach it, or have thought that they
strove, or have pursued something else, when this
was that after which they really aimed — reading
in history, too, and in his own experience, the
danger of looking upon men in any light but as the
appointed means of transmitting the gifts of God
to man, which is the idolatry of other creatures,
—and the misery of refusing to look upon them
in that light — of wanting every thing immediately, and for our own purposes, which is self-
idolatry—which two evils, have been in every age
the great obstacles to finding that whereof we are
in search ;—reading in history, and in the experience of his own life, the mischief of looking
upon natural things as good in themselves, and
not looking at them as good and precious when
honoured and set apart by God and to Him,—
first, is disposed humbly to submit to the method
of this institution, because it is a prescribed one ;
and, secondly, humbly and devoutly to honour it,
because God has permitted him some glimpses
into its wisdom.   But while the idea of the elder
church thus beautifully corresponds to all the
cravings of a later period, whatever of confusion
in those points which concern not the transmitted
faith, but arose only from the lack of experience
in those who received it, were easily obviated by
the English Reformers, instructed in the evils
which these innocent confusions had brought
forth, and as keenly alive as any men of their
times to the necessity of asserting the freedom

and justification of the conscience. And here, again, we may perceive how remarkably, while they took away that of which their own age had perceived the danger, they were hindered from taking away that of which future ages would perceive the want. How the notion of a vicarious dignity in the ministers on the one hand,—of a substantive virtue in the elements on the other, had destroyed the very life of this Sacrament, by making it in very deed cease to be a Sacrament, I have partly explained already. It was impossible that the early church could foresee this danger; and that while they spoke of the glory of those human agents, who were set apart for this service, and of those natural creatures which were consecrated to it, they should not have used many warm and passionate phrases, to betoken that which they understood to be through them transmitted. But, did cautious coldness save the foreign Reformers from the peril of setting too much store, either by the visible man or the visible bread? In the case of the Lutheran, we have seen that it did not. Even Calvin, for the sake of averting the worse evil of losing the whole blessing, was forced to speak in such phrases, as led one cautious historian to accuse him of being at times half a Romanist; nay even Zwingle, when he hoped to escape the whole peril, did .in fact only introduce it afresh in another way. The memorial feast, despoiled of every sacramental association, must have acquired a glory of its own, most dangerous to the heart of

the communicant, most likely, as your friends,
who were chiefly brought into contact with English Zwinglians discovered, to degenerate into superstition. There was but one way of deliverance
from this natural danger, and that was to establish the idea of a real presence; to believe in an
actual communion between the Living Head and
and his members; and so to make every person
and thing connected with the service, precious
only as steps in that ladder. This course our Reformers adopted; they regarded Christianity itself
as a great Sacrament, and thus they were positively precluded from the temptation of assigning
a separate and independent value to that by
which they might, nevertheless, in speaking to
honest ears and humble hearts, express all its
value.

By putting the idea of Communion as the final
cause of all acts of Christian devotion, our Reformers,
however, did much more than merely explain the
nature of those acts, and justify the arrangements
which the direct words of Christ, or the authority
of the church, had settled for the performance of
them. They threw a broad and brilliant light upon
the connection between these acts and those more
transcendent acts, of which He in his own person
was the only author and finisher. What perplexity may have occasionally haunted the minds
of men in the elder church, while they dwelt on
the idea of a finished sacrifice to put away sin,
and yet felt the continual presence of sin,—how
this perplexity deepened into error, and what

practical fruits it bore, when men began to reflect more deeply on the operations of their own
minds, I showed in my last letter. I showed how
the notion of acts, still to be performed in order
to complete that justification, which something
within them that they could not gainsay, told
them was in some very practical sense not complete,—became gradually stronger, and invented
expressions for itself in innumerable arbitrary
mortifications and penances, but especially in the
innovations which crept into the service of the
Eucharist. It was comparatively easy for the
Reformation to sweep these away, and to prove
how fearfully they outraged the dignity of that
Divine Atonement which they professed to honour. Merely to confront such impositions with
the express language of Scripture, and then to
appeal directly to the conscience, whether it did
not find that deliverance and purification from the
reception of the simple declaration of God, which
it had not obtained from all its own experiments,
was all that the case seemed to require. And
yet, by degrees, the Reformers discovered themselves, — their successors have discovered more
certainly since,—that in some way or other the
feeling against which they thought they had provided so successfully, did again and again recur
in the minds, not of the unlearned only, but of
the wise—not of the disciples only, but of the
teachers. Protestants had need of their casuists
to track the windings of the hearts of men, as
much as Romanists. Protestants, who had most

thoroughly informed themselves on the doctrines
of their faith, who could argue most successfully on
the shame and impossibility of looking to any source
of pardon and peace but the Offering once made
for sin,—found themselves in solitary hours, in
midnight watchings, haunted by the same perplexities and terrors which they had deemed to
be the exclusive portion of the unhappy creatures
who had sought refuge in material and outward
consolations.   Protestants were found, secretly
introducing,—not penances and mortifications of
the flesh,—but acts and efforts of the intellect, or
experiences of the heart, as necessary accompani-
ments or prerequisites to the simple recognition
of an accomplished deliverance.   Protestants were
obliged to qualify their assertions with phrases
and adjectives, which went near to reduce them to
utter vagueness and unmeaningness : Faith justified, but it must be a living faith ; it was a sin to
doubt the full atonement of Christ, but then you
must be sure that you took it in the right sense.
And then the fierce reaction against such equivo-
cations,—which, let them come with what show of
moderation or learning they may, earnest men
will not bear, on matters so nearly concerning their
life,—was a hard, desperate Antinomianism, restoring those phrases which had been gradually pared
and smoothed away to their original roughness
and simplicity, but setting them up in opposition
to teachings that were intended to promote holiness and purity of life, and therefore imparting to
them a deadly meaning and effect.

Now, by that one simple method of proposing communion with the Holy God, as the end of all Christianity, the object to which all the divine plans have been directed, and to which all human desires must be directed, if man is to realise the purpose for which he is constituted; we say that the church relieves us from both these perplexities, each so deeply rooted in our nature, each sure to present itself in different predicaments of our mind and feelings, each in turn perceived and condemned by those who are the victims of the other, each pitied and justified by those who feel how prone they are to both, and feel inwardly what truth lies hid under both, each needing some kind mother and teacher, instructed and appointed of God to remove it, not by cold rebukes, but by tender and loving instruction.

Can the stoutest Antinomian express himself in stronger language respecting the full, perfect, and sufficient satisfaction for sin, than that which is adopted in our Communion Service? And yet, who does not feel that the words in the two cases, not merely do not lead to the same result, but lead to the most directly opposite result? The church had no need to weaken the statement respecting the freeness of salvation; she had only to state, broadly and plainly, what salvation is; she had no need to say something was left undone on the part of God in order to make His creatures happy; she had only to proclaim what the highest happiness is which God can bestow, or the creature can enjoy. If it be a state of com-

s 5

munion with God,—the resemblance of his character, the fulfilment of his commands,—it must
be a state of action, and a state of continual obedience.   To bring us into the condition in which
we can behold His countenance and live, in which
we can receive from Him all the power to will and
to do, was His act, accomplished once and for
ever.   To raise up the hearts of man to that contemplation, to bestow upon him that will and
power, is His continual act.   Now, does it need
any balancing phrases, is it any thing but the
carrying out of this idea, to affirm that *not* to
behold, *not* to will and to do, is to be miserable?

It is nothing to say, all this has been repeated
again and again in books of argument and
devotion.   I acknowledge it cheerfully, I acknowledge it in a larger sense than those who ask
for the acknowledgment would be at all willing to
believe.   Not only Protestants, but Romanists,
holy Romanists, perhaps, as clearly as holy Protestants, have again and again confessed to the
truth of all these propositions.   But it is another
question altogether, whether in their arguments
and statements of doctrines they have not, one as
well as the other, often practically subverted the
principles which, in the best and highest moments of their lives, they showed to be so near
their hearts.   It is a very different question, whether their disciples taking their notions as the
standards of their faith, and interpreting all devotion and all ordinances by means of them, have
not habitually sunk into one or other of the errors

from which their masters were preserved by their
devotions and these ordinances; and therefore it
is a very different question, whether these truths
have the same power and effect when they are ex-
tracted from the books of men uttering their most
inspired thoughts, amidst a mass of matter that
seems to the common reader much more directly
and formally to contain their judgments, or are
compounded out of confessions of doctrine that
are always intended to discriminate what is wrong
rather than to assert what is right, as when they
are set down for the deliberate and practical exposition of a Sacrament in which, its partakers
believe, that the most essential riches and the
most substantial blessings of God are stored.

If you do not yet apprehend the difference, I
will illustrate it in reference to two or three other
points. A man is justified by faith without works.
Can faith save a man? Is not faith without works
dead? Here are the great paradoxes of divinity,
which give rise to controversies and divisions, to
violent actions and violent reactions, which the
learned teacher sets himself to harmonise by help
of careful distinctions, addressing themselves to
the understanding merely, which the eager man
disposes of by appeals to the affections of his
hearers, availing just so long as those affections are
in their right tune; which the violent man gets
rid of by denying the one or the other; which
the moderate man escapes from, by reducing
both into equal insignificance. Where have these
sects learned the importance of each of these

principles? Where has the great doctor acquired
his distinguishing faculty? Where has the earnest
preacher been taught that the heart must be
called in to the solution of the difficulty? where
has the dogmatist been taught, that one truth is
so precious that the other cannot violate it?
Where has the man of moderation got his dream,
that they are capable of a practical as well as a
doctrinal reconciliation? I answer, in this Sacrament. That nothing but faith can join him to
the Living Vine; that no fruits which he bears to
himself, and not in virtue of that union, could be
good for anything in the sight of the Great Hus-
bandman; that it is not the act which joins him
to that Vine, but that it is the richness of the sap
from the root, circulating through all the branches,
which is the source of all blossom, and flower,
and fruit, and perfume—here is the great, living,
whole truth of the Sacrament, embodying and
concentrating those half-truths which the lagging
intellect staying at the foot of the mountain, on
which the spirit is gone up to worship, contrives
to cage in its formal and logical propositions.

This thought suggests a world of reflections
upon the universality of this Sacrament, as belonging to high and low, learned and unlearned,
which I must for the present suppress; till we
have considered it in another light, as obviating,
in the same grand and practical method, those
dark notions respecting sacrifice and satisfaction,
to which I adverted in my first letter; against
which I admitted that your friends had most rea-

sonably protested, but which, I believed, that
both they and some of our own communion had
not escaped from without a perilous loss of living
truths. As it is, the idea of the service that communion with a Being of perfect holiness and love,
is possible, and is the great blessing intended for
men; every condition which it sets forth as necessary to the attainment of that end, must necessarily be contemplated with reference to it.
Now you will see, with a very little reflection,
that it is not mainly with reference to this end,
that those have spoken of the sacrifice for sins
who have described it, as offered up by the arbitrary institution of an arbitrary Being, to appease the wrath which had been excited in Him
by the transgression of his creatures. The relief
of the conscience, goaded by the sense of committed evil, is all that they contemplate in their
view of the Divine proceedings. They wish to
believe that God does not regard with wrath, but
favour, those who are united to Christ. They
embrace the declarations of Scripture, which assure them of this truth; they feel the comfort
flowing from it in their hearts. Beyond this, all
with them is vagueness and speculation; their
understandings are restless and at work; and they
must find out the how and the why of this transcendant satisfaction. They see that there is
something in Scripture upon this point, something which tells, not only of a reconciliation effected, but of that way being the only possible
way, the only one well-pleasing to the Most High.

But these passages mount above the level of their conceptions. There is nothing in the scheme of their divinity to interpret them. The obvious resort of the carnal understanding, its resort in all ages, is to analogies from human procedure—to a method tacitly assuming that God is altogether such as we are; even while it pays the most apparent and affected homage to His transcendant supremacy. Then the law courts begin to be ransacked for precedents to explain and justify the Divine government; those very law courts which, in better and simpler days, were felt not to be the fountains from which theology is to borrow her maxims, but to derive all the health and soundness of their principles from her teachers; then Commecre to all the other corruptions with which she has infected national life, adds this, yet above all,—that she infects the dialect and the habits of that study, by which alone her secularizing influence can be counteracted, her gold and precious stones converted into something better than ornaments of the Temple of Mammon and the decking of his priests. The reports of the King's Bench, or oftener the judicial acts of furious Autocrats, become the hornbook in which we are instructed in the awful principles of that reconciliation which God made with his creatures. The Stock Exchange becomes the school in which we are taught to apprehend the wonderful nature of His covenants; and this, too, by persons who were all day long crying that the Bible, the Bible only is the reli-

gion of Protestants, and are sworn that the voice
of saints, confessors, and fathers of the church in
all ages shall never intrude itself to disturb their
pure and simple hearing of the word. Oh, grievous condition, miserable blindness! when pride
leads men into the lowest depths of humiliation ;
when they fancy that they are in danger of every
evil but that which is ready to destroy them.
Meanwhile, the church has been bearing a calm
and steady witness as to the transcendant worth
and meaning of sacrifice, which, if they had
heeded it, might have saved all her sons,—which
has saved numbers of them either from yielding
to those dishonourable misrepresentations of that
Name, to hallow which is our first duty and our
earliest prayer, from yielding to the unbelief, into
which some, by indignation at these cold and
crud interpretations, have been driven. Without
a sacrifice for sins there could be no communion
between God and his creatures. His sacrifice re-
moves those impediments to the communion,
which the blood of bulls and goats, sacrifices of
mere arbitrary appointment, though most precious as instruments of moral and spiritual education, could not possibly have removed. Until
One appeared who said, "Lo! I come, in the
volume of the book it is written, to do thy will,
O God,"—until He offered up himself as a perfect
and well-pleasing sacrifice to God, how could
there be perfect contentment in the mind of a
holy and loving Being, how could a perfect communion exist between Him and man? And thus

the church, taking the Epistle to the Hebrews for
her classic, and giving, not a literal, but a living
exposition of it, teaches us that a sacrifice, a real
and spiritual sacrifice, was necessary to the atonement of God and his creatures ; that this sacrifice
was offered up once for all, and was accepted for
the sins of men ; that the consciences of those are
purified from sin, who by faith receive this sacrifice as their reconciliation to God; that this
purification is itself only a means and preparation
for our drawing nigh unto God with pure hearts
and faith unfeigned, through Him who is the
Priest, as well as the sacrifice, the ever-living Mediator of a covenant which is established, not in
the law of a carnal commandment, but in the
power of an endless life.

And if by this method the church has rescued
spiritual life and truth from one tyrannical im-
position of the understanding, which intruded
rashly and audaciously upon the counsels of God,
she has no less delivered us from another, which
has in all ages been most destructive to union
among men. By making communion with God
the end of all Christianity, and the sacrifice of
Christ the communion point, the only means to
that end, she has at once overleaped those deter-
minations of the Calvinistic system, which to the
mere logician seem, and are, so clear and irresis-
tible. The Calvinist affirms, that there is no medium between the most utter indistinction and
those broad black lines which he has marked out,
between the elect and the reprobate. We affirm,

that his distinctions, for all that they seem so well
defined and accurate, are practically effaced by
continual alterations and allowances, are proved
to be practically ineffectual by the confusions and
perplexities in which they terminate. We demand more close, delicate, subtile distinctions
than he has ever been able to devise; and yet,
distinctions which shall be found at last, far more
real and practical. And such distinctions, we say,
this Sacrament, as expounded by our church,
provides us with,—distinctions which do not
destroy unity, but sustain it. The full, sufficient,
and perfect oblation and satisfaction, we declare,
has been made for the sins of the whole world;
all whose parents, by Baptism, have claimed that
regenerate state for them, which Christ claimed
for them by taking their nature, dying in it, and
rising again; all who, by refusing confirmation,
have not declined to say, that this state is their
own; who do not wish to disclaim it, by refusing
this ordinance, we invite and invoke to come to
it. To what do we invite them to come?—to seek
for fellowship with perfect truth, and holiness,
and love. To what do we invite them to come?—
to participate in that sacrifice which Christ offered
upon the Cross, that they may offer themselves as
sacrifices, holy and well-pleasing to God. To
what do we invite them to come?—to receive that
spirit of purification and life which it is promised
shall be renewed continually in those who seek it.
And, forsooth, it is dangerous to offer men
these rights; to put them in possession of these

privileges, is accounted a horrible confounding of the church and world, by those who will accept certain formal professions, certain verbal descriptions of experiences and struggles, as a satisfactory index of men's Christianity and purity. Our offence is, that we take to ourselves that which we see has always been given us, the right to cut off or prohibit those who, by outward and flagrant acts, have shown to men that they despise their birthright; and that we conceive the discernment of the thoughts and intents of the heart, the dividing asunder of soul and spirit, joints and marrow, is too mysterious an operation for any but Him who claims this glory for Himself, who will perform his own work in his own ordinances, and who will be avenged of those who have said Peace to those to whom he has not said peace, and have made them sad whom God has not made sad. I conceive, then, the distinctions in *practice* are far more successfully secured by our method than by theirs. The distinction in *principle*, that he who seeks this communion will find it, and he who seeks any other object, here or elsewhere, as his final end and satisfaction, will be as when a hungry man dreameth and behold he eateth, but he awaketh up and his soul is not satisfied; that he who seeks this, must seek it in feeding upon that Sacrifice, with which alone God is well pleased; that it must be with the spirit, and not with the flesh, that we feed upon a spiritual sacrifice — these are mighty and living, and, as mighty and living, are realised in

acts, not in words, the truth and fineness of which
all dogmatic artifices shall vainly endeavour to
reach.

In all those cases, you will perceive, our
Reformers, who stood upon the old catholic
ground, were able far better to oppose the errors of
Popery than those who abandoned that ground.
This difference was remarkably illustrated in another point. A communion between the seen and
unseen world,—between the spirits of the just
made perfect, and those who were still wrestling
between flesh and blood,—had always been regarded as one of the privileges which had been
asserted for us by the incarnation, death, resurrection, and ascension of Christ. Without such
an idea, the whole language of the 11th and 12th
chapters of the Epistle to the Hebrews,—language
which seems to be adopted for the most directly
practical purposes,—is only the flight of an extravagant fancy. How this idea was perverted into
the miserable notion of intervening mediators between man and his Lord, I have explained already. But when the Protestants threw off these
notions, the truth which it had hidden almost
perished with it. For the satisfaction of the individual conscience was now regarded as the end of
Christ's work upon earth, and, as a necessary consequence in every Protestant body, the fall of Adam
was regarded as the first doctrine of theology,—
the incarnation and sacrifice of Christ, as only
the provision against its effects. What followed? The heart of man has no satisfaction

in such a system,—it still asserts the possibility of fellowship with those whom it has lost; and it falls into all fantastic notions, as to the nature and manner of this intercourse,—into imminent peril of that very error which was the source of all Papal confusion,—the error of believing that the sympathy of friends and fellow-sinners, is more precious and intimate than that which exists between the members of the body and their Lord. We say pure Protestantism made no provision against these deceptions of the heart, because it does not recognize the truth which the heart requires. It left innumerable loop-holes through which Popery might steal in, in those very walls and buttresses which it raised for the purpose of excluding Popery for ever. But, if you consider you will see, that the real barrier against it was that very truth which the Protestant system asserted so weakly, and threw so much into the shade. If an actual union had been established between God and man in the person of Christ,— if he was actually God and actually man,—if on this rock his church stood, — and it was against this rock that the gates of hell could not prevail, —all fancy that there could be any other ladder to ascend into the presence of the Holy One but through the suffering man who had borne our infirmities, and carried our sicknesses, was idle and profane; and yet this same truth set out with the power and clearness with which it is stated by the Apostle in the beginning of the Epistle to the Hebrews, involves that belief of a communion be-

tween all redeemed creatures, militant and glorified, which the Papists corrupted and the Reformers forgot. Our Anglican Church embodied,
in her Communion Service, the very fullest and
highest·form of this idea of communion between
earth and heaven, and made the grounds of it the
more firm, by removing from it every notion
which could possibly make it unsafe. In her
service we are taught, that it is not through communion with the creatures that we ascend to
communion with God; but that, the highest communion is the foundation of all other, the fellowship with God, is the ground of fellowship between men. Their translation affects it not, so
long as the objects of both,—those on this side
the grave and the other,—are the same; if they
have the same delights, the same occupations,
if there is one centre to which all eyes are turned,
one food by which all are sustained, conditions
of space or time cannot affect their union, or
hinder the blessings of it.

Thus the effects of the fancy, often mischievous,
and always deceitful, are precluded by a truth
which transcends them. And this truth not only
lifts its head above the cloud-land, into the serene heaven, but has its foot firmly fixed on the
common earth. In the infancy of the Reformation, its teachers delighted to expatiate on the
Christianity of common life; they asserted constantly, that it was a sin to shut it up in clois-
ters,—a sin to deny that, in all the commonest
transactions, God might be as much glorified as

in the most elaborate exercises of devotion. But such sentences, while they might give freedom of spirit to many, did not in the issue produce the effect at which they aimed. Again and again Luther had to complain, that the farmers liked the Reformation very well, because it set their consciences free from priestly exactions, and seemed to leave them the liberty of oppressing their labourers as they listed. Again and again he wept and lamented, because the people fancied that he was giving them a licence to be secular, when what he wished was to persuade them, that in all things they ought to be religious. When the deliverance of the conscience was the end so exclusively kept in sight, I see not how it could have happened otherwise; nor when, at any particular crisis, or by any sudden movement, the attention to religion revived, do I see how it could have failed to happen, that the old Popish notions should be reproduced in Protestantism; that men should have begun to regard religious studies and ordinances, as entirely separated from their ordinary life,—and should have looked upon that life, which, in their practice, had been utterly worldly, as such by its very nature and principles. Then, instead of cultivating that hatred of father and mother for the sake of Christ, which is the relinquishment of attachment based on an insecure selfish ground, for the purpose of rebuilding it on its true safe ground,—they learned to regard those relationships which Christ himself hath established, as in some sort interfering with his prerogative,—then the new-fledged Christian thought, that the nest in which his wings had grown, was to be discarded and despised,—then all citizenship and political life began to be looked upon as profane,—then order, and simplicity, and homely duties, and child-like obedience, were strangely set in contradiction with the faith which alone can foster them,—then conceits, and towering imaginations, and a desperate self-will, and a cunning self-indulgence, began to flourish under the name of that Gospel, which is to bring every thought into captivity. And where was the cardinal error? Or is it not a more important inquiry, where was the cardinal truth, by seizing which the error, that seemed so skilfully composed of what was old and what was modern, of Protestant and Popish inventions, might be subverted and effectually warded off? We say, that our Reformers were taught by a wiser spirit than their own, to declare both the truth and the error, not in discourses delivered to the ears of their own generation, but in forms appealing to the hearts of ages that were to come. Admitting a holy order and constitution in Christ, the national life, the family life, being, as they deemed, holy and divine ordinances, were of course esteemed parts, though subordinate parts of it. The church-life was in one sense the flower and consummation of all the rest. In one sense it included them all, —it might be spoken of as root, and stem, and flower; for the church was the great kingdom which God had set· up on earth; grounded upon a fellowship established with himself in the person of his Son ; and this kingdom ruled over all; and this communion involved the principle of all rule and all subjection between rulers and people, masters and servants, fathers and children,—redeemed every sovereign injunction out of the circle of tyrannous acts; caused, that dutiful homage should never be confounded with slavish fear; drew, with exquisite subtilty, the lines which distinguish the law, which knows no relaxation or mercy, from the Sovereign Mind, which is the seat of reason and equity, yet upheld each as necessary to the other ; qualified the strict order of the state with the gracious order of the family, without abating the strength or consistency of either ; offered, finally, the only realization of that dream of a family love, for the sake of which the raving fanatics of Munster in the 16th, and of Amsterdam in the 17th century, would have rent society in pieces, and driven meekness, charity, and religion out of the world.

The last remark suggests another, which I have hinted at already, but which has not been brought out as its importance deserves. The Sacrament of the Lord's Supper, thus explained, presents us with a view of moral evil, as awful as ever overwhelmed the mind of the most wretched speculator,—more awful than such a man ever conceived, because far more practical, and yet one that can never create a moment's hopelessness. The horror of thick darkness which comes over the spirit when we contemplate a black

ground of sin, relieved, or rather made more
frightful by a few specks and spots of sunshine, is
surely something very unlike that feeling to which
God is seeking to awaken us, when we look upon
the disorders and miseries of the universe. If
you know any person in whom that habit of
mind is very predominant, I think you will agree
with me, that though it may have grown up
among the kindliest and most generous sympathies, and may even have been fostered by the
indulgence of them, yet is it continually interfering with their wholesome and comfortable exercise, is fatal to all sustained benevolence, and
threatens ultimately to create a perfectly heartless
character,—for heart and hope never have been,
and I suppose never can be long severed from
each other. If it be so, there must be some radical error in such persons. It cannot be merely
that they dwell too fixedly on a painful object.
Who could recommend them to wink and close
their eyes for a little while at a truth to which
they must at last awaken? But is it a truth,—is
not their chief hypothesis a lie? Does not God
from first to last teach us to look upon sin as the
violation of an order? And is not this the view of
it which every Christian, in every earnest moment of practical life and meditation, inevitably
adopts? But so deeply is Manicheeism rooted in
the corrupt nature; so readily is it deduced from
every examination of the mere *facts* of the world's
history, unassisted by illumination from above respecting its *principles,* that men fall into a habit

T

of speaking of the constitution of things around us as evil, thus actually justifying that constant tendency of every man to violate this constitution, which is the great sign and symptom of our depravity and fall. To illustrate this habit and its effects, would be to make an exposure of half our modern philosophy, politics, and divinity; but to show how it may be avoided, would be a far more mighty task, if it were not for the help which this grand ordinance, as expounded in our Communion Service affords us. There we find sin presented to us as the setting up of the self-will which separates man from God, and separates man from man,—this sin, as put away by a divine and perfect sacrifice, uniting God to man, binding men to each other; participation in this sacrifice, as the destruction of that self-will in each man, which is his own curse and the plague of society; the final extinction of it as the triumph of God over Satan; of order over anarchy; of life over death. And out of this great political truth another is instantly evolved, that a Christian's conflict is with a power which is striving to separate him from a happiness already won for him; that a Christian's prayer is, that himself and all the creatures of God may not resist that will which is striving to bless them.

If I am not mistaken, the more you meditate upon our Communion Service, and upon the observances connected with it, taking the few inadequate hints I have thrown out for your guide, the more you will be convinced that the principles

of Christianity, cannot be expounded fully or satisfactorily, except, if I may so express myself, in
the terms of this Sacrament. The truths of Christianity are deep, practical, universal.   That which
expresses them should combine all these characteristics. Does a theory or a book of dogmas combine
them ?   Can a hortatory address combine them ?
Can a mystical rapture combine them ? No; if you
would have dogmas useful, if you would have sermons useful, if you would have raptures useful,
you must find some language more comprehensive,
more expressive than any of them.   Does any one
say, " The Bible is such an expression," I hope I
shall by and bye prove that I am not second to that
objector in my reverence for the Bible.   But before I can set up the Bible against ordinances, or
speak of it as superseding them, I must be sure
that the Bible does not speak of ordinances, and
presume those whom it addresses to be partakers
of them.   It would be a poor way of showing our
reverence for a book, to set aside its very words.
Ask yourself then solemnly and seriously,—' Can
I find Christianity,—the Christianity I want,—a
Christianity of acts, not words, a Christianity of
power and life, a divine, human, Catholic Christianity for men of all countries and periods, all
tastes and endowments, all temperaments and necessities so exhibited as I find it in this Sacrament.
And if so, have I not an *à priori* evidence of its divine original and truth, which it must take a mighty
array of positive proofs against it to overturn ?
   That I have carefully abstained from setting

forth anything of my own on this subject, you will allow; but you may think that I have somewhat too much magnified the forms of the Anglican Church. Do you mean, some one may ask, that these forms are above all forms; that the Anglican Church is identical with the Universal Church? This is a question which I am not careful to answer; because when the terms of it are understood, it answers itself. I am setting before your friends what I believe is a safe refuge from the confusion and divisions of the sects. I am endeavouring to convince them that this refuge is the Catholic Church. The moment such a proposition is stated, the cry is raised,—" The Catholic Church, forsooth! And what and where is that? A dream! A nonentity! It is anything, everything, nothing. All the sects are the Catholic Church; all believers are the Catholic Church. If you are an honest man, tell us what you mean? Give your idea a ' local habitation and a name.' " Well, I will endeavour to comply with your wish; and, as it seems the more regular and customary course not to examine the distant till we have considered the near—as it seems time enough to look at the condition of things a thousand miles off, when we have fully sifted and been thoroughly dissatisfied with that in the midst of which we are dwelling, I thought it would be as wise first of all to see whether the forms which are used in every parish of the land four times a-year, and much oftener, I hope, in most, do or do not embody anything like the principle we are in search of. Now, whether this be the case, whether these forms do give a fixed expression to the idea of a church—do reveal its meaning—do not offer a refuge to them who need one,—is a fair question, which I have endeavoured to discuss fairly, and which, I shall heartily rejoice if any one will discuss with me. But, whether these forms are the best imaginable, is a very silly question, which no man in his senses will waste his time in debating. Men of business, men who are earnest, first ascertain what they need, and then to him who brings it are thankful; men who are not in earnest, mere talkers and cavillers, may talk and cavil till doomsday, if they will not insist upon our being listeners. As to the demand, whether we mean to confound the Anglican with the Catholic Church,—to those who have done me the honour to attend to the remarks I have been making on our position at the time of the Reformation, it will seem nearly as unreasonable as the other. I have shown wherein our church differs from both the Papist and from the Reformed bodies; that it is not a compromise between the two, but asserts that which is most precious in each more strongly than either. But what is the idea which it asserts so strongly and practically, and which all those bodies whereof we speak, have asserted poorly and ineffectually? I answer, the idea of *Catholicity*. We say that we offer a firm ground for universal fellowship, and that the Romish Church, by reason of its local and visible dominion, the Reformed Churches, because (omitting other reasons to be considered hereafter), they put the profession of a dogmatic or experimental religion in the place of sacraments, are necessarily exclusive. If of any particular body you allege this not to be the case, bring forward its pretensions, and we will either cheerfully acknowledge it to be as sound a part of the Catholic Church as our own, or will show you wherein we conceive it to have a more partial and narrow foundation. In the former case, your practical conclusion cannot be in the least affected by our candour, for no one will go to Germany or America for that which he has at his own door; in the latter, we shall no further assert the superiority of the Anglican Church, than as we prove it to have a wider platform of truth, and to be less arrogant and intolerant than others.

But the arguments require me to show, not only that this Sacramental view of Christianity is in itself more perfect than either the dogmatic or the purely spiritual; but also to prove, that both systems of divinity and Christian life have suffered, when Sacraments have not been made the ground-work of them.

To illustrate this point, I will first, for two or three minutes, call your attention to the object and construction of our Thirty-nine Articles, as contrasted with those which were compiled about the same time, and are in use among the other Reformed bodies. From what I have said already, you will easily see, that these definitions of doctrine can never be used in the Anglican Church

as tests and prerequisites to Communion,— can
never be imposed upon the body of the people.
They are employed for the education of our ministers and learned men, for whom they chalk out the
method of study which they are to follow, and
whom they warn of numerous errors, both scholastic and popular, which they are sure to meet
with while they are seeking truth in their studies,
acting upon it in the world, or communicating it
to their fellow-men. For this end, I conceive,
precise, formal, dogmatic articles became essential
at a certain period of the life of the church, after
men had been taught by experience the evils to
which the understanding and heart are most
prone, and had arrived at that stage of growth in
which the intellect requires a discipline and method as well as the affections; and they cannot, I
conceive, cease to be necessary, until the evils
against which they are intended to guard, have
ceased to be dangerous, or till the intellect
shows that it can flourish in strength, and do
no mischief to the other parts of our nature,
when it is left unwarned and untrained. If the
question be started, whether some other articles
should not be substituted in our education for
those which have been established about three
centuries, it becomes those who answer that question in the affirmative, to do one of two things.
either to allege some reasons why a better system
of articles, that is to say, one better fitted for the
purpose for which articles are designed, is likely
to be framed now than at the time of the Reforma-

tion; or else, by examination of our existing articles, to show that they do not answer their professed object.   On either of these pleas, we should be ready, at a proper time, to join issue with them.   But perhaps, before either of them can be well argued, it might not be unadvisable to ascertain what is the form and method of those articles which, for their actual deficiencies, or the possibility of an improvement in them, are to be so summarily disposed of; and this, as I said, is a point which throws light upon our present subject.

You have heard often of Lord Chatham's oracular declaration, that we have a Popish Liturgy, Calvinistic Articles, and an Arminian Clergy. In each of these positions there is that glimmer of sense and truth, which is all that a rhetorician cares for, and which serves better far than naked falsehood to bewilder the understandings of those for whom he speaks or writes.   What measure of meaning there is in the first member of the triad, we have considered already ; we may try hereafter to find a meaning for the last clause; at present I will, with your permission, investigate the soundness of the second.   And here our former remarks will be a great help.   Just in the same sense as we have a Popish Liturgy, we have, I conceive, Calvinistic Articles.   If we found good prayers which had been poured forth in the infancy of the church, before men began to argue and speculate, we did not discard them because they had been used by Romanists ; if we found

good and accurate distinctions taken in that age
in which men became capable of distinguishing,
we did not consider them spurious because they
had been noted or adopted by Calvinists; we did
not go to the Reformers for our forms of worship,
for we found them very cold; we did not go to the
early church for intellectual niceties, because we
found them sometimes obscure and declamatory.
There 'is no defending our Reformers from the
charge of profiting by the gifts which God gave
to each of the ages; it was their principle, — a
principle which it was very natural that statesmen should not understand, because it is one on
which they so rarely act. In this sense, it is true,
that as accurate distinctions were the peculiarity
of pure Protestantism or Calvinism, and as accurate distinctions are precisely what are needed in a
system of articles, our articles were Protestant or
Calvinistic, and not Patristic. But the orator may
be justified still further. We have seen that certain
facts, relating to the condition of man as he finds
himself in the world, had been comparatively
overlooked in the first ages, (except when the particular heresy of Pelagius brought them to light),
had been subjects of anxious speculation afterwards, and had finally been set in a clear and
strong light at the time of the Reformation. Such
was the fact of the depraved nature of man—of
the incapacity of his will—of his justification being by the righteousness of another—of all good
deeds being the effect of union with that righteous Lord—of the impossibility of supererogatory

T 5

acts—of the impossibility of any particular man, *as an individual*, being sinless—of the nature of repentance, as applying to the conscious acts done after Baptism—of the duty of each man to refer his personal life and holiness to the will and purpose of the Father in Christ—of the name of Christ, and not any set of opinions or notions being the ground of salvation. All these facts, we cheerfully acknowledge, are asserted in our articles, just as formally and explicitly as in any Reformed Confession. What more does Lord Chatham want fully to justify his assertion? A little more yet: The name Calvinistic articles ought to mean something more than that we assert certain facts which the Calvinists assert; it ought to mean that we adopt the Calvinistic method; that the relation which these facts bear to the rest of our theology, is the same which they bear in these systems, which are confessedly Calvinistic. Now, by way of bringing the question to a test, whether this position be true or not,—place our Articles side by side with the Confession which the Scotch preachers, in the time of Knox, drew up for the use of their church. No one doubts that this Confession is Calvinistic; no one who reads it can doubt that the men who compiled it were able, as well as honest men. There is a spirit and a life in it, which distinguishes it strikingly from the hard dogmatism of the Westminster Assembly, and all the formularies of the next age. Now what is the method of this document? The first article corresponds with the first in ours. Both

are on faith in the Holy Trinity. But look at
the second. In the English scheme it is on the
Word made flesh; in the Scotch it is on the fall
of Adam. Here is the key to the whole difference
of the systems. The Incarnation of Christ,—
Christ becoming perfect man,—is the central point
of ours; this is the ground of our idea of humanity; this is the foundation of our church. Sin,
evil, apostacy, are the foundation of theirs. What
is the necessary consequence? The articles which
follow immediately in their Confession are on Election and the Kirk. In ours the Catholic doctrines,
— the truths of Revelation; the authority of the
Scriptures wherein they are evolved historically, of
the Creeds wherein they are enunciated absolutely,
—are set out in the first eight titles; and it is not
till the ninth that we enter upon the Fall, and that
series of experimental facts which *constitute* almost
the whole Calvinistic theology. And it is not till
we have finished these two portions, — that I
mean, which sets out the transcendant parts of
theology, (that which, strictly and purely, *is* the-
logy), and that which deals with the actual condition of men,—that we proceed (from the nineteenth
article to the end), to develope the idea of a church
as founded in these Catholic truths, and implying
these human conditions, as being an exhibition of
the true form of redeemed and regenerate humanity, as having its power and life in Sacraments, a
pure Word and an Apostolic ministry, and as being
intended to enter into relation with the kingdoms
of the earth. After what I have said on the Sa-

cramental idea of a holy constitution, and of all
evil as a departure from it, you will not be at a
loss to perceive, that this difference must be a
most radical one, even if you did not reflect that
as articles are intended expressly to develope a theological *method*, their order becomes
part of their very substance. And, (what is far
more important than the blunting of Lord Chatham's point), you will acknowledge, I hope, that
the Scotch or Calvinistic dogmatic system is a
system merely; that the English dogmatic system
is one which all along presumes and recognises
Sacraments as the full enunciation of those truths
which it can only prevent from being confused or
counterfeited.

But this dominion of Sacraments over dogmas
was not to be maintained without a desperate
struggle. There was one nation on the Continent
which was circumstanced somewhat differently
from all its neighbours. Holland had not, like
Switzerland and Bohemia, been merely quickened
by the Reformation : it was born of the Reformation. It had no past to rest upon,—no discipline
of centuries to prepare it for the shock of this
age; its inhabitants dated the commencement of
their political and moral being from the shock,—
all behind was dreariness and desolation. But
the infant was no feeble and shivering bant-
ling; it put forth gigantic powers while it was
yet in its cradle. And if these powers had been
exerted only in strangling the serpents of Spain,
a wise bystander might have rejoiced and trem-

bled. But when the young republic threw its arms across the seas, when it became, at the very dawn of its existence, a great commercial potentate, who could consider without dismay what might be the consequence of such precocity upon those principles which give strength and heart to a nation ? With thankfulness we own, that the dark auguries which a thoughtful statesman might have formed from such observations, as to the permanence of this state, have not been accomplished; that the series of troubles and calamities which it was appointed to endure from the conflicts of its hereditary chieftains with the able champions of mere democracy, and subsequently, from the ambition of Louis, seasoned and disciplined the character of its institutions and inhabitants, and enabled it to assume and retain a great and honourable position among the Continental governments. But the immediate effects of the singular rise and education of this people, upon their theological views, which is the only point that we are concerned with, was not one whit less disastrous than the most gloomy seer would have foretold. It was scarcely possible that a country, starting into life, when struggles concerning the intellectual part of Christianity were at their height, and owing its deliverance to their struggles, should not have produced men full of speculative zeal and activity. It could not be a very wonderful circumstance, if even its princes felt it no departure from their province to enter with ardour into these discussions. Nor should we, .

perhaps, have had any difficulty in predicting
what direction the speculations both of one class
and the other would have taken. It was tolerably
certain, that the questions which interested that
age, not the truths on which former ages had
dwelt, would engage the greatest part of their attention. It was tolerably certain, that that which
bore upon the actual condition of man would become uppermost in their minds, and that all the
more transcendant truths would be considered only
in their relation to these. Nor need you wonder that, while the practical part of Christianity
was nearly forgotten in these disputes, they should
have *seemed* to assume a peculiarly practical character, — a much more practical character than
theology had ever taken before,—for these Dutch
divines were also Jurists ; they could talk as
learnedly about commercial law as about divine
law. Every thing in the circumstances of the
time and in their position, tended to give the
writers and the controversies in this new country
a prominence to which, when we look back upon
them from a distance, we cannot conceive how
they were entitled. And thus it came to pass,
that the link between the old Catholic Church and
the Protestant bodies, which Luther had wished
to preserve, which Calvin had not wished wholly
to break, was in Holland snapped violently as-
sunder ; and at the same time, Holland being
quieter than the German states, more conveniently
situated than Sweden, and more important than

Switzerland, became a sort of centre for Protestantism.

And now then began, inevitably began, that dreadful warfare which for two centuries and a half has rent in pieces the theology and the philosophy of Europe, has led the students of both to scoff at principles in their books, which they are obliged to acknowledge in their lives, and has left those poor people who need the truth of both systems to nourish their hearts, and want not the distinctions and subtilties of either, to complain, in bitterness of soul, that when they have asked for food they have received a stone; when they cried for fish they were stung by a serpent. For now, a man being no longer taught that he has a nature to be crushed, and a will to be delivered and united to another, if he would be a free and happy man, and that the freedom itself, and what desires there are excited in him after it, — what method he finds established for its attainment, are not of himself but God, whose love originates, and constructs, and moves everything that is not out of order and tune, and brings into order whatsoever will yield itself to him,—this instruction being not new and nice enough for these scholastic wits, they must enter upon disputes about the freedom of the will, without any reference to the conditions of its freedom or the causes of its bondage; upon the election of God, without any reference to that which is elected, or to the fountain from which it arises, or to the end of attaining the likeness of

divine love wherein it terminates. In which hard
and dreary arguments, much may well be said on
each side, that is most precious and heart-stirring,
because there must be a generous and divine
glow in asserting that which has been disparaged,
and which, by the highest witness, you know to
be true; and this may be at one time more in the
one party, at one time more in the other, according as the writer had more of true sacramental life
in himself, or as that which he vehemently proclaimed was more unpopular, and likely to be
forgotten, and needed, therefore, that God should
raise up some prophet on its behalf; but yet,
with all these occasional inspirations, there is
such frequent barrenness, such a contradictory
temper, such unworthy artifices, such twisting of
Scripture, such exaltation of the human judgment when it favoured, such affected disparagement of it when it crossed the conclusions just
then to be established, that but for the promise,
" All things shall work together for good to them
that love God,"—it were a hard matter at times to
believe that these debates were not wholly mischievous. Still harder is it for an Englishman,
taking the view of our Liturgy and Articles
which I have set forth in this tract,—to excuse
our divines for engaging in it, and ranging themselves under the banners of those Dutch doctors,
who were fitter, one would have thought, to be
their pupils.

But no man who cultivates historical candour
and impartiality, and believes not only that they

may be attained without the sacrifice of truth, but are necessary to the maintenance of it, will rudely attack the wise and good, whom he reverences, for not entirely resisting the influence of their age. We have enough to console us in remembering that the English divines, whom King James sent to the Synod of Dort, strong predestinarians as they were, maintained a higher position than any of the other deputies to that unhappy assembly, that, in spite of all their own personal tastes and predilections, the influence of our forms and articles was so strong upon them, that they asserted, one and all, the doctrine of Universal Redemption against the foreigners of their own party, and declared, moreover, (which some of their brethren abroad acknowledged), that we had maintained the order and constitution of a Catholic church, not only without running any risk of falling into Popery, but so as to be more effectual witnesses against it. I do not say that these facts, coupled with their abstinence from all those shameful proceedings consequent upon this Synod, which ought to make Protestants blush when they pretend that Rome has any monopoly of the persecuting spirit, were a compensation for the mischief of our taking part in the controversy at all; but at least they show how forms act in controlling the minds and judgments of men, and what a healthy influence they have sometimes exerted. And even when these disputes began to occupy all thoughts and tongues in England,—when our clergy began to be called Arminian or Calvinistic, — and when their errors were discoursed of in the edicts of monarchs and the votes of parliaments, it is interesting to observe how that feeling of the church being a kingdom, and not merely a sect professing certain dogmas which I have traced through our history, gave a new form to their controversy, and connected each side of it with the assertion of great practical principles concerning the life of men and the order of society. The Arminian, fixing his thoughts chiefly on the acts of human creatures, and what was necessary to influence or control them, became the supporter of outward, positive, formal rule; the Calvinist, dwelling most on the divine arrangements and provisions, connected his tenets with the idea of an invisible, spiritual order. The first had always a tendency to uphold arbitrary power; the second self-will; and both tendencies were sure to express themselves in a multitude of acts, while neither could, in truth and fairness, be said to be more characteristic of the respective parties than affectionate loyalty was of the one, and a reverence for the majesty of unseen law of the other. This is the conflict to which I alluded in the beginning of my first Letter. I recur to it now, because the history of the battles of actual church order and government with the attempt at something more divine, is necessarily interwoven with that question as to the relation of sacraments to dogmas, to spiritual life, and to the whole principle of Christianity which I am endeavouring to examine.

I hinted that at the Reformation the character of Henry was · a blessed security, not indeed against his assuming the spiritual prerogatives of the Pope, but against his claim to them obtaining any credence. And thus, I said, that the truth of Christ's true universal kingdom was brought out with peculiar power just at the time when so many circumstances seemed to threaten the belief of it. But a century had passed away, and during that century various circumstances had arisen to make men desire, as the Jewish people desired in the days of Samuel, to merge the theocratic principle in the dominion of a visible ruler. Notions and opinions were so rife and various that they seemed to turn us into a set of mere sophists and dogmatists; and faith, as we know, must be very strong in men, before they can be brought to think that God will provide for his church better than they can by their cunning devices. Now to heighten this danger, the sovereign in whose reign such feelings began to prevail, was of a character altogether the reverse of Henry's, one eminently calculated to win the hearts and devotion of his subjects. I must believe, then, without imputing bad motives to any one, that the church was at that time in the greatest hazard from her friends,—the hazard of being supposed to want the aid of kings and statesmen to uphold her, when it should be the doctrine of all who really believe her to be a divine institution, that they need her help to support them. Looking at things in this light, I am not only not concerned to defend the measures of Laud and of Charles (at the beginning of his reign), I am concerned, upon church grounds, to put in as strong a protest against them as is made against them on other grounds by the Puritans. And I am not only not concerned to prove how it was possible that the Episcopal Church should have been brought into such deep waters as she afterwards was, I am bound to think that they were intended as well for her own purification as for the illustration of the real principle on which she rested. But if I think this most important lesson and warning is to be gathered from the proceedings before the rebellion commenced, what lesson shall we learn from its success? I have no need to teach it,—you will find it in the pages of Harry Vane, John Milton, George Fox. They will tell you what were the blessings to the conscience and spirit of man when the church idea, which they found so intolerable, was subverted. Milton, above all, who on his return from Italy poured forth all his eloquence in support of the ten Presbyterian ministers, — Milton, who saw the dawn of a brighter era so near that his words burst into poetry, as he invokes the Prince of all the kings of the earth to come forth from his bridal chamber and put on the robes of his visible Majesty,—before many years had to lament, that new presbyter was but old priest writ large, and to confess, tacitly if not openly, that the forcers of conscience under the Long Parliament were more galling to him by far than the prelatists had ever been. It is difficult to imagine what must have been the feelings of men like him, when they saw, in place of the beautiful order which their pure spirits had imagined rising out of the wreck of forms and systems, the most organized scheme of dogmatical despotism that the world has perhaps ever witnessed. That Laud's schemes to prevent men from dogmatizing and arguing were most vain and arbitrary, I freely confess; but surely if the spirit of man smarted under his rods, it groaned more deeply under the scorpions of the Westminster Assembly. The obligation never to put forth a formal proposition upon any manner of doctrine, is not so dreadful as being compelled to convert all thoughts, feelings, aspirations, into propositions.

To those who examine the writers of that age (I do not mean the Episcopalians), there is evidence that the self-imposed yoke was a most fretting one. But what course remained?—they had thought the discipline of the prelates unbearable; they now ascertained the discipline of the Presbyterians to be so. Where should they go next? Milton and Fox (that I may join together the names of two men who, as a member of your Society once remarked to me, were the most dissimilar in all outward qualifications and accomplishments, the most like in some of the habits of their minds, and eventually in their creed),— Milton and Fox, the one secretly, the other before

the world, proclaimed that ordinances and dogmas
had been both weighed in the balance, and found
wanting, and that what remained was either to
maintain a hermit life of spiritual contemplation,
or, if it were possible, to build up a society of which
this should be the end, and which should throw
aside all those outward forms and notions that
had hindered the attainment of it. Here, then,
was the commencement of another great moral
experiment, of which it behoves us shortly to examine the results.

But first, let me ask you to reflect for a few
moments upon the position which Fox must
have assumed before he *could* decree that the
Sacrament of the Lord's Supper was not essential
to the constitution of the Christian church.
You are apt, I fancy, to set the question before
yourselves in this way :—" It is very true that on
a certain solemn occasion, the most solemn that
has ever occurred in the history of the world, our
Lord did take bread, and break it, saying, ' This
do in remembrance of me ;' but there is little said
respecting the appointment; there is nothing positively to determine that the words extended beyond the immediate friends of our Lord, who were
sitting with him at that table. That three of the
Evangelists should record the event may be singular; but why is there no allusion to it in the
fourth, the most spiritual of all the Gospels, the
one written by the beloved disciple ? That some
memorial festival is alluded to by St. Paul in the
11th chapter of the First Epistle to the Corin-

thians we admit, and that there is a kind of allusion to its having been a part of a revelation to
himself; but here again the ceremony may have
been connected with the regulations of a particular church; there is no distinct assertion of its
universal obligation, still less of that obligation
extending beyond the Jewish period, and it seems
to us that the whole character of the Gospel dispensation, as a spiritual dispensation, is hostile to
.the continuance of a mere outward ceremony, after
the principle of it has been once established and
received into the heart."

Now attend to your own last words. You admit that it is a dispensation,—that there is something wonderful and peculiar in Christianity, —
that it was the crowning point and consummation
of a former dispensation;—you admit that the
one had something to do with the other, by the
very language which asserts their difference.
Having this common ground to go upon, I am
bound to tell you that your way of putting the
question is a most inadequate and deceitful one.
It is not merely that in the judgment of all former
ages our Lord meant to institute a ceremony
which should continue in his church, and that
George Fox, having great spiritual illumination,
saw that the words had no such meaning; but it
is that the church in all former times, looking at
the whole of God's revelation, connecting the
Jewish scheme with the Christian scheme, the
root and stem with the flowers and fruit, had decided, that in this institution is contained the

spirit and form of Christianity, as in the institution of the Passover was embodied the form and
spirit of Judaism, and that George Fox, upon his
own responsibility, set at nought this conclusion.
The whole church acknowledged as strongly as
he could, that Christians are brought into a
spiritual world, into the holiest of holies, not the
figure of the true, but the very presence of God
himself.   But they said, this institution just as
much embodies these higher privileges, and is as
necessary to the full enjoyment of them, as the
elder ordinance was necessary to the enjoyment of
the privileges of the second court into which men
were .at first admitted.   They said, without this
institution the distinction between our privileges
and those of the Jew will be lost sight of, we
shall as surely sink back into a condition no
higher than theirs, as they sunk back into a condition no higher than that of the Gentiles, when
they forgot the ceremonies of the elder worship.
They said, if you consider the circumstances
under which this feast was instituted, — if you
consider who it was that instituted it, and the
words in relation to the Passover which accompanied it, you cannot conceive a more solemn
obligation of the one ordinance, or more solemn
substitution of the other.   The words could not,
did not *mean* to the Apostles more than they
meant to us; they meant less.   The words of the
institution were to get their life from events to
which those who first heard them had not yet
been witnesses; and this being premised, it was

so far from being puzzling to the church that the
Apostles should have been the first to receive the
gift, and that no particular phrase should have
been used to declare it of future validity, that
they could not understand how the ordinance
should be what they believed it to be, if it had
been delivered in any other form.   If the church
was to be built on the foundation of the Apostles,
they were to acknowledge themselves, and evidently did acknowledge themselves, stewards, who
received every mystery in trust for the use of that
and of every future generation.   To deny this
was, according to them, to set aside the idea of
the dispensation, — to turn the doctrine of a
kingdom set up upon earth into a dream and a
nonentity.   Then Fox was bound to believe, that
the church is not a kingdom,— not a body built
upon the foundation of the Apostles ; that the
spirituality of a dispensation consists, not in the
circumstance of our being admitted into closer
communion with God, but in the circumstance of
our being without visible ordinances.   In one
word, he was obliged, in the very act of asserting
a Christian dispensation, to deny it the character
of a dispensation, — in the very act of proclaiming spirituality as all-important, to reduce it into
the low and negative notion of something which
excludes what is visible.   But once more, the
elder church believed that the outward and visible
elements proclaimed, by their very outwardness
and visibility, a most precious principle, — that
not only the soul, that which thinks and judges,

U

but the body also, that which sees, and hears, and smells, and tastes, and handles, is the subject of Christ's redemption, was raised up with him when he left the grave, was glorified by him when he ascended, and shall in each man be redeemed out of the bondage of corruption, and enter into the liberty of the children of God. Supposing a mere spiritual act were all that is necessary to share the blessings of the moral and intellectual redemption, what is there to testify for this redemption, and that it only is obtained and realized by union with the Son of God?—and yet, without this belief, not only do men very imperfectly honour the gracious designs of God, but they are continually apt to adopt stoical notions, leading immediately to great glorification of the intellect and powers of man, and often ultimately to great sensual impurity.

Let us consider whether the constitution of your Society, and its history, confirm the judgment of the church or the judgment of Fox.

No one — I have admitted it again and again, not reluctantly, but with the greatest satisfaction — no one could be more anxious than he to assert that a spiritual life is intended for man,—that fellowship with a Being above us, — is one of the conditions implied in our very constitution; nor could any one proclaim more fully than he the mighty obstacles which our nature opposes to the attainment and enjoyment of this, the great end of our being. The principles on which he based these assertions, I vindicated in my first Letter against the cavils of your own members and of other sects. But how can I defend his consistency in working these principles into an actual system? What has Christianity according to your founder done to establish that fellowship with God which he felt to be so all-important, — to remove those hinderances to it which he acknowledged to be so tremendous? The right of drawing nigh with pure conscience and faith unfeigned to the Father of our Spirits, — that right which stands foremost in the charter which Christ brought down from heaven and sealed with his blood, your founder, instead of maintaining with greater boldness, went near to take utterly away. I know well how many excuses even in the sight of man, and I cannot doubt in the sight of Him who sees with clearer and more equitable eyes than man, he had for his language and conduct in this matter. I am well aware how that holy awe which he cherished in his mind of the nature and the majesty of God, were shocked by the irreverent exhibitions which in that day of religious profaneness he was continually called to witness. That the High and Lofty One who inhabiteth eternity was not to be addressed in phrases which an earthly king or father would have repulsed as insolent, which an earthly friend would have thought to be coarse, he felt in his inmost soul, — all honour to him that he did feel it! But when the child was hindered from approaching the presence of a Father, who had invited and commanded it to approach Him, and

warned it of the danger of living out of His sight,
till some impulse, — which a hundred physical
circumstances might check or modify,—which a
thousand moral circumstances might misinterpret,
— indicated His will that it should do so, I must
maintain that his sense of awe inspired a practice
which outraged the very principle that gave it
birth, and inevitably led to the very superstition
and familiarity from which it sought to deliver us.
Here, then, is the first test of the soundness of
your doctrine and of ours. By the Sacrament of
the Lord's Supper we have asserted the privilege
of men to hold communion with God, and have
assisted them to enter into the full realization of
it, yet by its deep mysteriousness, by the severe
simplicity of its ceremonies, by our accurate preservation of strict forms in the observance of it, we
have upheld the awfulness of that which, at the
same time, we affirm to be so necessary. You,
abolishing the use of that Sacrament, have been
unable to proclaim the blessing as obtained for man,
without which you declare that he cannot live;
—that you may not lose your fears you abandon
your confidence. And since this fear is preserved
by living in the presence and atmosphere of
holiness, and not by refusing to enter into it,
you run a mighty hazard of parting with the one
as much as the other. I do not wish to urge you
too closely; it is not for me to say how far this
danger has been realized; but I ask you frankly
and fairly, what your own experience and your
knowledge of Quaker history testify on the sub-

ject? And this is perhaps as safe for you, and quite as pleasant to me, as to produce the complaints and confessions of your own members, living and departed; whereof, nevertheless, if it were needful, your archives would supply me with a very ample store.

But again : I have shown you how this idea of the privilege of communion is connected in our minds with the idea of *Sacrifice*. On this point, as I hinted in my last Letter, your Friends have spoken largely, and I did not scruple to add, beautifully. To give up self, — to annihilate self, — to be crucified, — are the great aspirations of all your devouter members, the necessary steps, as they affirm again and again, to the realization of spiritual life and happiness. But what is it that gives the reality and possibility to such sacrifices ? What is it that makes them self-sacrifices indeed, and not the subtlest acts of self-exaltation ? If Revelation did not answer the question, history would. Let a man fancy that he is to purchase a blessing by these sacrifices,— be it the most spiritual blessing conceivable ; and in the first place, he shall experience an intolerable bondage, while he invents one Papistical or Brahminical contrivance after another to bring him into lower and lower depths of abasement; and secondly, he shall find, in the lowest depth, that his pride is most rampant and obstinate. Set before him the Head of the family offering up a sacrifice once for all to reconcile him to God, and inviting him and all men to be partakers of his

death and resurrection, and the casting away of
selfishness is but the removal of a filthy garment,
which is inconsistent with his new and glorious
position, — is but the deliverance from a monstrous anomaly, which hinders him from being
what he is meant and created to be. It cannot
be effected at once, and without many a struggle of the evil nature, and Christianity should
show us how it may be effected. But still it is a
natural death not an artificial death. It is the
death of a plague and pest which we hate, not a
tearing in pieces of our own proper being (which
is the notion that so many of the mystical writers
give us of this self-annihilation); it must be won
surely by submission to God's plans, not by
devices of our own. Here again your founder
defeated, it seems to me, his own principle; he
wished, I fully believe, to pay some higher honour
to the sacrifice of Christ than that which is implied in the notion of its being a mere type or
symbol of what is to take place in us; but he
could not find his way to the expression of what
he wanted. He believed the Calvinistic dogmatists around him were destroying all idea of the
sacrifice required of each man, by the hard, dry
language in which they asserted the sufficiency of
Christ's sacrifice; and he bent the staff violently
the other way till it snapped. And so he might,
and so have others in all ages done before him,
and perhaps have been raised up for the very purpose of doing it, that they might counteract a
prevalent evil; but then they did it under cover

of a church ordinance, which stood forth the
abiding witness for the truth which they disparaged, — the reconciliation of it with the truth
which they asserted. Fox would not have that
ordinance, and therefore his notion of a sacrifice
became the highest which you could reach; you
are taught to regard it as the highest which God
intended you to reach. Have you gained by this
belief? Are you gaining by it now? Do all the
exhortations of your older members to the young
and discontented Friends (sincere exhortations, I
believe, necessary, I doubt not), to be humble,
and sink themselves in the dust, and wait for
teaching, profit in the very least? No, you know
they do not. A feeling has arisen in their minds,
that there is some pretence and deceit in all this
language; they fancy that it does not mean what
it seems to mean, — at any rate, while they think
so, they cannot and will not wait to see whether
they are fairly dealt with or no. I have no wish
to foster this restlessness, — I tremble when I see
it, — I tremble lest they should part with precious truths, and learn to despise humility; but
I tell you that you cannot allay it. You have no
words with which you can charm the spirit which
has been raised among you to rest. You cannot
restore the unity which has departed from you, —
you have destroyed that ordinance which is the
centre of unity, — which keeps doctrines from
perpetual clashing with each other, and men from
being the slaves of doctrines.

And this is the third point on which I would

beseech you to consider what you have gained by
defying the judgment of the Universal Church, on
the great practical question. Fellowship between
men, I have shown you, is the third great element
in our sacramental idea. Now, no one ever asserted so solemnly as your founder, that communion between men must be spiritual; that formal
bonds could never knit them together; that the
Holy Spirit of love and unity, can alone make elements naturally unsociable, completely and permanently to cohere. It was a glorious proclama-
tion. Therefore, continued Fox, we want no
outward feast to bind us in one. No! but you
want external signs of dress to bind you together; you want outward formalities of conversation to bind you together. Consider—if you part
with these, your wisest and most thoughtful men
believe, (and believe, I am convinced, rightly),
that your existence is at an end. You have parted,
then, with a feast, which the church says is established by God as a bond between heaven and
and earth, and between all the members of Christ
here on earth ; a feast which connects together
the ages present with ages past; a feast, in which
you cannot deny that hundreds and thousands of
sincere men and women have believed that they
found spiritual life and peace; you have parted
with this, because it is too carnal to be a link between men who have the Spirit; and you think
the fashion of a coat no unapt condition and upholder of that fellowship! I suppose you will not
say,—' This is only our witness to the world.'

You must be prepared for our answer. You must know that we should say at once,—' Then you would rather men of the world should infer the spiritual character of Christianity from your symbol than from ours; from a difference in vesture than from a feast, which professes to speak of a fellowship of love between a Heavenly Father and his family.' To sum up, then, the whole difference, —you assert a high spiritual life, as that which is the privilege and glory of a Christian. We bear witness that this spiritual life is not merely a name, not merely something resident in the man who enjoys it; but that it is the effect of an actual communication between God and man. You say that man must sacrifice himself in order to obtain this spiritual life, we bear witness that one who is both God and man has sacrificed himself, in order to bring God and mankind into union, and that we are privileged to partake of this sacrifice, and so to receive afresh every day the spirit which prompted that sacrifice. You say that men have fellowship one with another, when the Spirit comes upon them and quickens them; we bear witness that the Spirit of him who raised up Christ from the dead, doth dwell in all who will come and submit to him; and that this Spirit binds men to each other, by binding them first to God. Which is the fullest and more spiritual faith? — which is the most practical?

I do not touch upon other points, on which I might perhaps have some right to enlarge. You seceded, and formed yourselves into a society

to be witnesses against the worldly and secular
spirit which you thought pervaded us. I do not
ask you have you escaped it? But it is a question
which it is of great importance that you should
ask yourselves. You like plainness. Set the matter plainly before youselves thus :—" The great
abomination of the age in which we live,—that
age from which we by our habits are separated,
and against which we are protesting, is its mo-
ney-getting spirit. Have we expelled it from
ourselves ?"

" Why beholdest thou the mote ?" you may
be tempted to exclaim. I answer,—I do not
look for the mote in your eyes; I exhort you
to look for it in yourselves. And I most sor-
rowfully confess, that there is a beam in our
own eyes which must needs be most frightful,
because we have had such wonderful instruments
for removing it which we have not used, such
a glorious light continually about us, which we
have excluded. But if you fancy that the deep-
seated corruptions which we have to deplore,
are the effect of our Sacraments, and not the effect of neglecting them, I think I shall be able to
show you in a few moments, that you err grievously ; that our body-politic has become sick
and faint, because it has invented food for itself,
instead of receiving that which God has provided
for it; and that if we will now repent, and receive
that food as medecine, it will heal us and restore
us as no nostrums of human invention ever can.

I. First, then, you will not, I think, deny — as

Quakers you should not,—that a spirit of restless excitement is one of our saddest religious characteristics. If we look at the symptoms of this disease in individuals, we find violent convictions of an evil nature, alternating with a lazy subjection to it; the sudden discovery that the past life has been selfish, leading to acts not less selfish in their object, and scarcely more benevolent in their effects; an apparent warfare with the world around; a real entertainment of some of its worst tendencies; to sum up all, a fever in the heart, a confusion in the understanding, an irregular and inconsistent practice. I will not go farther; I will not ask how often utter indifference or complete infidelity is the reaction from these religious fits; I could say some awful words on that subject, but the hint is sufficient. If, again, we look at the society of which these individuals form the elements, we shall find by what a number of stimulants this temper is created; how much religious machinery is at work to produce benevolent or religious impressions, or to keep them alive; how little, in directing the movements of the machinery, I do not say the more delicate tastes and apprehensions of the spiritual man, on whom it is meant to act, are heeded; but how constantly even that sense of straightforward honesty, which used to be thought an essential part of the Christian character, is insulted and outraged. It seems to be considered the all and all of religion, to produce a tremendous startling effect; and how long that effect shall last, or by what means it shall be

produced, or how much it shall tend to the glory
of God, are questions not worthy of a moment's
consideration.

Now that feelings such as these should be much
at war with the idea and principle of ordinances,
that their very name should be irksome, as implying something regular, appointed, and, therefore, according to modern notions, unspiritual;
will not, I think, surprise you. I want no better
testimony to their preciousness than the fact,
that they worry and torment this temper of our
age, and give birth to passions which are just able
to find a decent vent in warnings against the
danger of Popery, the horror of substituting the
form for the spirit, the delusion into which persons may be led by mistaking sacraments for faith
and holiness. To the mere arguments contained
in such solemn sentences, it is sufficient to answer,
that Popery is a horrible evil which we are most
anxious to avert, and which we believe is rushing in
upon us by means of religious meetings and revival
schemes, and whatever else excites religious anxieties and cravings, and does not satisfy them,—for,
that of such anxieties and cravings, dishonest
priest-craft in every age has availed itself, and
will undoubtedly avail itself again. But of the
temper of mind which such warnings imply, we
offer ordinances, and especially the Sacrament of
the Lord's Supper as the only remedy; for not
only does the idea of a settled state, established
by baptism, wherein this other sacrament is
to preserve us, by continued new supplies of

life, remove that notion of getting ourselves
into some state by self-willed exertions, which is
the parent of all restlessness,—not only does the
idea of communion with God, as the end of all
Christianity, set aside those selfish ends and principles, which this excitable religion affirms and
sanctions,—not only does it give a new view to
our conflict with the world, showing that it is to
be carried on day by day, in our own hearts, with
the principles, and habits, and maxims of the
world, and especially with that, its most prevalent
tendency, the wish to choose paths and courses of
action, instead of entering into those prescribed
by God; not only in all these ways does it com-
bat our worst tempers, and tend to cultivate
a serene and a Christian habit of self-denying
action or suffering, but also it satisfies most remarkably the very cravings which seem to oppose it.   The feeling of the necessity of society
to keep alive our religious dispositions, here
acquires its strict and highest interpretation;
that feeling of a warfare against principalities
and powers is here defended, and placed on its
stable ground; that feeling in the heart, that
faith and charity should live together; that what
we receive, we should impart, hath here been
asserted and vindicated from generation to gene-
generation. A person, then, feeling his lot cast in
this age, and considering, first, how it may derive
the full benefit from those lessons which God is imparting to it, and how it may hinder these lessons
from being turned to the devil's use, will, in this

Sacrament find exactly that which he desires, to secure the blessings, and avert the danger.

II. That feelings, such as I have described, should produce more conflicts of *opinion* than have existed in any former age, a wise man could have conjectured. A mind disorderly and tumultuous will needs lay eager hold of one portion of truth, and as readily insult what to him, in his ignorance, seems to oppose it. And thus, out of the very heat of that furnace which should seem to make reasoning and speculation impossible, shall come forth more various, unhewn masses of dogmatism, than the most scholastic and speculative period hath ever originated. That these divisions should set at naught the idea of a universal fellowship, and should convert this Sacrament into the mere symbol of party-life, is a fact which, however fearful, is nowise surprising. Yet, as I ventured to hold, (with some diffidence, because it is scarcely safe even to think how past evils, which God hath permitted, for greater good, might have been averted), that one of our great controversies,—that which is in some measure the centre of all protestant controversies, might never have arisen, had the communion been regarded more as the centre of Christianity ; so I am, with much greater boldness, ready to maintain, that the course which that controversy, and others have taken in later days, proves conclusively, that in this Sacrament they may find, and here only can find, their adjustment. The Calvinistic system, as I have shown you, began in the honest desire to protest against the naturalism of Popery, to assert a spiritual principle of man, and that with this, and this only, God can hold converse. Hence the denial of the patristic doctrine of the baptised church, as chosen of God, to be the receivers and witnesses of his grace ; hence the magnifying of individual election ; hence the assertion of the fall, and not the Incarnation, as the ground of divinity. In the next age, I remarked, the controversy took a new form. There arose two sects, not one asserting the Catholic principle, and one the Calvinistic, in which case our articles could have offered them reconciliation; but both alike renouncing the Catholic principle, and debating whether the individual man is chosen to salvation by a mere decree of God ; or whether his own will originates the acts and means which tend to his salvation. In this century the word Salvation begins to lose the meaning which it had in Calvin's mind. It is no longer identical with deliverance from sin and admission to holiness, as I conceive it always seemed to him ; it begins to be used like an algebraic symbol, without much recollection of its meaning. And, therefore, this stage of Calvinism prepares the way for a third, in which the existence of a will, or spiritual principle, in man, is entirely denied; in which man is supposed to be moved as a log of wood or a stone is moved. This is Edwards's Calvinism. Can there be anything more directly opposed to the Calvinism of Calvin himself? And yet the progress from one view to the other has been so gradual, I might add so inevitable, that few persons

even suspect, that while they are using the same
words, they are holding an entirely different thing.
What then? Have not we a proof that the controversy is worn to the very bone? Now, must not
Christians begin to look about them and inquire,
" How may I maintain the existence of that great
fact, that man is not a mere natural thing, for the
sake of which Calvin was led to differ so widely
from the old church? I cannot maintain it by the
dogma which bears his name. Can I maintain it
by dogmas at all? Or can I maintain the calling
and election of God, in the sense in which I wish
to maintain it, by dogmas at all? Am I not in
continual danger; has not the danger been
shown, by the experience of three centuries, of
converting man into a mere natural agent, the
living God into another name for Necessity?
What must I do? How can I fly from these horrors?" I say this Sacrament offers you a refuge.
Here you have all life and acts referred to God.
He gives the food and the appetite, the sustenance
and the power of receiving it. His creature hath
been formed by him with capacities for enjoying
this communion; hath been formed in his own
image; is spiritual, as he is spiritual. But that
spiritual life he only enjoys, while he submits to
the Lord of his spirit; his will is only free when
it obeys the Supreme and Perfect Will.

Ex hoc disce omnia. If there be a sacramental
resolution of this controversy, surely we need not
despair of any other. And can anything be more
likely or reasonable, than that the same ordinance,
which is meant to be the bond of all hearts,

should be the reconciliation of those differences which have kept them apart? But I must not stay to follow out this delightful conclusion into a number of tempting illustrations. I must hasten on to another characteristic of those times, which is suggested by what I just said respecting the Will.

III. The denial of a spiritual principle, which the physical studies of the last century promoted, lingers among us still; but it cannot be said to be a marked feature of the most energetic and thoughtful of the young men of this day. This habit of mind, as I expressed myself just now, wore itself to the bone, and at length there arose men of logic, more austere than Edwards, and even less prone than he to enthusiasm, to assert, by the clearest and closest argument, that there must be something in man which transcends sense and experience, something which is presupposed in all the conditions of the intellect, and cannot, therefore, be subject to them. This faith has taken hold of numbers who do not acknowledge or understand the data on which it is founded. It is making its way gradually and steadily into the minds of thinking men, and has all the more likelihood of resting there because it has had to encounter much mockery from within and without. No one can trace the progress of this silent revolution in philosophy without perceiving that it must affect men's theological views and apprehensions much more remarkably than any which has occurred since the time of Lord Bacon. A person who maintains that our understanding is not a court of ultimate appeal, — that the very constitution of our being, involves that of which it can take no cognizance, will not of course speak of mysteries as essentially impossible or worthy of contempt. The tone in which the writers of the last century treated them, will seem to him not profane, but ridiculous. He will smile with great exultation and self-complacency at those who thought themselves privileged to smile at every one else. But it may be pretty surely conjectured, by those who know anything of themselves, that with a tone of considerable contempt for certain kinds of philosophical infidelity, and of occasional compliment to the grand ideas of Christianity, there will be mixed in such thinkers no slight infusion of self-idolatry, — no slight dislike of anything that savours of humiliation. For all that he stands proclaiming that the reason lifts a man out of himself, and demands the infinite for its satisfaction, — for all that he looks into the dark abyss of the will, and feels that it requires the ground of a Supreme Will to rest upon, — you will find that he is very apt to make this necessarily self-dissatisfied reason, this necessarily dependent will the real objects of his wonder and his worship. Still more apt will you find him to believe that these conclusions and discoveries respecting the reason and the will, are the highest and most amazing developement of the religious principle; that Judaism and Christianity were but vestibules to the inner shrine of the temple; that all the facts of both were well contrived to embody so much of those principles as men could apprehend (being important possibly as facts, till an age of greater illumination), and that their mysteries are exceedingly interesting studies for a person who has investigated the laws of his own being.

That the feeling which dictates such kind of language as this, must look upon ordinances with more indifference and disgust than any other part of Christianity, because they indicate more practical submission, — something prepared for us, and not perceived by us, — is very obvious.   Nor dare I pretend, that on persons thus infected and possessed by the spirit of self-glorification, they could act even medicinally. A philosopher must be first well seasoned by poverty, or sickness, or an agonised conscience, — must first have been knocked and bruised, and taught to feel himself a beggar and a fool, before the very notion of coming to eat and live will be anything to him but a theme for fine speculation and frothy talk. But when he has received these terrible castigations, and is thus made to understand the monstrous impertinence of his former thoughts, will he not perceive that they are as much at variance with the particular truth that appears to suggest and warrant them, as with the condition which he now finds is his own, that of a poor sinful man? Will he not see that his proud notions were, in fact, the most absurd contradiction to the doctrine to which they were linked? — that the whole virtue of that doctrine consisted in its affirming that the deepest and most radical part of man is also the most universal, — is that which belongs to learned

and unlearned, high and low alike, and that upon
this sound and glorious discovery he had built up
an edifice of esoterical pride and self-conceit, such
as could only *become* those who fancy the variable
faculty of the understanding the rule and measure
of truth? And will he not then, when his heart
is brought to the same level with his intellect,
confess that he wants something more than these
discoveries to keep him from the most flagrant inconsistencies of life and practice, — to make him
an honest man — confess that if man has within
him that which will not be satisfied with earthly
food, it must be sustained from above by heavenly
food, — confess that if that food be given, it is a
mercy to which he has no right or claim, — confess that he must eat as one of a family, and cast
to the winds all pretence of being better or wiser
than the very meanest of them all. Thus, in this
instance again, we find this Sacrament coming.in
to encounter one of the characteristic diseases of
the age, and that by supplying the organ which
the disease has attacked with its needful aliment.

IV. But, lastly, I would advert once more to
that which is the most remarkable and portentous
peculiarity of this age, — the disposition to combine, not on a family or national basis, but in one
that aims at being universal. The French Revolution brought out this tendency in all its naked
power; it was held back for a while in our own
land by the religious feeling which had been recently excited in the poorer classes, by that regard for the forms of our national life, which
Burke's writings converted in the minds of

thoughtful men into a deep, intelligent reverence;
and, lastly, by the atrocities which accompanied
the first manifestation of the new principles. But
the influence of that religious excitement has
passed away; the events of the French revolution
are forgotten or not connected with its creed; national institutions have lost their hold upon the
multitude, and the principles which their great
defender asserted are little remembered by the
statesmen who have succeeded him. Meantime
the restless desires which began to put themselves
forth at the end of the last century, are becoming
stronger every day; if their outward exhibition is
checked for a moment, you may see that they are
working more securely underneath. Here is another habit of mind, then, which must have tended
to produce a great impatience of ordinances; a
contempt because they seem to have no outward
result, — a hatred because they are fixed forms,
and not the work of our own hands.

And yet, if you consider again, where will you
find anything so suitable to meet this state of
mind, and, if God will, to make it sound and
healthy, as a bold declaration of the meaning
and power of this Sacrament? We cannot raise
again the dormant national feeling; to attempt
it seems to be spending our strength for nought.
We cannot reproduce that kind of religious excitement which the Methodists were permitted
and ordained, for merciful reasons, to be the
means of creating; see how abortive and mischievous all attempts of the kind have proved. You
cannot excite horror of a past evil. Alas! history

had never much influence on men's minds, and
we have used the facts of it so dishonestly, for
such low, mob purposes, that now it has less than
ever. But you can meet men who are longing
for a universal fellowship and say, — " Here is
one, and here are the symbols of it, and you have
a charter of admission to it, signed and sealed in
blood. And this universal society is founded by
God himself, and it has stood for eighteen centuries, and in this Sacrament the Lord of this society has bound himself to its members, and they
to him and to each other ; and when they hold it
fast, he has enabled them to love him and love
one another; and he has never broken this Sacrament to any one man, but many have broken it
to him by not obeying him, and helping and serving
one another. And this disobedience is dreadful, and
shall meet its reward. But none who trust in
him, none who really join themselves to him in this
Sacrament, shall incur that danger. They shall
go from strength to strength ; they shall get the
better of every thing that divides them from him
and from each other, and from the whole family
in heaven and earth, till at last they shall all
come to know and feel that they are indeed one
with him, and one with each other, and that they
shall be so for ever and ever." We may declare
this to them, and we may tell them, that they
have tried other Sacraments, and they have come
to nought; they have sought to be brothers, without having a common Lord, and their hugs have
been death embraces. There is but this one left ;
but it is God's Sacrament, and nothing in earth

or hell has power to break it.   And if we speak
to them thus, I believe we shall act more wisely by
far, than if we try to rouse their consciences to a
sense of sin, or take any other course whatever of
our own devising.   For surely we are meant to
study the course of God's providence; what desires he awakens in man—these we whom he calls
to be his fellow-workers are meant to satisfy.
The individual consciences of men were alive at the
Reformation; to them the Reformers appealed;
the desire for union and fellowship is alive now;
to that let us appeal.   Only let us appeal to it as
Christians,—as men who would use what is holy
in men to further holy ends, not what is vile,—
as men who would do the will of the God of
peace and love, and not the will of the spirit of
division and enmity.

    To turn once more to you.   We are full of
personal restlessness, of religious dissension, of
philosophical pride, of political hatred.   But we
have within us, if we would use it, that which
would make our lives calm, and holy, and orderly; that which would heal our differences;
that which would humble us and satisfy us;
that which would make us a true and heavenly
family.   Come, then, not to make us glory in a
train of proselytes, but to make us ashamed, as
we behold how much they prize that which we
have counted worthless.   Come and tell them
who have thought Baptism an empty name, that
there are scales on the eyes of those who do
not submit to it; that it is the privilege of those
who receive the ordinance, to find them disap-

pear, and to behold their relation to Christ, and to all their brethren in him. Come and tell those who have thought that the gift of the Spirit is not really connected with this divine adoption and fellowship, that there is a mighty difference between the hope of sudden and casual visitations, and the belief of a power abiding with you by night and day, of whose presence sin may make you unconscious, to whose presence repentance may restore you, but of which it is a sin to doubt whether he is with you of a truth. Come and tell them who think that acts of self-appointed devotion may supersede the Holy Eucharist, that it is an incalculable blessing to feel that you are not seeking life to yourself, but that He is providing it for you ; that you are not engaged in a solitary exercise, but in an act of holy fellowship ; that your whole life, fashioned according to this model, becomes more and more that which the life of a translated saint must be,— a divine Sacrament, a thanksgiving feast, a holy communion.

Believe me,

Yours very faithfully.

* * * *

END OF VOLUME FIRST.

ERRATA.

Page 244, line 6 from top,—*for* this Sacrament, *read* those Sacraments.

Page 252, line 6 from top,—*for* it, *read* their authority.

Page 308, line 7 from the bottom,—*for* obligation, *read* abrogation.

CPSIA information can be obtained
at www.ICGtesting.com
Printed in the USA
LVOW10*1235110218
566112LV00011B/127/P